MATILDA INFANTRY TANK

1937 onwards (all marks and variants)

COVER IMAGE: Matilda Mk II Infantry Tank.
(Ian Moores)

© Dick Taylor 2020

All rights reserved. No part of this publication may be reproduced or stored in a retrieval system or transmitted, in any form or by any means, electronic, mechanical, photocopying, recording or otherwise, without prior permission in writing from the publisher.

First published in April 2021

A catalogue record for this book is available from the British Library.

ISBN 978 1 78521 644 2

Library of Congress control no. 2020947246

Published by J H Haynes & Co. Ltd.,
Sparkford, Yeovil, Somerset BA22 7JJ, UK.
Tel: 01963 440635
Int. tel: +44 1963 440635
Website: www.haynes.com

Haynes North America Inc.,
859 Lawrence Drive, Newbury Park,
California 91320, USA.

Printed in Malaysia.

Senior Commissioning Editor: Jonathan Falconer
Copy editor: Michelle Tilling
Proof reader: Penny Housden
Indexer: Peter Nicholson
Page design: James Robertson

Acknowledgements

Grateful thanks must be extended to the following people and organisations, without whom writing this book would not have been impossible, but it would be nowhere near so complete!
   Dafydd Ashton, Alastair Bowie, George Bradford, John Bryce, Bob Darwood, Simon Dunstan, Michael Grieve, Jonathan Holt, Jon Kneebone, Andy Lang, Robert Lockie, Shane Lovell, George Moore, Merlin Robinson, John St John Smith, John Tapsell, Tank Museum Curator David Willey, Head of Collections Chris van Schaardenburgh, photographer Matt Sampson and the staff of the Tank Museum Library and Archive.

MATILDA INFANTRY TANK

1937 onwards (all marks and variants)

Enthusiasts' Manual

Insights into the design, construction and combat use of the Matilda Infantry Tank – the 'Queen of the Desert' – the only British tank to remain in frontline service throughout the Second World War

Dick Taylor

Contents

| 6 | Foreword – David Willey, Curator, the Tank Museum |

| 8 | Matilda is born |

The 'Queen of the Desert' 10
Finance and rearmament 10
The waltz that led to the Matilda 15
The Vickers Medium Tank 16
Experimental medium tanks 20

| 26 | The infantry tank concept and the A11 |

The first Matilda – the A11 30
The A11 described 35
Arras 1940 40
Aftermath 40

| 44 | Design and development |

A12 Infantry Tank Mk II Matilda II 47
Armour performance 58

| 60 | Matilda at war |

Into action – France 1940 62
Back into action – North Africa 63
More action – USSR 67
Final action – the Far East 70

| 76 | Anatomy of Matilda |

General layout 78
Driver's compartment 82
Engine and transmission 85
Starting-up procedure (cold engine) 94
Suspension and tracks 95
Electrical supply and equipment 99
Radio 99
Weapons 100
Turret layout 105
Ammunition, stowage and tools 108

| 110 | Marks and modifications |

Calling a spade a shovel – the story of the name 112
Crossing trenches 114
Increasing the ground clearance 115
Sunshield 115
Canal Defence Lights – CDL 119
Mine-clearing Matildas 123
Australian modifications 126
Miscellaneous variants 130

| 134 | The story of the restoration |

Chris Van Schaardenburgh, Head of Collections, the Tank Museum 135

| 152 | Matilda walkaround |

| 168 | Endnotes |

| 169 | Bibliography and sources |

| 170 | Index |

OPPOSITE **The French tank museum at Saumur holds a Matilda II, in good condition but unfortunately wearing an inaccurate depiction of the famous Caunter camouflage scheme** *(Courtesy John Bryce).*

Foreword

David Willey, Curator, the Tank Museum

This volume adds to the series of Haynes Manuals with another classic tank of the Second World War – the Matilda II. For a period, the Matilda II enjoyed a dominance on the battlefield that is so often associated with later German tanks that get much more attention. As Dick Taylor so ably shows in the text, the Matilda II was the result of a sometimes-muddled British design process to meet the requirement for a tank to support the infantry on the attack. It only needed to advance at infantry pace and would therefore be a ready target and in consequence would need thick armour. The design was expedited by a hurried rearmament programme in the late 1930s as war in Europe loomed. The tank made it to the field army just in time to see action in France in 1940. Its contribution in the British counter-attack at Arras helped create a fear in the German High Command that, at least in part, caused Hitler to stop the German advance for 24 hours. That minor action leading to the infamous halt order gave a chance for the British to reinforce the Channel ports and rescue the army – a hugely significant moment in the war. Late in 1940 the Matilda II again proved a decisive weapon, this time in North Africa, with O'Connor's victory against the Italians in Operation Compass. The tank's armour proved impervious to Italian anti-tank guns but the chance of an overall victory in North Africa was lost when key British and Commonwealth troops were removed to aid Greece early in 1941. The arrival of German forces with the Afrika Korps saw the use of the 5cm Pak 38, the 7.5cm Pak 40 and the famous 8.8cm Flak gun used in the anti-tank role. The Matilda's reign of invulnerability was over – but there were still moments of success, such as the break-out from Tobruk as part of Operation Crusader. The complexity of the design and the inability of the Matilda to be upgunned meant it saw a relatively swift decline in use in the Desert War, and few were in service by the time of the Second Battle of El Alamein in October 1942. As part of the support to the Soviet Union, over 900 Matilda IIs saw service with the Red Army at a time when any tank was welcomed with open arms. It should be noted that later criticism of Lend-Lease tanks by Soviet sources has to be taken with a pinch of salt in the political bias of the Communist era. The Matilda also saw service in the Far East with Australian forces. The thick armour again proved effective against Japanese artillery. The close-support version of the tank fitted with a 3in howitzer proved effective against bunkers and an Australian conversion created a flame-throwing vehicle called the Frog. The Matilda also provided the hull for the British Baron and Scorpion mine flails, as well as the top-secret CDL (Canal Defence Light) tanks and it was, like many tanks withdrawn from frontline service, used extensively for training. This is the fifth in the series of tank manuals written by Dick Taylor, who has recently hung up his uniform after 43 years of service in the British Army. Dick started as a crewman in the 3rd Royal Tank Regiment on Chieftain and ended his career as a lieutenant colonel. As a tankie, he brings a wealth of first-hand knowledge of the subject to bear, along with his peerless research and deep interest in the topic as a whole. And what a topic. The tank as a weapon is now just over a hundred years old, a British invention whose aim it was to bring manoeuvre back to the static battlefield of the Western Front during the First World War. Before the end of that conflict the tank had been rapidly developed into a wide range of armoured vehicles with different roles; in fact, most of the types that are in service today can be seen to have a forerunner in 1918. However, it is the Second World War that dominates interest as this was the period when armour really came of age. The tank had a new and decisive impact on the battlefield; the numbers made, the variety of models and the rapid growth in capability, gun size, armour thickness, range and how they were to be used and by whom is a big subject area. As those who took part in the

ABOVE **The restoration of the Tank Museum's Matilda nears completion as the restored turret is lowered to re-join the hull.**

fighting inevitably disappear from around us, the fascination with the conflict and the wider period just seems to grow. This can be seen in media, arts and literature – look at terrestrial television programming and online media: it is stuffed with Second World War content – of varying quality.

From the public the interest manifests itself in many ways; for some it is sparked by family history research – the personal story of what it was like – while for other comes a fascination with the engineering and the technology involved. The traditional routes of interest such as the model maker, the war film fan, those with a passion for military history and so on, are now bolstered by those who love 'vintage' in its many forms: the re-enactor and of course the computer gameplayer. Millions now play online games with a tank element involved, and inevitably many want to learn more about the real thing. At the Tank Museum we try to engage with all these audiences, and our Matilda II restoration was filmed throughout and posted on YouTube in a series called the 'Matilda Diaries'. The response of the public in the comments section showed the level of interest in the conservation of tank history – feedback that was heartening to all those involved. The restoration of the Matilda II tank that can be seen in the pages of this book was carried out by a core team of staff but also with assistance from a team of volunteers. Grant money to assist the restoration was obtained from the Arts Council of Great Britain via their Prism Fund, and it has been the success of the Tank Museum being able to reach new online audiences with projects such as this that has led to further funding grants. To all those who supported the project, our grateful thanks.

For many, the best transfer of knowledge still comes from the written word and if you are like me, the delight of a real book in your hands is still something uniquely satisfying. So, sit back and engage and enjoy the Matilda tank and her history.

David Willey
Curator, the Tank Museum

Chapter One

Matilda is born

The birth of a new tank never starts on the day that the designer first sketches out the concept, but is shaped by experience and doctrine over many years. The Matilda was no exception, and owed its birth to many factors that influenced British tank development between the wars.

OPPOSITE Building Matilda tanks at Horwich, c.1940. From the London Midland and Scottish Railways at War series. Oil painting by Norman Wilkinson. *(Photo by Science & Society Picture Library/SSPL/Getty Images)*

The 'Queen of the Desert'

The Matilda II is without doubt one of the iconic British tanks of the Second World War, and for a short period it enjoyed an enviable reputation of being almost impervious to most enemy anti-tank guns. One commentator looking back on its contribution stated that at the time of its introduction into service 'it was undoubtedly the best tank in the world'. It was not without its flaws, but nonetheless nearly 3,000 were built and it saw service in France in 1940, during the campaigns in Libya and Tunisia from 1940 to 1943, on the Russian Steppes and even in the jungles of the Pacific. It was the only British tank that was in frontline service when the Germans invaded Poland and was still in frontline service when the Japanese surrendered. Known by many as the 'Queen of the Desert', for about 18 months it was regarded by the Italians and Germans as a golem; it would not be stretching a point to suggest that in that time it was considered by its opponents as a sort of bogey-tank that was nearly impossible to destroy, much as the Tiger came to be regarded later in the war. However, in order to understand how it came to be built in the unusual way that it was, we have to first investigate the haphazard story of British tank development between the wars. To put this into the right context we must start by looking into the problem of money.

Finance and rearmament

Probably the biggest constraint to any form of rearmament in Britain in the 1920s and into the early 1930s was the Ten-Year Rule. First applied in August 1919, this was a general rule that stated that Britain would not expect to fight a major war for the next ten years. It stipulated that 'The British Empire will not be engaged in any great war during the next ten years and that no Expeditionary Force is required for this purpose.' In effect this meant not before August 1929, and if any conflict was detected after that point, there would be plenty of time to rearm. In July 1928, as the rule was nearing the end of its life, the Chancellor, Winston Churchill, persuaded the Committee of Imperial Defence to amend the meaning of the rule to read: 'It should now be laid down as a standing assumption that at any given date there will be no major war for ten years from that date.' This much more specific version was in effect a rolling rule applied on a day-to-day basis that meant until someone rescinded the rule, the next ten years could be considered to be safe. This was applied, as most decisions by Chancellors are, for purely budgetary reasons. Until the rule was cancelled there could be no serious rearmament for any of the services. It was to remain in place, despite the frequent and vocal objections of the service chiefs, until 23 March 1932; ironically, this pre-dated the appointment of Hitler as Chancellor as it was fear of Japanese rather than German aggression that finally caused it to be rescinded.[1] It did much harm, and Churchill's 'lone voice in the wilderness' warnings in the 1930s must always be weighed against the harm he did to the services by his amendment to the rule in the previous decade. However, it is critical to realise the impact that it had:

> *It is difficult to estimate the damage caused by the Ten-Year Rule. All three services were affected. The Army was hit hardest of all. . . . The greatest danger of the rule lay in its assumptions: that Britain's decision makers of the future would be able to identify any potential threat in good time and that the transformation from a process of disarmament to one of rearmament would be swift . . . the policies to which the rule gave rise brought about the atrophy of frameworks for military development and production.* [2]

The tentative decision to begin rearmament was taken within government much earlier than many people realise; the end of the Ten-Year Rule in 1932 allowed the potential, if not the reality, of some rearmament to begin. It was only begun in earnest in 1935, and slowly gathered pace – this affected the army much more than the other services. The word 'slowly' is used advisedly, and it is necessary to understand the limiting factors that severely affected not only the pace of the rearmament programme, but also the priorities that became necessary, and which had such a major impact on the production of an armoured force. Once the decision was taken, the ability of Britain to rearm was restricted by several factors. Most obvious was the financial aspect, but also important was the ability of industry to provide new equipment, which itself was a function of the availability of plant, skilled manpower, raw materials and time.

Until the First World War, London was the financial centre of the world, but the war had nearly bankrupted Britain, and there remained a desire to return to the pre-1914 position of eminence. Confidence, however, was low, and for the first time ever in peacetime, a balance of payment deficit was recorded in 1919, which was repeated in 1926 and 1931. The Wall Street Crash of 1929 had a profound effect on everyone involved with finance, and no one was prepared to take chances. Fiscal orthodoxy within the British government, whatever its political leanings, clearly stated that it was necessary to maintain a so-called 'balanced budget'. British policy held that in any given year, governmental expenditure must not exceed governmental income, and thus income would drive the total sum available to the Treasury for all national expenditure, including for defence. Taxation was necessary, but the level of taxation was an emotive subject, and it could not be easily raised without consequences. Inflation was viewed with something approaching horror. An adverse balance of payments situation was therefore to be avoided at all costs, and this, more than any other financial factor, severely limited the amount of money available for rearmament purposes; no one was prepared to borrow for warlike materials. Strong arguments had been successfully fielded by the Treasury that spending excessive (or even moderate) sums on rearmament would inexorably lead to financial ruin and, therefore, rearmament could only take place at a pace dictated by what was affordable. The resistance to using loans to fund defence was very strong, despite arguments that defence spending would act as a welcome stimulus to dormant sections of British industry. In fact, it was not until 1937, and for the first time in peacetime, that a government loan was taken out specifically to finance spending on

LEFT Winston Churchill naturally features a number of times in the Matilda story, including getting involved in its name!

armaments. This was a huge moment in the rearmament process, particularly considering the fragile financial state and the widespread objection to 'militarism':

> *Within the country as a whole military expenditure in peace-time was regretted. . . . No better illustration of this can be found than the almost total absence of any examination by General Staff or technical experts among the general public of the equipment lessons of the 1914–18 war. ... Experience of the 1914–18 war had been very ill-digested at the War Office, [and only] small efforts were made in the 1920s to master its lessons.*[3]

BELOW A Mk V tank in 1918: advanced technology for its day but only ever intended as use in the infantry support role.

RIGHT The Wall Street Crash of 1929 led to even less money being available for the army, with new technologies – including tank development – suffering the most.

BELOW Destruction of the 'New Model Army' – a Whippet fast tank is broken up for scrap. This tank was the first to feature the mud chute design later used on Matilda. *(TM0899E6)*

Every year the Treasury allocated a sum to each service – in effect forcing each one to cut its coat according to the cloth available – to prioritise its programmes. On a yearly basis, the services would submit their initial bids for the next financial year, known as the estimates. After a protracted round of often highly charged bargaining, the final sum to be made available for the next financial year was decided by the Treasury. Money thus allocated could not be carried over from year to year, so any unspent sum was lost.

And then there was the problem of industry. In the years following the Armistice, Britain had systematically and deliberately dismantled its armaments industry. As Christopher Price correctly noted in his book, *Britain, America and Rearmament in the 1930s*: 'Lost productive capacity is [in effect] lost forever. New capacity can be created only when new capital mobilises resources.' In 1937 the sum of £34 million, which had been allocated to armament programmes, remained unspent, as there was insufficient plant within the industrial base to make use of it. The funds had been allocated for direct military expenditure, and it does not appear that there was any suggestion to apportion the unapportioned millions to investment in plant or training. As even the limited amounts available could not be spent fast enough, in late 1937 it was reported that although £81 million had been made available for the so-called deficiency programmes, only £35 million of contracts had so far been placed. The reason given was that spending the full amount would have interfered with normal (*ie* civilian) industrial production.

When Sir Thomas Inskip, Minister for the Coordination of Defence, submitted his 'Final Report on Defence Expenditure in Future Years' in February 1937, he recommended that rather than simply allocate funds to programmes deemed to be a priority in terms of foreign policy or military objectives, those programmes which would result in an increase in manufacturing capacity over the next two years should be fully funded, and that spending must be related to maximum production. In effect he was arguing for the bulk of the money allocated over the coming five years to be spent within the next two. This was a far-sighted policy designed to provide the maximum enhancement to Britain's military strength and which would thus support appeasement efforts, but which meant that programmes that could not demonstrate an increase in production would struggle for inclusion.

In actual fact, by 1937, just as money was becoming available, industry generally was enjoying something of a boom, and many firms were fully occupied making commercial and household items. This meant that only a handful of failing companies were available for the new task of building tanks prior to the outbreak of hostilities:

> *The North British Locomotive Co, for example, registered losses for every year between 1921 and 1937 . . . this firm, along with others like Fowlers and the Vulcan Foundry Co, was probably saved from extinction by tank orders.* [4]

Vulcan Foundry features prominently in the Matilda story, as we shall discover. In the context here, though, the important point is that an early decision to employ any spare heavy industrial capacity to begin to adapt to the task of making tanks would have borne fruit later, as many of the birthing pains would have been dealt with before the war started, and thus should have led to a much more efficient tank production base earlier in the conflict.

The additional money requested by the army for armoured fighting vehicle (AFV) *development* – as opposed to building new service tanks – were as follows:

LEFT **The Vulcan Foundry of Newton-le-Willows was a near-failed locomotive builder that was rescued when it was given contracts to build tanks. This is the company's logo.**

May 1936	£12 million	(none)
Nov 1936	£23.7 million	(none)
May 1937	£29.7 million	(£3.5 million)
May 1938	£22.7 million	(£5.5 million)
May 1939	£36 million	(£10 million)

The figures in brackets are the actual allocations. These increases were primarily intended to fund the infantry tank programme which had priority and had little to do with cruiser tank development. It was one of the great tragedies that when money did become available it was unable to be spent fast enough. As the tank design facilities and expertise in the country were so limited – in effect this meant the design team at Vickers plus a handful of civil service and military individuals at Woolwich – there was no one to design experimental models to allow experience to be gained or new theories to be tested, and this lack of capacity was to prove costly in subsequent years. Not only could new components and systems have been designed and tested, particularly engines, but this knowledge could then have been passed on to the inexperienced companies who were being pressed into the tank design business, allowing them to concentrate solely on building tanks to someone else's design. As an indicator of how far behind Britain had fallen, the following table is instructive:

World tank state in 1936			
	Light	Medium	Total
France	500–600	180	c700
Germany	1,600	300–400	c2,000
Italy	600–800	0	c700
Japan	450	150–200	c650
UK	209*	166#	375
USA	135	19	154
USSR	2,000	4,000	c6,000

Notes:
* ⅔ obsolete (older light tanks)
# 164 obsolete (medium I/II tanks)

Initially as a result of Italian aggression in Africa rather than because of a clear understanding of a growing threat from Germany, in 1937 the sum allocated to AFV development was increased to £3.5 million. The following year this rose to £5.5 million and in 1939 it was set at £10 million. It was not until 1940 when all the financial shackles were finally removed that the sum allocated was sufficient, a huge £200 million. The realisation that war was all but inevitable came late, not only to the public but also to the government; it probably sank in for most people only in spring 1939, once Hitler had annexed the rump of Czechoslovakia. Until this mental transition had been made, peacetime practices would continue, industry would see the commercial imperative (profit)

as their overriding concern and the attitude of the government remained hopeful that their stated aim of avoiding war through deterrence and diplomacy might still prevail. There were undoubtedly thoughts of the assessment of summer 1914 in the politicians' minds: the orthodoxy was that the 'arms race' had contributed massively to the outbreak of the First World War, and this catalyst had to be controlled. The July 1939 report of the Economic Advisory Council's Committee on Economic Information to the government concluded: 'Our defence programme has nothing to lose and everything to gain by the adoption of remedies less drastic than those required in war, but appropriate to a time which we dare not regard as peace.' But that was in the future. During the years 1927 to 1936 the sums available annually for new tank development in Britain varied between £22,500 and £93,750 – hardly generous when one remembers that the design and manufacture of a single handbuilt experimental tank might cost anything up to £30,000. By the mid-1930s one source indicates an annual total expenditure of only £400,000 was allocated for the production of new armoured vehicles, including spare parts. Most of this would be for light tanks, armoured cars and carriers, not genuine tanks. Using common car prices for comparison, a Crossley Manchester in 1925 cost £925, while a top-of-the-range 1926 Sunbeam 30HP cost around £1,295. J.D. Scott summed up the interwar pre-rearmament tank development policy nicely in *Design* and *Development of Weapons*:

> Since the finance allocated for development in the inter-war years did not allow the production of more than about one pilot model per annum, the possibility of a highly experimental tank proving a complete failure was an exceedingly grave risk. Everything was against the genuine research project. It was a system which provided some very fine pieces of mechanical engineering, but it did not provide [. . .] any considerable body of theoretical knowledge about the tank as a weapon. The system, indeed, was associated with the tendency to regard the

BELOW Although the majority of the First World War tanks were scrapped within months of the end of the conflict, some experimentation continued against a background of ever-increasing financial constraints. This is an 18pdr gun transporter of 1922, with a typical multi-bogie suspension layout incorporating mud chutes.

tank as a composite of gun and vehicle, and not as a unique entity with complex engineering qualities of its own.

Colonel Justice Tilly, the Chief Instructor at the RTC depot in Bovington, had a revealing conversation with a War Office (WO) financier in 1936 who said that he was 'quite willing to find whatever money the tank people needed if only the General Staff could make up their minds what they wanted'. If only both parts of that statement had been true.

The waltz that led to the Matilda

The tank was invented during the First World War for one reason only – to allow the infantry to get through barbed-wire obstacles and on to an objective, and then to support them as they fought into and through it – but not beyond. Therefore, in essence all tanks in that conflict were simply support weapons to allow the infantry to break in and break through, which would then allow the cavalry to conduct the breakout, thus restoring manoeuvre to the battlefield. For the majority of armies looking at the potential of the tank in future conflicts, that was how it was still perceived after the war; indeed, there were some who believed that the particular conditions of the war were a one-off and that nothing like it could happen again, and therefore the tank itself was an anachronism and could be disposed of. The cavalry in particular developed a protective mechanism to explain the war, and the term 'Back to 1914' was used by them to make clear their preferred stance. In a lecture entitled 'Possibilities of the Next War' delivered only one year after the Armistice, the speaker, General Sir Louis Jackson, claimed that 'The tank proper was a freak. The circumstances which called it into existence were exceptional and are not likely to recur. If they do, they can be dealt with by other means.' What those 'other means' might be was not elaborated upon. In the 1920s General Seely, a cavalryman, could not even bring himself to mention the word tank, preferring instead to call them 'those petrol things'. Not helping this was the unbelievable slowness of the British military at the highest level to properly evaluate the lessons of the conflict. Incredibly, the Kirke Report, the official assessment of the lessons from the First World War, was only published in October 1932 – almost exactly 14 years after the end of the conflict!

In opposition to this paralysis of thought, some visionary thinkers saw in the tank much more potential than a mere lumbering beast tied to the infantry. They perceived it as not only the weapon that could assist with break-in and breakthrough, but saw that it could be the weapon that allowed the breakout, in effect becoming the arm of decision, combining the attributes of cavalry (mobility) and artillery (firepower), both within an armoured carapace (protection). For those who took this thinking past its logical endpoint and into the realms of technical make-believe, the tank could replace all other arms and become the decisive, nay only, weapon in the future. In the 1920s this was Wellsian fantasy, in large part because the engineering and technological means did not exist to make tanks mobile and agile enough, carrying sufficient protection to make them all but invulnerable, with lethal firepower, a large range (or radius of action in the terminology of the day) and the communication means to control them both tactically and operationally.

It is sometimes said that defeat is the mother of reform; it might be contended that, in Britain at least, victory is too often the father of stagnation – the Kirke Report being a prime example of this. In the meantime, the Tank Corps had officially been entered into the order of battle and gained a 'Royal' prefix (becoming the Royal Tank Corps, RTC, on 18 October 1923), although its permanency could not be absolutely guaranteed. RTC officers needed to be alive to the need to take every opportunity to prove the worth of the new arm; initially they did not even belong to the Tank Corps, as did the other ranks, but to their parent regiment. The biggest problem that the army faced in the 1920s was not so much doctrinal – although this was an issue – as financial, and this would greatly hinder the development of the new, immature, somewhat unproven and frequently unpopular arm. This was simply because to develop new tanks with cutting-edge technology that could be employed to demonstrate the proposed capabilities required amounts of money that simply could not – would not – be made available. A general rule applied at this time was that to build a tank cost £1,000 per ton, this in the days when the defence budget was measured in millions, not billions. This rule of thumb was known to the Treasury, which often argued that many small tanks represented a better investment (in their eyes anyway) than fewer larger and heavier ones. The world financial crash of 1929 exacerbated financial stringency still further. There was a widespread political agreement to this approach as well, which, with typical weasel words, could portray the nation as having many hundreds of tanks, ignoring their actual military capability. And there were even some generals who agreed with this, taking the stance that having more tanks allowed more crews to be trained and large-scale tactics to be refined, as there would be plenty of time to rearm the RTC with genuine modern vehicles if war again threatened – after all, the country had managed to produce the first tanks from a standing start in a few months in 1915/16, so building new tanks was clearly a rapid process, wasn't it?

Many in the RTC could see the possibilities in developing tanks that possessed the full range of capabilities – a higher top speed, decent acceleration, better range, more armour, greater firepower, vastly increased reliability, easier control, as well as the hard to define and elusive 'fightability' – which would allow tanks to become much more than an adjunct to infantry assaults and be decisive weapons in their own right. This would see the RTC becoming in effect the perfect combination of the capabilities independently provided by the three traditional fighting arms of infantry, artillery and cavalry. But there was neither the military will to push this revolution through, nor the funds to develop new tanks with the perfect blend of these capabilities. In any case the search for perfection would have been hindered by the limitations of available technology, which of course persists to this day. As a result tank development in Britain in the 1920s and '30s was handicapped, as it tended to concentrate on developing only one (if that) large tank prototype each year, while maintaining the existing and ageing medium tank fleet procured in the early 1920s, and only buying in anything approaching quantity new (and cheap) light tanks that had utility in policing the empire. By way of example, in 1929 the army annual budget for petrol – for all motorised vehicles, not just tanks – was a paltry £27,000, whereas £607,000 was allotted to the purchase of fodder for horses.

As a result of the huge reduction in the size of the Tank Corps immediately after the war, by the early 1920s only six battalions remained: the 1st Battalion became the unit that ran the Tank Corps Depot at Bovington and Lulworth and was responsible for trade training, the 2nd, 3rd, 4th and 5th Battalions were the only operational units, and the 6th became briefly the RTC Workshop Battalion, but this was disbanded in 1925 when the Royal Army Ordnance Corps (RAOC) took over its functions. At the same time, although diminished, the cavalry still had 20 regiments – and they did not abandon the lance until 1927.

The Vickers Medium Tank

As soon as the Armistice was a certainty, the monumental plans to build a huge tank army for the 1919 campaign were shelved, and the majority of the tanks that had fought in the war, including many newer models that were under construction, were retired and broken up for scrap. Although much experimentation continued, the main equipment of the Tank Corps for the next nearly two decades was to be a tank that started life as a private venture by the major arms manufacturer Vickers-Armstrongs (V-A), intended to combine the very latest technology into a tank that was in many ways revolutionary. This was interesting as V-A had not had very much to do with tank development during the conflict, and this came about because almost all of the First World War weapon manufacturers went back to their pre-war businesses, leaving V-A as the only major arms manufacturer in the country. What V-A delivered was a tank that provided much of what had been needed during the last conflict and solved many of the problems identified during it, but which also looked forward to the future. This was the Vickers Light Tank Mk 1,

ABOVE Medium I 'Blair Athol' of 2RTC leading a pair of useless tankettes and a half-tracked lorry. This tank represented a genuine advance in design, including a fully revolving turret. *(TM6209B4)*

brought into service from 1923 and later renamed the Vickers Medium when the army decided that it would classify tanks by weight – there was no requirement to classify them by role, as there was only one role. The system used was that tanks under 10 tons were light tanks, those above 20 tons were heavy tanks, with those in between called mediums. In other words, whatever new capabilities the Vickers tank possessed, it was still viewed by most in the army as being useful only in terms of the role that 'Mother' had been built for in early 1916: infantry support. However, the RTC proponents of the idea of the tank as the decisive weapon saw in the medium tank the capability to achieve much more. They viewed it, and used it on exercises, both for supporting the infantry and also in independent operations or, better still, as part of a genuine all-armoured mechanised army. (In 1924 General 'Boney' Fuller had noted that it should be looked upon as a 'universal tank, one which can be used for all tactical purposes'.)

The original design of the Light Tank Mk 1 was given the project number A2E1, indicating that the requirement had come from the army staff, but it came to be known as the (Vickers) Medium Mk I, with 30 being procured.[5] The tank featured a driver in his own compartment (or cab) at the front, a separate front-mounted air-cooled engine, sprung suspension and a fully revolving turret mounting a 47mm 3pdr gun capable of firing HE (high explosive) – in theory at least, as no HE rounds were actually issued – with a total of two Vickers and four Hotchkiss machine guns (MGs) mounted around the hull and turret. It is probable that the choice of main gun, which had a higher muzzle velocity than the wartime 6pdr, was very deliberate and that it was intended to allow the tank to defeat enemy tanks, the MGs being the weapon of choice for suppressing and killing infantry. Although the tank represented a massive step forward in design, overall it was simply a large box at the rear

BELOW Typical construction for the time, the Medium II was made up of a series of flat plates bolted or riveted on to a steel frame; this added weight and was only suitable for a basic box design. The Matilda did away with such a method, and instead used the armour plates and castings to provide a rigid structure.

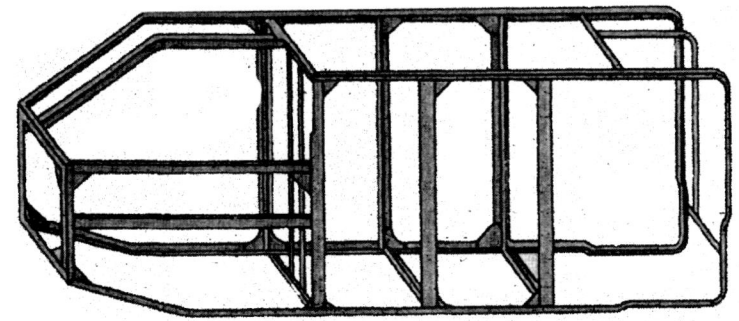

with the turret mounted above it, and the driver alongside the engine at the front.

It was, however, much faster than the First World War series of tanks, being capable of an impressive 15mph, tweakable by a knowledgeable driver to quite a bit faster than this, and was considerably lighter, weighing in at under 12 tons. One of the main reasons for the low weight was that the armour plating was exceptionally thin at only ¼in, but it did feature sloped plates in some places, which had the effect of increasing the thickness slightly – even if not intentionally.[6] It had a crew of five, with the commander in the turret at the highest point of the vehicle, very important for efficient command and vision. Two of the tanks were built as close-support (CS) versions with a 15pdr 3.7in low-velocity mortar replacing the main gun, intended mainly for laying smoke. The track did not run around the track frames at the top of the hull as had been the case with the First World War tanks, and the suspension units were somewhat exposed. A major twin preoccupation of British tank design that lasted for 20 years was about to surface, which was how to prevent mud clogging up the tracks and suspension, and how to protect the suspension (known as the running gear) from enemy damage. To deal with this it was decided to put angled mud chutes between the top and bottom runs of track, just above the suspension units, with the intention that the track in contact with the ground would invariably pick up mud, but when it rattled along the top run and around the track support rollers much of this mud would be shaken loose, and the angled chutes would then carry the dislodged mud outboard of the vehicle and away from the suspension. In order to protect the alarmingly exposed multiple suspension units and wheels, it was reasoned that bulletproof armour skirts would also be required.

A key point about this tank was that no prototypes were built, so in effect the original design was simply a short production run used as a starting point, which exposed many flaws that could be sorted by tinkering with the design incrementally.[7] And so from 1924 an improved version, the Mk IA, was purchased, which had a better (and safer!) design of driver's vision hood, an anti-aircraft MG mounted in a bevel at the turret rear and slightly more armour (⅓in in some places, still very thin, based on First World War experience). The next model, the IA*, again sought to make more improvements based on

BELOW 'David' of 4RTC, a Mk I Medium mounting a CS howitzer. As there were not enough of these, other 3pdr-equipped tanks were marked with the letters CS and their gun barrels painted white to simulate these vehicles on exercises. *(TM)*

ABOVE The boxy Medium II was a development of its 1923 predecessor. This one has bitten off more than it could chew, and it looks as if the driver is being rescued. It was not uncommon for drivers to be knocked out cold while driving. (TM1589D1)

the experience and feedback from the users and consisted not of new tanks but a series of modifications made from 1928 to the Mk I and IAs that were already in service; as a form of modern shorthand for what happened later we can refer to these as the 'Star modifications'. This included new tracks, a proper rotating cupola for the commander known as the 'bishop's mitre' due to its shape and the provision of a canvas sling commander's seat, something he had previously lacked.[8] In many ways the key improvement in the IA* was modifying the 3pdr mounting so that a third Vickers MG (the Hotchkiss MGs were deleted) was placed alongside the main gun in what came to be called a co-axial mounting. It was the first tank in the world to display this feature, which soon became standard on almost every tank built thereafter. This allowed the gunner to use the same controls and sighting gear for both guns, representing a major advance.

The next production order came in the mid-1920s for 100 new models, based on the Mk IA* but incorporating yet more improvements. This was the Mk II, the tank which was the mainstay of the RTC until just before the outbreak of the next war, and which saw service as a training machine into 1941 at least; a few even saw some limited operational service during the early months of the Libyan campaign.

It retained the air-cooled 90hp Armstrong Siddeley V8 engine; the use of air cooling was seen as advantageous as it meant that there was no water-based coolant to boil dry in the heat or to freeze in the winter. Externally the key modification was the use of armoured skirting plates to protect the suspension units, fitted with hinged access panels. The position of the driver was altered to give him better visibility, while a longer barrel was used on the 3pdr to increase the muzzle velocity slightly. From 1927 the tanks began to be equipped with the Laryngaphone (sometimes referred to as the Checkophone or Parlaphone), a voice

RIGHT A new-looking Medium II showing off the radio box or 'bustle' attached to the rear of the turret. Britain led the world in the use of radio to command and control armoured formations. *(TM1588B5)*

BELOW The Laryngaphone speaking tube system, here shown dismounted from a Medium II. *(TM10759-004)*

tube communication system based on naval technology and allowing the commander to control the driver, but which was not compatible with the use of radio. The original Mk IIs were then modified with the same set of 'Star modifications' around 1930, resulting in the II*. From 1931 another world-leading change happened when some tanks, known as Mk II**, were fitted with early wireless (radio) sets.[9] These were distinguishable by a large box housing much of the equipment and mounted on the turret rear.

Experimental medium tanks

Although the Vickers Medium Mk II tanks were the mainstay of the RTC, with lack of finances precluding the purchase of anything better, experimentation and development continued concurrently with them, albeit at a very limited scale. The first of these was designed by Vickers to the General Staff (GS) specification A6, of which three were built, all of mild steel as was commonplace for prototypes. The first two versions, A6E1 and A6E2, were completed at Sheffield in September 1927, the differences mainly being in the engines and transmissions used. The third, A6E3, was completed 13 months later. Known colloquially as the 16-Tonners, these were intended to be larger and more capable machines than the in-service mediums, with the top weight set at 15½ tons in order not only to be able to use the current army mobile bridges but also to stay within the limit being proposed at various international disarmament conferences. At the suggestion

ABOVE The A6E1, also known as the 16-Tonner. This was a more modern, rear-engined design that represented a major move forward in tank development. (TM0094C1)

BELOW The A6E1 front-on, the oval disc announcing that it had been built by Vickers-Armstrongs Ltd, at their River Don works in Sheffield in 1928. Note the twin machine-gun sub-turrets either side of the driver, intended to be the main weapons for killing enemy infantry. (TM1632C5)

of the designers, three small 'sub-turrets' were to have been fitted for mounting machine guns, but one of these could not be included without going over the specified weight limit, as the WO insisted that the suspension must feature mud chutes and be protected with 6mm bulletproof plates, as used on the Medium Mk II. Vickers protested at the weight penalty involved but the WO was insistent, telling the company to reduce armour elsewhere to compensate. Instead the front of the hull saw two MG turrets fitted, one either side of the central driver's cab, each carrying a pair of Vickers .303in MGs in the E1 and E2, and a single gun in the E3. Such sub-turrets were an ergonomic nightmare for the crewmen occupying them, but a doctrine that emphasised the necessity of having multiple machine guns meant that they were a common feature for the next decade.

In many ways the A6 tank resembled a smaller version of the Heavy Tank A1 (known as the Independent and then in development) and was intended to rectify the shortcomings being discovered in the medium tanks in service, including the lack of armour, with 14mm being specified. It certainly looked modern, with a rear-mounted engine separated from the forward fighting compartment by a bulkhead, and the petrol tanks were mounted externally, unlike

the in-service mediums where fuel was carried inside the rear of the fighting compartment. Technically the 16-Tonners were a huge step forward, particularly by the standards of the time. They were capable of nearly 30mph on the road, with cross-country speed measured at 19mph. Much of the experimentation on these tanks was concerned with trying out different transmissions, as well as various suspension arrangements, in order to make full use of the speed and provide a stable gun platform. One report notes that in 1934 'entirely new suspension units built by a firm specialising in this type of work proved satisfactory'. If they were such specialists, one wonders why they were not used earlier. Although frustratingly not named, this was probably a reference to the Slow-Motion suspension company. Each A6 tank cost £16,000, in accordance with the costing rule of thumb.

Concurrently with the early stages of A6 development, in 1929 the Medium Tank Mk III was ordered; this was in no meaningful way related to the Medium I or II but was a new design, which would incorporate certain features of the A6; the designation indicates that it was hoped that it would be the replacement for the Medium Is and IIs in service. Similar in general layout to the A6, once again the driver was positioned on the centreline of the tank, which was extremely useful for judging width when passing through obstacles, crossing bridges and so on. The turret rear incorporated an extended rear or 'bustle' in which the radio equipment was mounted, another innovation that would become a standard design feature of many tanks thereafter. It also featured proper seats for the three men in the turret; amazingly enough this was the first time that this had been done. Although only 10mm of armour was carried, it was of a new specification called CTA (cemented tank armour), later known as face-hardened armour (FHA), which was the equivalent of 14mm of the earlier type, and thus a lot of weight was saved without reducing protection. Only three prototypes were built from 1933 onwards and, despite being cheaper than the A6, financial stringency stopped the tank entering service.

The next – and final – attempt to produce a modern medium tank was the A7, sometimes called the 10-Tonners although they were – no surprise – quite a bit heavier than that when

RIGHT The A1E1 Independent was a heavy tank that was designed for operations independent of the infantry, but represented what the British Army needed in 1917, with a long hull to facilitate the crossing of wide trenches, a revolving gun-armed turret and positively bristling with machine guns. Most tank designs of the inter-war years anticipated the return of trench warfare.

built. These differed from the A6 and Medium III in that the design came from the Chief Superintendent of Tank Design rather than V-A; initially two examples were built, E1 and E2, this time at the Royal Ordnance Factory (ROF) at Woolwich. Weighing about 14 tons, the design featured a strange hull front; not only was the driver offset to the left, his view to the right was completely blocked by a single MG sub-turret. There was also a large access hatch in the nose which did nothing for structural rigidity or armour protection – and would be the last exit point that a crewman bailing out in action would choose to use. It is probable that this was done for ease of manufacture and maintenance rather than for practicality once in service. Both tanks were used extensively to trial different transmission and suspension arrangements, without great success, although it must be presumed that lessons were constantly learned, even if those were how *not* to do it. At least some of the weaknesses were identified with improvements incorporated into the third and final model, the 18-ton A7E3 which appeared in 1936. This featured the by now *de rigueur* mud chutes and suspension armour, but this time including small access hatches which allowed the crew to service and repair the components behind. The turret also featured a new design of turret front with a curved mantlet that not only added additional protection to the area of the tank most likely to be struck by enemy fire, but also allowed bigger guns to be mounted. In

ABOVE LEFT Inside one of the A6E1 MG turrets. The effects on the gunner of firing two Vickers MGs together were catastrophic in terms of noise, heat and especially toxic fumes. *(TM1632E1)*

ABOVE The Medium III ran to three versions, this being the final one of those, the E3 variant. An advanced tank in many ways, it displays features that were to find their way on to the Matilda II, including the central driver's position, the mud chutes and the track plate design.

LEFT A 1939 recruitment poster featuring the Medium III, issued just after the formation of the Royal Armoured Corps, which prompted the renaming of the RTC to the RTR.

ABOVE The next attempt at producing a general medium tank was the A7 series, often called the 10-Tonners, although in reality they often weighed in nearer 14. This is the A7E2. The driver's view to the right was obscured by the single MG mounting. *(TM10759-001)*

ABOVE The A7E3 was the best all-round tank built before the Second World War. Although the strange decision to include a front-mounted escape hatch persisted, along with the hull MG turret, the tank possessed many virtues. *(TM10759-002)*

BELOW A7E3 from the side. The turret design was very similar to that adopted on the early cruiser tanks like the A9, but the suspension shared commonality with that later used on Matilda II, including the mud chutes and access hatches. *(TM10759-003)*

order to give the tank sufficient power a pair of (different) AEC water-cooled diesel bus engines were mounted side by side. Pairing two engines together to give the same amount of power as one larger unit had been tried before (in the Whippet of 1918) and was certainly innovative, but it was technically complex and required extra components just to mate the two units together. It also featured a vacuum-assisted pre-selector gearbox, which was popular with the drivers. One unwelcome feature of all the tanks was their unreliability, and the twin engines of the A7E3 meant that the drivers and mechanics had to service two engines per tank, greatly increasing their workload and complicating not only repairs but also the spare parts chain. The next experimental medium tank, the proposed A8, was never built and so the A7E3 represented the final attempt to build an all-purpose tank. In any case, doctrine was already in the process of changing in a way that would create specialised tanks meant for specific roles. Although far from perfect, the A7E3 was viewed by many in the know as a very good design; in April 1938 the Mechanisation Board forbade the Tank Design Section at Woolwich to refer to it during discussions, as its potential was something of an embarrassment to the Board who had failed to develop it further.

Not without their faults and bearing in mind that they were all little more than experimental machines, the 16-Tonner A6, the Medium III and the A7 all represented genuine advances in tank design. The basic layout and some of their features were copied by the Russians and the Germans, and importantly for the Matilda story being described here, many found their way into both the cruiser and infantry tank families developed from 1934 onwards. Unfortunately, they all shared one common vice, in that they all were powered by available commercial engines rather than developing an engine specifically for the extraordinarily demanding environment that battle tanks operate in. This was almost certainly as a result of the usual financial pressures, as there were never enough funds to build both a new tank and a bespoke engine to go in it. This oversight would dog British tank design for most of the war.

MEDIUM TANKS BETWEEN THE WARS			
Type and mark (built as)	Registrations	Qty	Remarks
Medium Mk I	T1–14	14	T1 mild steel. Batch made by ROF Woolwich
Medium Mk I	T15–30	16	T15 mild steel
Medium Mk IA	T31–41	11	
Medium Mk IA	T42–58	17	
Medium Mk II Hybrid	T59–60	2	AKA Indian pattern
Medium Mk II	T61–115	55	
Medium Mk II	T116–156	41	
Medium Mk II	T169	1	Australia
Medium Mk II	T192–205	14	
Medium Mk II	T206–220	15	
Medium II Special	T221–224	4	Australia
Medium II Command	T236	1	AKA Boxcar
Medium II Command	T349–352	4	Probably not built
Medium Mk II**	T363–365	3	
A6E1	T404 (ML8698)	1	Mild steel. AKA 16-Tonner
A6E2	T405 (ML8699)	1	Mild steel. AKA 16-Tonner
Medium Mk IIA	T418–427	10	For service in Egypt
A6E3	T732 (MT9637)	1	Mild steel. AKA 16-Tonner
A7E1	T816 (MT9639)	1	Mild steel. AKA 10-Tonner
A7E2	T817 (MT9640)	1	Mild steel. AKA 10-Tonner
Medium Mk III E1	T870 (MT9707)	1	
Medium Mk III E2	T871 (MT9708)	1	
Medium Mk III E3	T907 (MT9709)	1	
A7E3	T1340 (BMM117)	1	Mild steel. AKA 10-Tonner

Chapter Two

The infantry tank concept and the A11

British doctrine classified tanks into two main types, Cruiser and Infantry. The Matilda was one of the latter, designed to be well-armoured but slow and intended purely for infantry support, although the chaos of battle saw it used in many other roles.

OPPOSITE The A10, here in prototype form, was an attempt in 1934 to uparmour the A9 and turn it into an infantry tank, although even with the new armour it was underprotected and shared the poor reliability from its cruiser heritage. It was reclassified as a heavy cruiser and saw action in France, North Africa and Greece, but was never liked by its crews. *(TM3469C6)*

Due to muddled thinking over doctrine resulting from conflicting theories of armoured warfare, and also due to concerns that the medium tank concept had produced tanks that were not ideally suited for any of the roles they were asked to do, it was decided to develop three very different types of tank to be used by three different types of tank units. The inability to produce a good all-rounder between the wars resulted mainly from the problems identified in Chapter 1. If there was one single organisational reason, it was that the lack of funds had not allowed for technology to be advanced. The greatest technical error was not developing bespoke and reliable powerplants, capable of moving heavily armoured tanks at speed. The three categories of tanks required were as follows: light tanks were to be used for reconnaissance by the mechanised cavalry units and were viewed simply as the modern replacement for the horse; they were cheap and would also have utility in policing the empire, particularly in India. They also had the advantage of simplicity, which generally aided reliability. Cruiser tanks would be lightly armoured but fast, suitable for the exploitation role; and the final category was infantry tanks (often abbreviated to I-Tank).[1] These would be slow but heavily armoured, and only used to support infantry attacks at the speed of the infantryman crossing contested ground on foot.

The perceived need for this specialised category of tanks intended just to support infantry attacks was clearly heavily influenced by the experience of the role of the tank in the First World War. With the benefit of hindsight such distinctions were clearly artificial, as they relied on commanders being able to control the chaos of warfare in order to ensure that the right type of tank, in the right numbers, was always available at the right time and place. Moreover, in an attack, it required the infantry supported by I-Tanks to make the break-in and breakthrough, with the faster cruiser tanks then pushing through the breach and into the enemy rear. In 1934 when the policy was conceived, many – but not all – senior RTC officers could see the faults inherent in the categorisation of tanks by role, but they were silenced. By 1943 the problems with this flawed system had become apparent to most and work finally started on a tank that was capable of fulfilling all roles, the so-called universal tank. But that was in the future and the realisation only came at the cost of much blood and treasure.

On 25 April 1934 a meeting of the Chief of the Imperial General Staff's research committee confirmed the notion that a specialised type of tank called the infantry tank was urgently required. The draft specification for an I-Tank that emerged from the meeting included a minimum of 1in of armour all round, either a 2pdr gun or a .50in heavy machine gun for engaging enemy tanks plus one or two .303in MGs for dealing with enemy infantry, a speed of 5mph cross-country and double that on roads and a maximum weight of 18 tons (in order to cross existing military bridges). Army Training Memorandum No 13, released in 1934, confirmed the doctrine that 'infantry would require the support of an I-Tank able to operate in an area defended by anti-tank weapons without undue risk'. Typical for the British military establishment, two schools of thought then developed as to the form such I-Tanks should take. One school favoured a small number of heavy machines that carried a gun and the maximum amount of armour protection possible, the other school preferred a large number of small and hopefully inconspicuous machines carrying machine guns that would overwhelm enemy defences by being difficult to spot and shoot at, allied to sheer weight of numbers. And, of course, the argument was, in 1934, still strongly influenced by the prevailing financial limitations, army rearmament not yet being under way. Both tanks would share one common feature: the need to carry sufficient armour to make them impervious to the small-calibre anti-tank guns that were beginning to be produced by all nations for use by the infantry, and which immediately called into question the 1in (25mm) of armour proposed. And to muddy the waters even further three different views on the tactical employment of I-Tanks also emerged. The first view was that the tanks should be used much like an artillery creeping barrage, moving forward at a set (meaning slow) rate governed by the pace of the infantry who followed along immediately behind them, much as was done at Cambrai in 1917; one commentator described this as tying a 20mph machine to the belt buckle of a 2mph infantryman. Another view was that the tanks should cover the ground as fast as they could, dealing with any enemy strongpoints on the way, leaving the infantry to move up as fast as they could behind and then mop up. The last school of thought was to use the tanks entirely on their own to suppress all enemy MGs, operating without infantry support, who would not be committed until the tanks had destroyed the opposition and who would simply occupy the ground gained.

As a result of the decision to create a specialised tank unit just to support the infantry, the Army Tank Brigade (ATB) was created – in theory only at this stage – with the intention of being 'a supporting arm to assist infantry onto a position'. It was noteworthy that the supporting role was re-emphasised. In advance of actually receiving any I-Tanks (which, of course, had not even been designed yet), in late 1934 the 4th Battalion RTC stationed in Catterick were converted into an experimental specialised infantry support battalion, which led to it being renamed as 4th (Army) Tank Battalion RTC, still using its existing tanks. This unit was to be the first of many, the intention from late 1934 onwards was to eventually to provide an I-Tank battalion to each infantry division.[2] In order to carry out the infantry support role, which was much more limited in scope than the forward-thinking and imaginative RTC battalions were used to and desired, it would be necessary to equip it with specialist tanks designed for the task. The thin-skinned mediums still in service were designed to be general dogsbody tanks and were clearly not the answer. A new design was required.

During 1934 the lessons learned from the experimental medium tanks did lead to one sensible attempt by Vickers to produce two versions of the same basic tank, allowing economies of scale and training, and simplifying production . . . if it could be made to work. The A9 was intended to be a cruiser, and its close relative the A10 was meant to be an infantry tank, with the same engine and suspension as the A9 but much more heavily armoured. The A10 was requested in May 1934 with a contract awarded in November. Vickers' chief tank designer, Sir John Carden, was entrusted with the project. One contemporary source referred to the A10 as 'the original I-Tank', which is certainly correct, although few histories seem to have recognised this point. Weighing in at 14 tons it could manage a respectable 16mph on roads. Unfortunately the 25mm of armour specified for it, probably because of the April 1934 meeting, was only able to stop a .50in armour-piercing (AP) bullet, and in any case the additional protection was provided by adding extra plates over the thinner 14mm base armour of the A9 design. The trouble was that this novel composite armour solution was swiftly overtaken by advances in small and mobile anti-tank guns with calibres of 25–40mm that could penetrate much more armour, and so the A10 was rapidly outgunned to the extent where it was clear that it could not be used in the I-Tank role. It was reclassified as a heavy cruiser, which was a designation made up to cover the embarrassment of a design made obsolete even before it entered service. Although in many respects a modern vehicle and better in many ways than the experimental mediums, neither the A9 nor the A10 could be made sufficiently reliable and by the end of 1940 advances elsewhere had rendered them all but obsolete. This early failure of the A10 project to produce a large, well-armoured I-Tank with a gun was to lead to the procurement of the first Matilda, the A11. (As a by-product of the A9/10 development, Vickers designed a new commercial tank around the same suspension, which would eventually see service as the Valentine.)

This doctrine of operating different types of tank with very different tasks and physical and technical properties was confirmed and codified in the 1935 edition of the army's main doctrine publication, *Field Service Regulations*. Unfortunately, this document confused the lessons of the First World War with the potential for the tank in the future, and, in the words of the eminent historian David French, 'FSR 1935 codified a bifurcation in British armoured doctrine and unintentionally impeded combined-arms cooperation. It was to bedevil armoured operations for much of the war.'[3]

The first Matilda – the A11

Even as it was becoming clear that the A10 was failing, another I-Tank had already been conceived of. This was the Infantry Tank Mark I, later named as Matilda,[4] and later still as Matilda I (once the Matilda II had been produced).[5] This tank was ordered at the very start of the rearmament period, when it was still hoped that peace in Europe could be maintained, but a little more money was made available for the army to partially modernise – but not enough to really go to town. Conscious of this, Carden made a proposal in October 1935 to develop a new two-man I-Tank for around £15,000 in development costs, and from this he thought that he could build service tanks for about £5,000 per unit. This tank clearly fell into the alternative school of thought for I-Tanks: a small, cheap and inconspicuous machine. Carden knew that this would be attractive to many as it would be affordable – surely it was better to have large numbers of half-decent tanks than none at all? His handwritten proposal, first made in Chertsey, the location of the Mechanisation Experimentation Establishment (MEE), in mid-October, indicated that the tank could be delivered inside six months ('certain'), would have a small cast turret, a top speed of 5–8mph, use no wireless or lookouts (meaning vision devices or cupola) and be armed with a single .303in MG. The maximum armour at the front would be an incredible 60mm, and this would render the tank all but invulnerable to the anti-tank (A/T) guns of the day – as long as it

RIGHT Sir John Carden's notes on what would become the A11 infantry tank, written in October 1935. It was intended to be simple, affordable (meaning cheap to make it attractive) and based on existing components wherever possible.

BELOW LEFT Carden's sketch of his A11 proposal, which he prepared before his meeting with the WO, shows the theory of the tank crossing a trench . . . *(TM10511-003)*

BELOW . . . which can be compared with the reality, as one appears to come to grief. Crossing trenches remained an obsession with many of the military, and this led to modifications being made to the A11's successor, the A12 Matilda II. *(TM6427B3)*

was hit there, and not in the less well-armoured places which were as thin as 10mm and only designed to withstand a rifle bullet.

Clearly Carden's view that development costs could be kept so low and the tank made within such a short timeframe relied upon using existing technologies, in effect by taking parts already produced by Vickers or readily available from other suppliers and throwing them together into a 'new' design. His sketch indicated the use of four double-roadwheel suspension units of the type already developed for light tanks. The contract for one mild steel prototype was issued on 25 January 1936 and the vehicle was given the official designation A11E1. Casting a small cylindrical turret just large enough for one man plus a machine gun was easily done, and the lack of anything resembling a technical feature made the design fast to complete and gave it a degree of reliability, one of its two redeeming features, the other being protection. By fiddling with the 'cheat device' on the Zenith governor fitted to the Ford V8 petrol engine it could be made to travel at almost 11mph, nearly twice the official top speed and more than enough to keep up with a charging infantryman – the tank was only meant to be capable of 7mph on a level road. Carden's proposal was accepted 'with alacrity' by the Director of Mechanisation, Major General Alan Brough, and supported by his deputy, Colonel Studd, an RTR officer. Many thought that Studd should have known better: writing in 1945, Brigadier Edward Custance of 8th Armoured Brigade considered that 'this sort of tank, and indeed the idea of

an AFV without a gun was severely criticised by many thinking tank officers at the time . . . it doesn't pay in the long run [just] to save a few thousand pounds'. Nevertheless, the prototype was ordered.[6]

The A11E1 prototype was ready for trials at the MEE by that September, indicating not only Vickers' ability to turn work around quickly, but also the reliance on using existing parts wherever possible. The front of the hull featured an innovative pointed nose, shaped not so much for ballistic advantage as to keep unnecessary weight down in order to allow the maximum thickness of armour to be carried. The nose was shaped to encompass (just) the legs of the seated driver. Following the trials only a few modifications were deemed essential: redesigning the turret, replacing the unnecessary toothed front idler with a plain wheel, moving the suspension and tracks further outboard of the hull, removing the rubber tyres from the rearmost roadwheels and providing a periscope for each crewman. The track pins caused many problems as they

ABOVE The prototype A11, with the original toothed front idler, low-mounted rear sprocket and early design of turret.

LEFT The simplicity, even naivety, of the design is apparent, being nothing more than a simple armoured structure just large enough to encase two men, the engine and the gearbox. *(TM1764A1)*

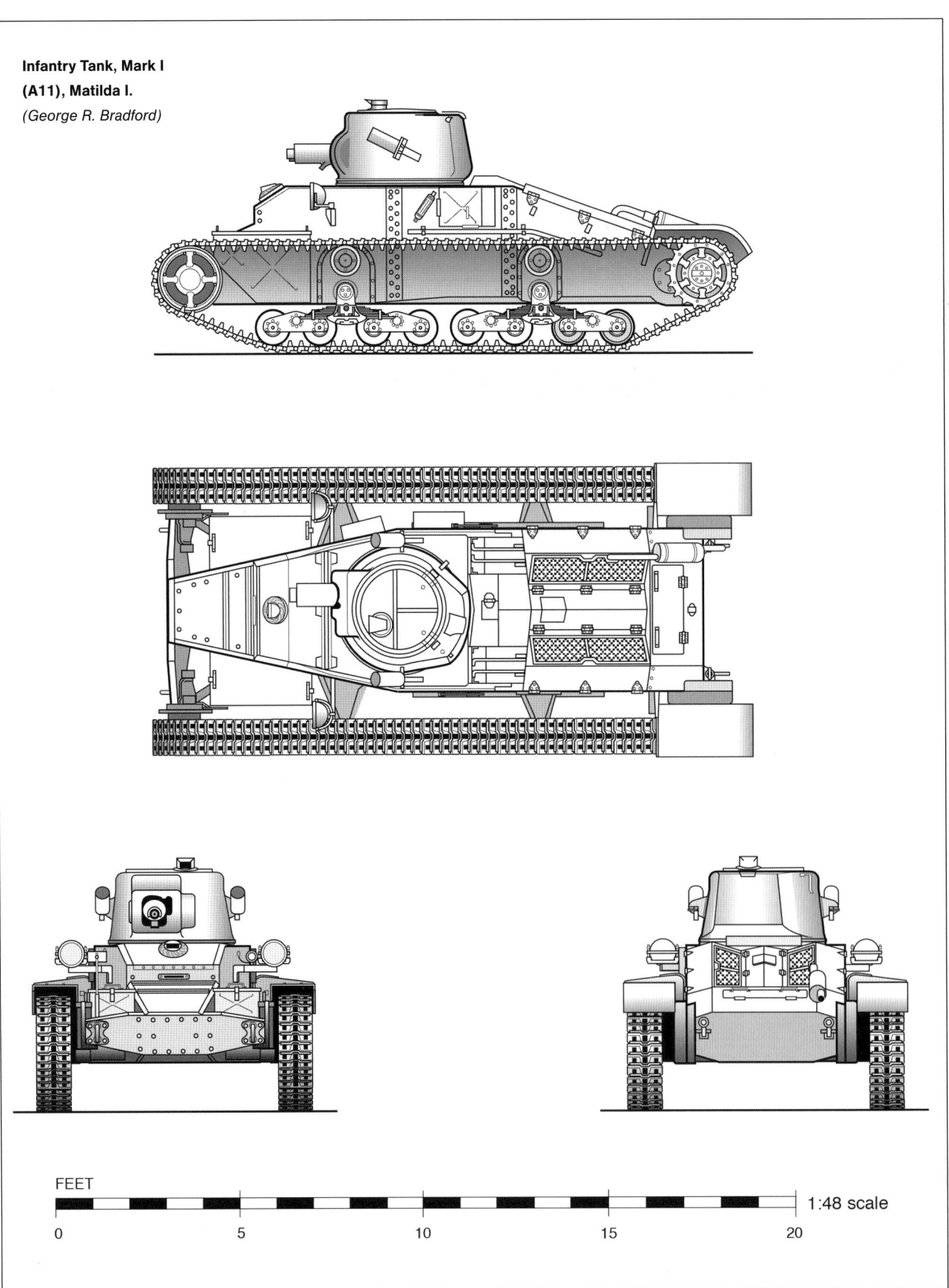

Infantry Tank, Mark I (A11), Matilda I.
(George R. Bradford)

ABOVE **The prototype, having been modified following trials, with the plain idler and amended suspension which increased the ground clearance. Tools and lights have also been added.** *(TM0148A4)*

kept breaking; after six months of trials the fault was traced to the design of the suspension. Lowering the rear suspension unit on each side had the effect of raising the rear sprocket by 5in, which in turn increased the ground clearance from 9½in to 15in and solved the track pin problem. Stowage boxes and lashings were also added internally and externally.

Production can best be described as leisurely; the specification for what the production version should look like was issued on 2 April 1937 following only about six months of MEE trials. However, for an unknown reason there was then a delay of a year before an initial batch of 60 were finally ordered over a year later in April 1938; these were completed by April 1939. Another 60 were then ordered the following month and completed in February 1940 and a final batch

Type	Military registrations	Civil registrations	Quantity	Remarks
A11E1 Prototype	T1724	CMM880	1	MEE trials commenced in September 1936.
A11 Initial Model (high headlamps)	T3433–3492	HMH788–847	60	Morris-type radiator used. Simple driver's vision slit. Contract T4319 29 April 1938. Built between August 1938 and April 1939. Majority lost in France 1940.
A11 Second Model (low headlamps)	T5551–5610	RMY905–964	60	Ford-type radiator used. Flap-type driver's vision device. Contract T5429. Majority lost in France 1940.
A11 Second Model (low headlamps)	T8101–8119	PMX458–476	19	Ford-type radiator used. Flap-type driver's vision device. Contract T6458 January 1939. Contract completed 2 August 1940. Majority remained in UK.

LEFT A11E1, showing off the distinctive pointed nose which, with modifications, would become a feature of the A12, although in cast rather than riveted form.

ABOVE The vehicle identification plate, which all tanks were fitted with either internally or externally. T8106 was not sent to France, and is one of the three surviving A11s all of which are part of the collection at Bovington Tank Museum.

BELOW No 4RTC (later 4RTR) were the first unit to receive A11 tanks at their base in Catterick, where their appearance greatly interested the German military attaché who repeatedly tried to get close to the vehicles.

of 19 (a strange number, presumably based upon a staff officer's military arithmetic to meet a specific organisational need) ordered in January 1939 with production being completed in early August 1940.

In August 1938 4RTC in Catterick reported that one of the German Army attachés was showing a great deal of interest in the first A11 delivered to the unit whenever it was driven out of camp. On one occasion the CO had to 'shoo him away' when he managed to get within 15 yards of the tank. Following this it was decided to keep the vehicles inside the barracks until the German's attention was diverted elsewhere. By 1 February 1939 a total of 37 tanks had been delivered: 1 to MEE, 6 to the AFV schools at Bovington and Lulworth, 20 to 4RTC, 6 to 7RTC and four to 8RTC. (The latter two battalions had been reconstituted in 1937 and 1938 respectively and joined 4RTC in forming the 1st Army Tank Brigade. On 4 April 1939 the RAC was formed and all RTC units henceforth became known as battalions of the Royal Tank Regiment, RTR.[7]) With the war in its second month, by 31 October 1939, 84 A11s had come off the production line. Some 97, representing 70% of the total built, were to be lost in action within nine months of the war starting.

ABOVE No 4RTR on their way to France in 1939; they were to spend an uncomfortable winter exercising for the anticipated German onslaught.

RIGHT Another image of the same journey. The troops are wearing the pre-war service dress, which preceded the much more practical battledress uniform.

The A11 described

As mentioned, the A11 was designed to be cheap, simple, quick to build and wherever possible, to use tried-and-tested components already in production for other Vickers tanks. Therefore, the suspension was taken from the artillery tractor Dragon Medium Mk IV (itself derived from the commercial V-A design known as the Vickers 6-Ton Tank), the biggest difference being that the two bogie units each side were mounted on to brackets rather than a through-hull axle. Each suspension unit comprised nine leaf springs. Funnily enough, one of the reasons that the British Army did not much like the 6-Ton when it tested it was because of concerns over the suitability of the suspension – this seems to have been (conveniently) forgotten when it was necessary to build the tank rapidly from existing components! The steering system came from the Light Mk VI series with the bevel box from the earlier Light II/III. The engine and gearbox were commercial Ford units.

The tank was of riveted construction, the armour thickness meaning that rigidity was achieved without needing a frame to bolt the armour on to, saving a lot of weight. Frontally

BELOW The rear engine deck of an A11, providing a peek at the commercial Ford V8 engine. *(TM3469E2)*

35

THE INFANTRY TANK CONCEPT AND THE A11

the tank used 65mm of armour, an incredible amount for such a small tank, and even on the sides 60mm was employed, twice that of the A10's – or indeed the latest German Panzer III's – frontal armour. IT80B machinable armour plate was used for the flat plates, with IT90B armour used for the cast turret. Despite being very small the turret had a hydraulic-powered traverse with emergency hand traverse, the gun being 'stabilised' in elevation by the commander using the shoulder pad on the MG mounting No 13 to allow shooting on the move. A single periscope was mounted in the roof for use when closed down, and a sighting telescope was fitted to the gun mounting, though using it for shooting on the move must have been difficult as a result of vibrations. Much of the limited turret space was taken up by the cooling system for the Vickers MG, whose breech accounted for another substantial chunk. A water reservoir and pump were mounted in the turret rear, with the piping going to the gun running along the left-hand turret wall, and the return pipe from the gun jacket back to the reservoir routed along the right-hand side.

Although most of the tanks used the .303in MG, some tanks were equipped with the larger-calibre .50in version of the Vickers, intended to be an anti-tank version of the proven MMG – this at a time when most tanks would only carry a maximum of about 12–14mm of armour. At one point during the early design phase the intention had been to mount the new BESA 7.92mm MG in the turret, but concerns were raised about the vulnerability of the external mounting to the anticipated amount of enemy fire that the tank would attract, and so the old faithful Vickers MG was specified instead, in the Mk VII configuration fitted with a conventional pistol grip and with an external armoured jacket. The .50in Vickers Mk II version was preferred by the army as it clearly had more 'punch', but it was feared that using this on all tanks would slow down production and so only some of the tanks mounted the larger-calibre weapon. Section officers were given the larger weapon, with the smaller gun used on the other two section vehicles. This led to another problem: although the .50in had more penetrative power, unlike the .303in version it was prone to endless stoppages in action, giving the poor section officer/troop leader even more to do. Captain Anthony Austin of 4RTR remembered that it was common for the officer to have to strip the gun down in action, handing the problem component, generally the feed block, to the driver for him to sort out as best he could – as well as driving the tank. Another feed block was fitted, and often as soon as the driver had fixed the initial one, the second one would fail, meaning that the whole procedure had to be repeated, leaving belts of ammunition strewn all over the fighting compartment. For local protection two 4in smoke grenade dischargers were fitted externally, one either side of the turret, with a cable firing mechanism which culminated in a trigger (akin to a bicycle brake lever, fitted with a safety pin and chain) in the left side of the turret.

Ergonomically the A11 was a nightmare, due largely to the need to keep size and weight down. Space inside was at a premium, particularly for the commander, who had to cram himself into an already small turret that, among other things, mounted the bulky machine gun, ready ammunition, traverse gear, MG cooling reservoir and pipes, MG tools and spares, the speaking tube mouthpiece, spare prisms for the periscope and smoke bombs. Although the driver had a little more room, the inside of the fighting compartment was filled with a No 11 wireless (radio) set[8] and power supply unit, a 6V radio battery, 14 boxes of MG ammunition, signal flags, rations, a 1-gallon water container and two water bottles, a first-aid box, spare triplex blocks, two fire extinguishers and a signal (Very) pistol in a leather holster plus cartridges. In order to tune the radio, the driver had to

BELOW HMH788 was the first ever service A11, being sent to MEE as a reference and trials vehicle. One can see how in certain positions the turret MG could prevent the driver from escaping via the front hatch. *(TM3469E1)*

collapse the backrest of his seat and lie on the floor, trying to avoid being kicked senseless by the ammunition boots of his commander in the process. If the electrical system failed, the driver had to start the engine using the starting handle from inside the tank, as it engaged through an aperture in the internal bulkhead. Communication from the commander to the driver was by means of a voice tube which the commander spoke into, the driver listening using headsets. Only the commander could listen and speak on the radio net. One officer commander later recorded the battalion's disappointment at the slow speed of the tank compared to the mediums that they were used to, although the thick armour was favourably commented on as it gave the crews greater confidence.

The specification called for the tank to receive one undercoat of Red Oxide paint (or 'any alternative approved by the War Office') and then two coats of KR5413 Khaki Green No 3. Internally the tank was painted with two coats of aluminium paint. (The same specification was later used on Matilda II, although the internal specification was subsequently changed to white because of shortages of aluminium.) Although not officially designated by the use of different marks, two distinct models of the A11 were built. The first batch of 60 was distinguishable by having its headlamps mounted high on the hull sides, while on the second batch the basic design was altered to allow a Fowler mine plough to be fitted, as well as using a different design of radiator. As early as January 1937 it had been realised that anti-tank mines were beginning to proliferate, and so two Fowler-designed devices were trialled, a plough and a roller. The latter was chosen for service and this meant moving the headlamps further forward and lower; the stowage arrangements and bins were also modified to suit the use of the Fowler device. Of course, one of the biggest failings of the design was that there were only two men to do everything between them, with the commander being totally overloaded. This went against all the doctrine that had been devised during the experiments of the 1920s. In other ways, the tank was surprisingly good, including in the field of reliability, where the policy of using known components and simplicity paid dividends.

ABOVE Anti-tank mines were developed between the wars, and much thought was given to how the threat could be dealt with. In 1937 MEE had developed the Fowler plough, which in 1939 was fitted to their A11. The frame in use was pivoted forward by a chain drive coming off the rear driveshaft to rest on the rollers, with five Coulter blades in an arrowhead shape which would lift mines and push them out and away from the tracks. *(TM2126D5)*

Specification	
Weight	11 tons (laden, with crew and armament)
Length	16ft 3in
Width	7ft 8in
Height	6ft 6½in
Armour	65mm front, 60mm sides
Armament	1 × Vickers .303in Mk VII MG (.50in Mk II in some tanks); 2 × 4in smoke bomb throwers
Engine	Ford Model 79F-6000BS 8-cylinder V-90° 3.62 litre (220cu in)
Power	70bhp @ 2,820rpm
Carburettor	Zenith 42VEIS downdraught
Governor	Zenith B3W with 'cheat' device
Lubrication	Forced feed wet sump with external oil cooler
Cooling	5 gallons water, 6-blade pulley-driven fan
Fuel	Petrol, 2 × 21-gallon fuel tanks either side of engine
Gearbox	Fordson Type 68-7204 clash 4-speed and reverse
Clutch	Borg & Beck 11in dry plate
Electrical system	6V, 2 × 80/100Ah batteries (one for radio, one for starting and systems)
Air cleaner	Vokes dual panel
Tracks	11½in-wide manganese steel, 115 links
Speed	8mph
Maximum climb	32°
Trench crossing	6ft 6in
Vertical step	2ft 6in
Ground clearance	15in
Range	80 miles (50% road, 50% cross-country)
Power to weight	6.3bhp per ton

AN ACCOUNT OF ARRAS 1940 BY DAVID WILLEY

The Matilda II had a pivotal role to play in the battle south of Arras on 21 May 1940, an attack – badly organised and co-ordinated – that quickly broke down as the British infantry lost contact with the tanks. It ended with the loss of most of the attacking force – only 28 tanks returned from the 88 that set out. Yet the attack at Arras had enormous significance as it almost certainly saved the British Army in France and allowed it to be evacuated from Dunkirk and live to fight another day.

At the commencement of the German attack in the West on 10 May, the BEF moved its armoured formations forward into Belgium along with French formations to create a blocking position along the River Dyle; Belgian neutrality meant that this could not happen until after the Germans had actually violated that neutrality. The Allies' expectation was that the main German attack would come through Belgium as it had in the First World War. In fact, the Germans pushed their Army Group A with its concentration of seven Panzer divisions (of the ten then formed) through the Ardennes Forest but north of the French Maginot Line to sweep west and around the rear of the Allied armies.

The German breakthrough at Sedan, allowing the Panzer divisions to speed ahead, was considered a 'miracle' by Hitler. But Hitler and much of the German High Command were nervous about the Panzer force advancing so rapidly while much of the remaining German Army struggled on foot or on horseback through the Ardennes. Hitler was acutely aware that his army did not match the propaganda images Goebbels so readily promoted; 45% of his soldiers were over 40 years old, and 50% of them had only a few weeks' training. Of his 157 divisions in May 1940 only 16 were fully motorised and, of these, only ten were his elite Panzer divisions. Most of the German Army marched on foot or used horse transport; the German military used 1.4 million horses in the First World War but 2.7 million in the Second. Hitler was also conscious that his enemies had more divisions and more tanks than his own army. The quality of German tanks was still in question as the tank-building programme had been a major struggle for German industry – the German Army had assumed it would only need to be 'ready' for a major war in 1943. The German Panzer IV had an armour thickness of 30mm compared with the 60mm on the French Char B and 78mm on the Matilda II. The firepower of the standard German anti-tank gun, the 37mm Pak 36 (that was also fitted to the Panzer III tank), could only penetrate 64mm of armour at 100m. Hitler had been a soldier during the First World War and remembered the rapid German advance in 1914 that came to grief at the Battle of the Marne. His belief that the German forces might be marching to a similar fate – or into a clever trap laid by the Allies – prompted him to call a halt to the Panzers' advance on 16 May, leading Heinz Guderian, XIX Corps Commander at the time, to resign in frustration (although he was quickly reinstated). When the German advance resumed, the 7th Panzer Division, led by a thrusting and ambitious Erwin Rommel, advanced to the south of the town of Arras heading west, with the ultimate destination of the coast. German forces reached the Channel late on 19 May creating a 200km-long pocket in which the best of the Allied armies were trapped. All it would take now was for the German tank forces to seize the Channel ports and the Allied armies would have no route of escape.

As the German advance continued, the French High Command broke down completely and despite British attempts to encourage a joint attack to 'pinch off' the advancing German columns with a co-ordinated attack from the north and south, little materialised. At Arras, which was a major logistical centre for the BEF, Major General Franklyn was placed in charge of his own 5th (regular) Infantry Division and Major General Giffard Martel's 50th (territorial) Infantry Division, along with the 1st Army Tank Brigade, to create 'Frankforce'. He was tasked to clear German troops from the south of Arras and to achieve this he brought together two infantry battalions from the Durham Light Infantry, 58 Matilda Is, 16 Matilda IIs and 14 Light Mark VIB tanks from 4th and 7th Royal Tank Regiments of the Army Tank Brigade. There were also to be two supporting artillery batteries and some anti-tank guns. The tanks had earlier advanced into Belgium as had been previously planned but after the German breakthrough at Sedan had turned around to travel back. Rail transport was disrupted so they travelled on their own tracks – some not arriving until the night before the planned attack on 21 May. Crews were already worn out and tanks badly required maintenance, but the pressing need for the attack to go in meant there was little time for rest or maintenance, nor indeed preparation for the battle.

The attack would take place with two main columns heading south to attack the advancing 7th Panzer Division in its flank. To the right tanks from the French 3rd Light Mechanised Division were supposed to attack in concert, but liaison was poor, leading to British and French troops firing on each other at the beginning of the attack. On the right (west) column, the tanks and troops had to advance through columns of refugees and had little time to orientate themselves before the official 2.30pm start. They quickly came under shellfire and left bodies of men to garrison the villages of Duisans, Warlus and Berneville. Tanks of 7th RTR reached the Arras–Doullens road, attacking transport and infantry of the 7th Panzer Division. Further on, tanks caused something of a rout in the SS Totenkopf Division. German reports later accused the SS troops of panicking and scattering, but these were likely to have been exaggerated by the German Army who already had their own suspicions and jealousy of this rival arm. On the left (eastern) column, enemy resistance was also quickly encountered, and infantry troops lost contact with the tanks. At Achicourt, six Matilda II tanks overran a line of German anti-tank guns but as the tanks continued to Wancourt, the attack became less cohesive. Tanks ran into a hastily prepared defence line with artillery and 88mm Flak guns which took a dreadful toll in a few minutes. Fighting was costly to both sides and by late afternoon the order was given for the British force to retire. Heavily bombed by Stukas as they returned, only two Matilda II tanks remained operational along with 26 Matilda Is. Both battalion commanders of the Royal Tank Regiments had been killed in the action, yet the attack had a profound influence on the course of the war. During the assault, the German forces were undoubtedly alarmed. A radio message from the 6th Rifle Regiment cried: 'Strong enemy tank attack from Arras. Help, help!' Despite such signs of panic, they quickly were able to deal with the situation. The highly ambitious Rommel had exaggerated the number of tanks he was being attacked with (he reported 'hundreds'), to emphasise his own achievement. This ultimately backfired as it caused Hitler to call Field Marshal Keitel, the Head of the Wehrmacht Headquarters (OKW) at 01.30am on 22 May to discuss 'the crisis at Arras', and he sent Keitel to the front to personally restore order. The Panzers were again to draw a halt, preventing their advance to the channel ports.

Overnight, on 21 May, Britain sent troops across the channel to Boulogne and Calais and reinforced Dunkirk. The Panzers were only ordered to resume their advance at midnight on 22 May, a crucial delay of nearly one day. Boulogne fell on 25 May, Calais on the 26th, but Dunkirk held out until 4 June and over 338,000 troops were evacuated. This meant although it lacked equipment, the bulk of the British Army remained to continue the fight from across the Channel. The 24-hour delay to the Panzers caused by the effects of the Arras attack, and the sterling effort of the Matilda II tanks and their crews, had an enormous impact on the outcome of the 1940 campaign and indeed the subsequent course of the war. The 'what if?' scenarios when looking at history are always problematic, but if the Dunkirk evacuation had been stopped by the earlier arrival of the Panzers on the coast, Churchill would have had the Navy and RAF to defend England, but little else. Without Arras, the British Army may not have been rescued and that would have meant in turn Churchill having to sue for peace.

BELOW T3444, also known as HMH799, takes cover behind a haystack; the small size of the A11 was one of its redeeming features, making it easier to conceal than most tanks.

Arras 1940

In 1939/40 only three battalions of the RTR used the tank in any numbers: 4th Battalion RTR received 48 of the type, followed by 7th Battalion which received 27; both were in the 1st Army Tank Brigade which deployed to France as part of the British Expeditionary Force (BEF). The third unit in the brigade, 8th Battalion, received some A11s but did not deploy overseas in 1940, and was then equipped mainly with A12 tanks. About two dozen of the remaining A11 tanks were sent to the BEF Base Ordnance Depots RAOC in France as replacements for anticipated losses, although most were then captured by the Germans without ever being issued; seven were issued as emergency reinforcements to 3rd Armoured Brigade as late as 7 June. The most famous action involving the A11 was during the Arras counter-attack of 21 May 1940 in which 58 took part, along with just 16 Matilda IIs and 14 light tanks.[9] The performance of the A11 fleet at Arras was not helped by the confusion that had followed the German invasion only ten days previously, as the Tank Brigade was not committed initially and was then forced to endure a 130-mile road march on its own tracks, not something designed to maximise the numbers fit and available for battle, or indeed to rest the crews prior to a fight. Over 100 tanks started the road march but many dropped out on the way.

Aftermath

Reports by two members of 4RTR recalled their memories of the A11 during the action:

I distinctly remember SSM 'Muscle' Armit with [his] .5in gun just ahead of me getting repeated hits on his tank turret . . . crossing a railway line [outside Achicourt] was tricky, fear of jamming tracks, but was safely negotiated . . . my driver was finding me targets quicker than I could myself . . . everyone was firing away briskly and I claimed a motorcycle and sidecar machine-gun outfit . . . I decided to polish off two lorries parked near where an anti-tank gun was placed. Next thing, a flash and a cloud of smoke. This had been an ammo lorry and its demise also stopped the gun . . . I could not see a thing as the corn was higher than the driver's visor ...

BELOW HMH830 was a Vickers-Armstrongs-built A11, which served in France with A Sqn 7RTR, and was known as 'Giggle'. The white squares are the BEF recognition sign.

suddenly the glass in my driver's visor shattered, we found afterwards that a shell had knocked a rivet clean out of the armour plating . . . to our great surprise we found that we had come straight into the flank of a German mechanised column . . . there was a glorious free-for-all. We knocked out quite a lot of their lorries, there were Germans running about all over the place . . . some of them had a go at jumping on our tanks and I remember that I myself had a German who climbed on the outside of my tank and looked in the periscope, then a neighbouring tank very kindly turned his machine gun on me and that removed my passenger. ... It's quite an experience seeing guns getting trained on your tank and wondering if the shell is going to come through. Several of our tanks seemed to be burning, but it was caused by sparks as the bullets passed through the non-armoured tool bins which had petrol stores in them, and it was these which caught alight.

The old A11 performed extremely well in the Battle of Arras in 1940. Its mechanical reliability was extremely good as for ten days we trekked 300 miles on Belgian pavé roads and had very few casualties. My own tank was hit twice by anti-tank gun fire which just bounced off. Another tank was hit fourteen times with no ill results.

The same officer went on to comment that the criticisms he had of the tank were threefold: that it was underpowered, it did not have a 'piece' (gun), and that it was 'a two-man job'. The tank was totally unsuited to the role that it had been used for, which doctrinally should

**ABOVE AND BELOW
Two views of 'Glenlyon', a 7RTR tank that was taken over by the regiment in November 1939 and lost six months later during the Arras counter-attack, where it was serving with C Sqn.** *(TM1764C1)*

RIGHT T5574 was the tank produced immediately before 'Glenlyon' but which was sent to France not with 1st Army Tank Brigade but as a replacement held by No 2 Base Ordnance Depot. It was captured, having probably never seen action, and suffered the ignominy of being used as one end of a German washing line.

BELOW A 4RTR tank being investigated by interested Germans, including Panzer crews in their black uniforms. One wonders what they made of the design.

have involved cruiser tanks, thus exposing the flawed thinking that had developed tanks with capabilities built around very different roles.

All 97 of the A11 fleet that deployed with the BEF were lost in France, leaving only about 30 or so in the UK.[10] The British appear not to have realised the prominent part played by the German 88mm guns in breaking up the Arras attack, and therefore the implications for the future style of armoured warfare and the changed requirements for tanks. Brigadier Pope, the BEF AFV adviser, wrote during the Dunkirk days that: '1st Army Tank Brigade walked through everything it met but mechanical failures have wrecked it.' There was a little more to it than that: during the retreat to the coast, crews were instructed that if the tank broke down and the repair would take more than two hours, the tank was to be destroyed, meaning that some tanks were set on fire in response to something as simple as a broken fan belt. On 28 June 1940 a WO conference examined the performance of the various British tanks used in France, although actual evidence was slim. The A11 was criticised for lack of hitting power, although it was praised for its armour as this caused 'alarm' among the Germans who encountered it. This was not enough to save the tank, and it was ordered that production should cease, which it did when the final tank was completed on 2 August. The remaining 42 tanks were initially used for anti-invasion duties, with 27 still in service with the reconstituted 1st Army Tank Brigade in February 1941. After being removed from front-line service later that year, they continued to be operated for training purposes until at least 1942. Three examples survive in the Bovington Tank Museum, including one used as a hard target. However, the next generation of infantry tank, which was also used but in even smaller numbers during the French campaign, was already in production. It was this tank that would be the one forever associated with the name Matilda. A.J. Smithers summed up the Arras action with these words: 'Matilda I was useless, but Matilda II was a winner.'

ABOVE Three A11 tanks still exist, all at Bovington. One is a runner, another is a static display item, and the third is the shell of a hull and turret which has been used as a hard target and resembles a colander. *(TM4769C3)*

RIGHT The start of the restoration: the turret is lifted from the Tank Museum's A12, better known as the Matilda II. *(TM)*

BELOW One of the three surviving A11s, all to be found at the Bovington Tank Museum, was used as a hard target and was clearly able to resist many of the strikes on its tough hide.

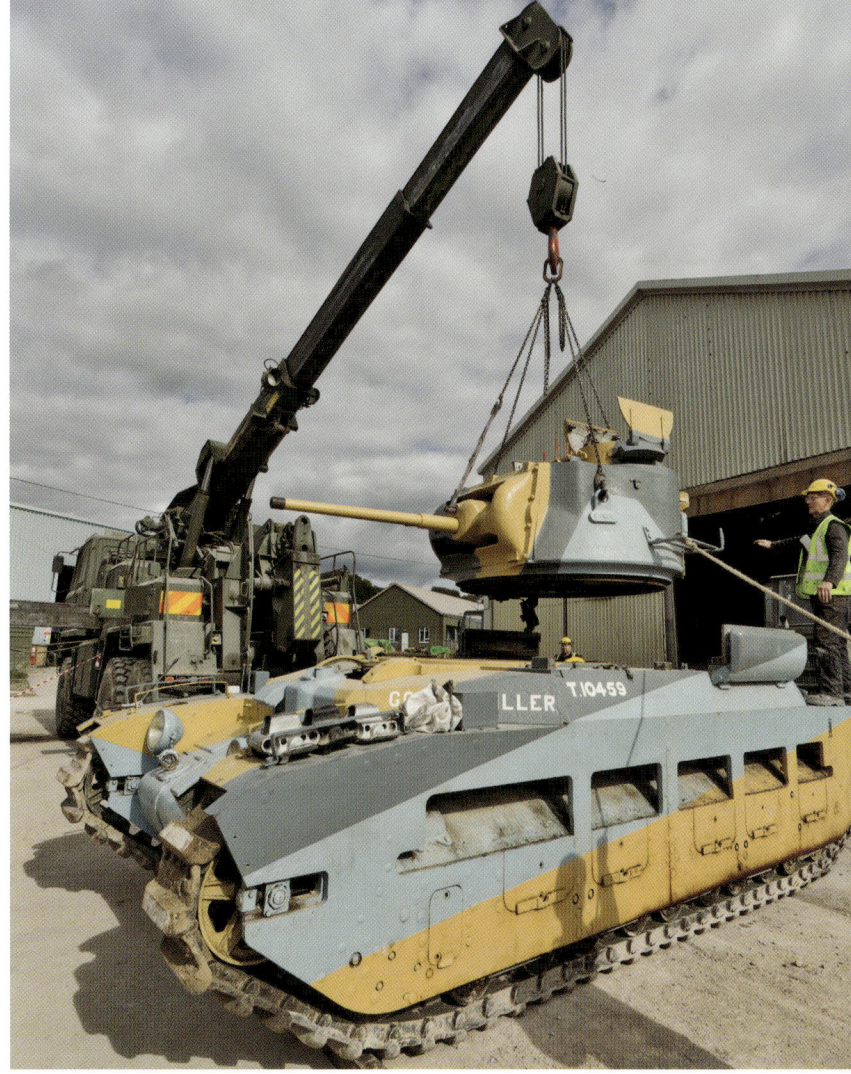

43

THE INFANTRY TANK CONCEPT AND THE A11

— THE VULCAN FOUNDRY LTD. —
TANK A.12.E.1.

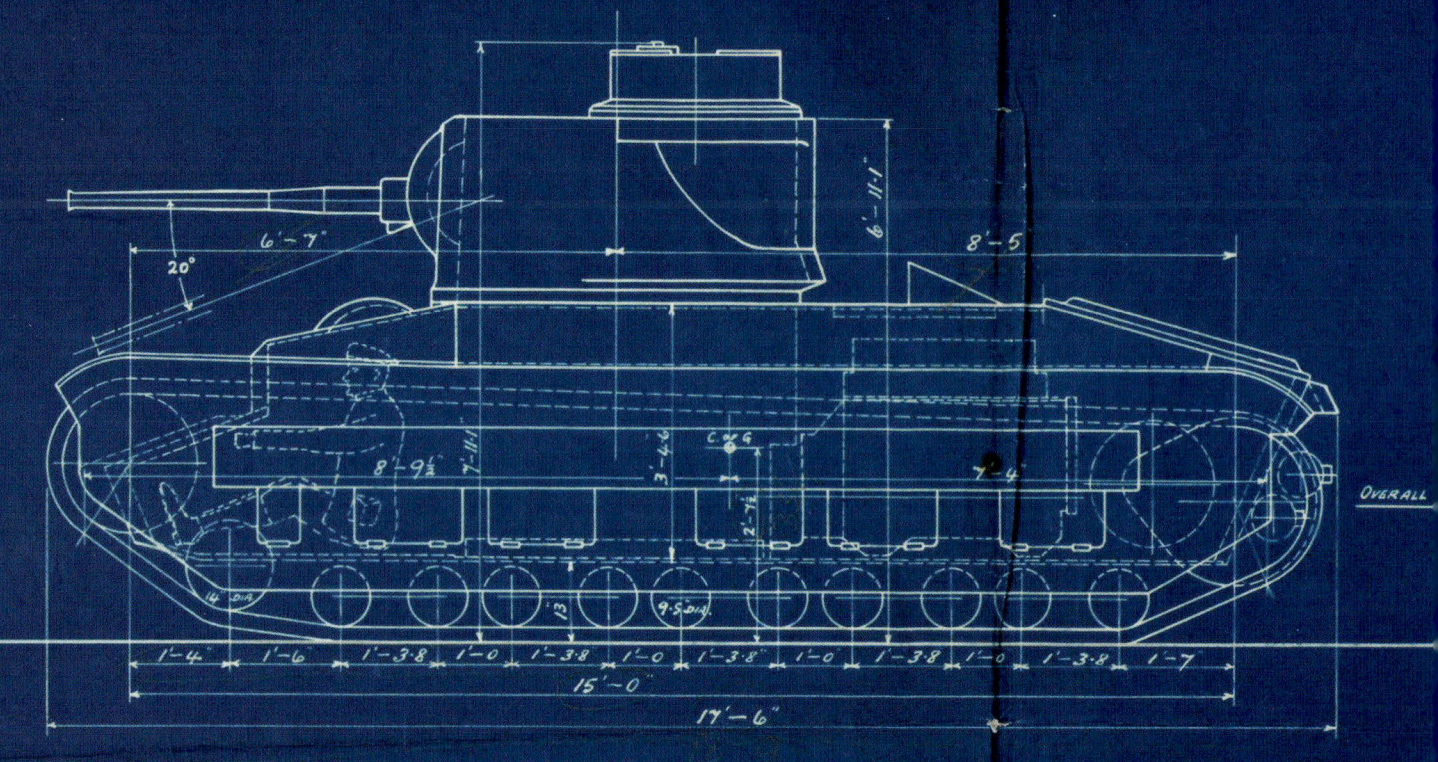

D.O.
2. APRIL

WEIGHT OF TANK 23 TONS
LOADING; SOFT GROUND 12·4 LBS. PER SQ. IN.

LEADING DIMENSIONS.____LENGTH OVERALL_____17'−6"
              WIDTH   OVERALL_____8'−1·5
              HEIGHT   OVERALL_____7'−11·1
              FLOOR OF VEHICLE FROM GROUND_____13"
ENGINES.__ TWO A.E.C. 6 CYLINDER OIL ENGINES EACH
      RATED AT 100 B.H.P. AT 2000 R.P.M.
CROSS DRIVE.____OVERSPEED RATIO ·8 TO 1. {ENGINE... 2000 R.P.M. / SHAFT... 2500 R.P.M.}
GEARBOX.____AIR "SERVO" OPERATED
      FORWARD DRIVE, 6 SPEEDS; RATIOS 2·64 TO 1, 3·56 TO 1, 5 TO 1,
            7·2 TO 1, 12·65 TO 1, 27 TO 1.
      REVERSE DRIVE, 1 SPEED; RATIO 16·6 TO 1.
FINAL DRIVE.____ RATIO; 4·85 TO 1.
STEERING.__TWO RACKHAM TYPE CLUTCHES WITH UNIFIED
      OPERATION OF CLUTCH & BRAKE
TRACK.____14 INCHES WIDE BAR TREAD.
SPRING SUSPENSION.__BELL CRANK COIL SPRING TYPE
TURRET.__THE POWER TRAVERSING TURRET ACCOMMODATES
      3 MEN & IS MOUNTED WITH ONE TWO POUNDER
      GUN & ONE MACHINE GUN ·303.
FUEL TANKS. FOUR TANKS TOTAL CAPACITY 46·5 GALLS.
      WHICH IS SUFFICIENT FOR APPROXIMATELY 50 MILES

COOLING SYSTEM.____FREE AREA AIR INLET_____900 SQ. INS.
            FREE AREA AIR OUTLET_____1020 SQ. INS.
AUXILIARY FITTINGS.
      TWO LUBRICATING OIL TANKS TOTAL CAPACITY 10 GALLS.
      WATER TANK
      ELECTRIC LIGHTING EQUIPMENT
      RADIATOR & FAN
      OIL COOLERS
      FUEL & WATER CIRCULATING PUMPS
      SET OF GAUGES
      WIRELESS RECEIVING SET
      AIR COMPRESSOR
      OIL PUMP FOR TURRET TRAVERSE
      TOOL EQUIPMENT
      AMMUNITION

PERFORMANCE.____MAXIMUM SPEED___15 M.P.H.
          TRENCH CROSSING_____8'−0"
          VERTICAL OBSTACLE_____2'−6"

Chapter Three

Design and development

The design and development of the Matilda II tank was entrusted to a failing locomotive builder called Vulcan Foundry, which, despite many problems, came up with a design that arguably made the tank the best in the world at the start of the war.

OPPOSITE A blueprint of the A12E1, dated 2 April 1937, and helpfully listing the major modifications introduced to the original design.

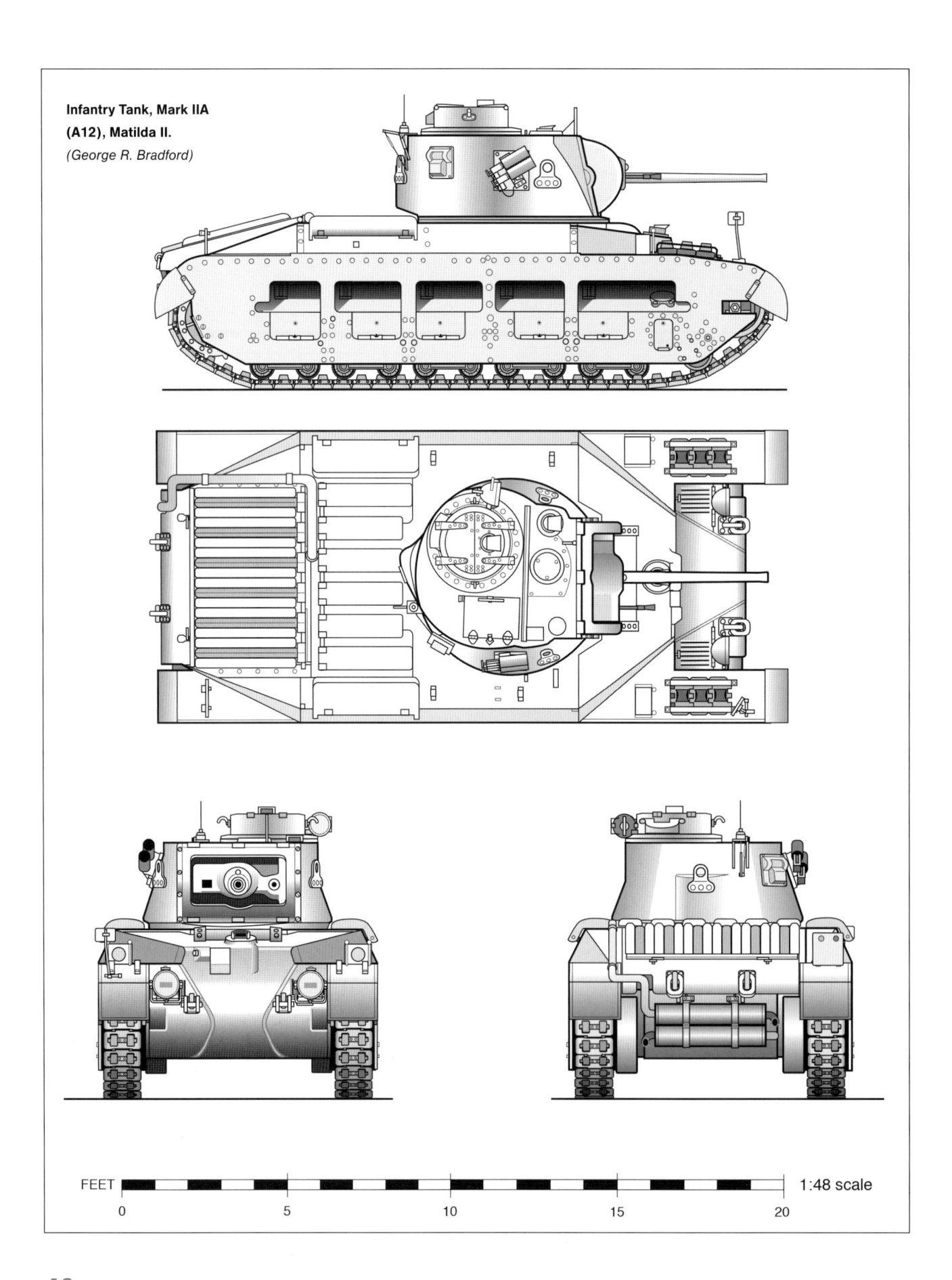

Infantry Tank, Mark IIA (A12), Matilda II.
(George R. Bradford)

FEET 0 5 10 15 20   1:48 scale

A12 Infantry Tank Mk II Matilda II

It will be remembered from Chapter 2 that in the mid-1930s many commentators in the British Army would have preferred a larger infantry tank than the A11, in particular one that was able to mount a gun. After having seen A11 and presumably not being totally impressed, the Master General of the Ordnance (MGO), Sir Hugh Elles of First World War Tank Corps fame – who was someone wedded to the idea of tanks as being simply an adjunct to infantry attacks – directed in September 1936 that a larger version of the A11 be built, capable of carrying a 2pdr gun, with a speed of 15mph, a separate MG turret and it was to use (unusually) a diesel engine in order to reduce a perceived cause of fires on tanks. In fact, wartime experience was later to prove that ammunition was the greatest culprit. In November, even as the specification was being refined, a trench-crossing ability of 8ft was called for (many still thought of First World War conditions when defining characteristics) as well as the ability to climb over a 3ft vertical obstacle. These demands meant that a much longer hull was needed, and thus a much larger tank overall.

The initial investigation into what would become the A12 tank started in late 1936, but was handicapped by the realisation that the usual port of call for designing and building tanks, Vickers-Armstrongs, was working at full capacity and therefore the army had to find a new manufacturer, one which would be able to both assist in designing the tank according to their particular capabilities, and then produce it in the quantities required. Not surprisingly, as rearmament was rapidly gathering pace, the choice fell to a company that was available, rather than one that was particularly suited to the task; most if not all of the best engineering companies were fully occupied in building items for the Royal Navy and RAF, whose rearmament was already well under way. The company with the spare capacity was Vulcan Foundry, located in the small town of Newton-le-Willows near Warrington, between Manchester and Liverpool. Vulcan was given the task in November 1936, having just been given a small 'educational' tank-building order to allow them to get used to the new requirements.[1]

Vulcan were first officially contacted with a view to assisting in designing and producing a new design of larger tank on 22 October 1936, with members of the Mechanisation Board visiting Newton-Le-Willows on 3 November. It was agreed at this meeting that Vulcan would prepare general arrangement (GA) drawings, followed by a wooden mock-up, and then, if satisfactory, they would make a number of pilot models from mild steel. In order to assist, reduce risk and to speed the process up, Vulcan were given the GA drawings of a number of existing medium tank designs, as well as a complete Medium II tank fitted with the so-called Japanese suspension (see p. 95), along with the suspension

ABOVE A Vulcan Foundry sketch showing the tank that would become famous as the Matilda.

BELOW A lack of skilled draughtsmen at Vulcan Foundry held up progress in the early stages of the design of the A12. It was not until September 1937 that eight draughtsmen were employed on the work.

drawings. Other sample components were also provided, including steering clutches, final drives and sections of track.

Having studied these examples, on 21 December, Vulcan started work and adapted the designs of the samples to meet the 'severe demands' of the new tank, meaning that many existing components had to be upscaled for the larger Matilda. On 5 February 1937 Vulcan delivered a ⅛-scale model to the Board, who examined it and then listed the modifications they required. To assist them, Colonel Hudson and his team at ROF Woolwich constructed a full-scale wooden mock-up of the front part of the hull which was sent to Vulcan on 1 April 1937; it was probably this model that defined the distinctive nose design of the Matilda. The Director of Mechanisation inspected a full-size mock-up of the vehicle (possibly only the hull) on 5 April, before Elles, the MGO, saw it 11 days later. There was general approval, and the decision was then confirmed on 16 April to build two tanks (these were not prototypes as such, but pilot models, implying the need for a rapid move into production vehicles) to the same basic design, with a cast turret being used. It was also at this point that the armament of 2pdr plus Vickers MG was confirmed, and the requirement for an MG turret in the hull finally removed. The manufacture of the two pilots, designated A12E1 and E2, was approved on 25 May 1937 and a contract was placed with Vulcan. A blueprint showing the A12E1 and dated 2 April 1937 listed the main modifications to the original design made on the 18th of the month, as follows:

- The engine lengthened
- Three belts instead of two used for the radiator fan drive
- The idler wheel diameter reduced from 21¾in to 17¾in, and the hub for the idler lowered by 2in
- The hull lengthened to allow for the longer engines
- The turret and driver's compartment moved forward
- The steering clutch brake bands widened by ¾in each, increasing the overall width to 8ft 3in
- 'The nose of machine to be of steel casting' – this comment indicates that the original design may have intended to use flat plates.

Clearly, designing any tank from scratch would be beyond the abilities of most firms, whatever their engineering expertise, and it must be emphasised that it was only with significant assistance from the Mechanisation Board that the tank was designed and produced; members of the Board were frequent visitors to Vulcan, although as time went by, Vulcan were expected to take more of a lead role. Developing the design was therefore increasingly conducted by the company, who initially were handicapped by only being able to find two skilled draughtsmen to produce the many detailed blueprints required, although by September 1937 they were able to increase this to eight. Another problem faced by Vulcan was the difficulty in getting components and parts from a range of subcontractors; it was noted that Vulcan lacked the 'clout' of bigger companies like Morris to put pressure on to difficult suppliers. The Mechanisation Board were also concerned that Vulcan, whose managing director was on sick leave, were not being entirely open and honest about the many problems they were encountering. Eventually the Director General of Munitions Production got involved, which appears to have eased the situation.

RIGHT The front cover of a Vulcan Foundry-produced instructional handbook dated 1939; the reference to AEC engines confirms that the introduction of the better Leyland engines was already under way.

As has been noted, the new design necessarily utilised a number of features from the experimental medium tanks that had been trialled previously – and in the case of the A7E3, had just appeared and was still undergoing formal evaluation. This tank provided many systems which were to appear, albeit in modified form, on the A12. The design for the tracks was taken from the Medium III, and the running gear and protective side armour were a natural follow-on from the medium tank development work of the previous 15 years or so. The use of mud chutes enclosed in armour plating to protect the suspension was insisted upon, and this gave the side profile of the Matilda a very distinctive look.[2] The bogies were of a bell crank[3] and coil spring design, one of the many suspension systems that had previously undergone trial-and-error development by Vickers. The mantlet was evolved from the new design used on the A7E3, and offered significant advantages over previous types, including a much wider spacing for the trunnions which allowed for better control in elevation/depression, as well as protecting the crew from bullet splash. The centrally placed driver's position meant that an MG turret could not be fitted to the hull front, which was a blessing as there was no way that a second crewman could have been sensibly located in the space available. The same lesson was later to be missed on the Nuffield-designed Crusader Mk I, which crammed an MG turret and crewman into the front hull to no good effect.

A major problem, as always with large tanks, was finding a suitable engine. A 'new type' of 6.7-litre AEC bus engine was selected, but in order to deliver the amount of power required two had to be used in parallel. A Wilson-type pre-select transmission system was also specified and in the words of an official report 'the rest of the tank was designed around it'. It was made by the firm Self-Changing Gears Ltd. The other systems were in effect sub-contracted out to various persons and agencies: a certain Captain Payne designed the cooling system, the Superintendent of Tank Design was responsible for the turret and the Mechanisation Board looked after the main design of the suspension and hull. At an early point during the detailed design work it was suggested that Matilda might use a fluid flywheel in place of a conventional clutch, with an automatic gearbox, but this idea was discarded 'due to production urgency'. Another idea for a fully cast hull was also not proceeded with for the same reason.

The armour thicknesses required for this new, larger I-Tank went beyond the experience of the tank designers who were used to much thinner plate, and so advice from the Admiralty was sought. It was the specific difficulties experienced in joining the very thick plates at the front of the hull that caused the Mechanisation Board to propose using a large cast nose – a new technique that had to be developed rapidly. This paid dividends not only for the Matilda but also on other tanks later in the war, including the Matilda's successor, the Churchill. The major steel company Hadfields Ltd of Sheffield supplied much of the plate and cast armour used on Matildas and also lent their expertise to Vulcan; it is probable that the cast armour sections for Matildas, including the turret shells, were made there and transported to the six firms that were eventually to build the tanks for assembly.

Despite all these problems, the two pilots, referred at that stage by some as 'Matilda Senior', were designed and built (from mild steel) in exactly one year, and began their trials as soon as they were completed in April 1938. As was the custom in those days, a lot of the tank was built first by hand using sketches

ABOVE A Matilda being painted ready for Russian service; the mud chutes gave the tank a distinctive but somehow antiquated appearance.

	A12E1 (original)	A12E1 (modified)	A12E2
Length	17ft 6in	18ft 3in	18ft 9in
Width	8ft 1½in	8ft 5in	8ft 3in
Height	7ft 11in	7ft 9in	7ft 11in
Ground clearance	13in	12in	13in
Weight	Not known	23.15 tons	25 tons
Engine	2 × AEC Diesel @ 100bhp each Total 200bhp	2 × AEC Diesel @ 82bhp each Total 164bhp	2 × AEC Diesel @ 94.1bhp each Total 188.2bhp
Gearbox	Wilson self-changing epicyclic; 5 forward speeds (plus emergency low) and 1 reverse		
Power-to-weight ratio	Not known	7bhp per ton	7.53bhp per ton

with close oversight by the design team, and only then were detailed drawings produced – reverse engineered in the modern parlance – from the pilot. Despite the potential for disaster the tank in its A12E2 guise turned out to be a sound design and required remarkably little in the way of modification before it was put into production. The engine output was increased from the original 82bhp each on the A12E1 to 94.1bhp on the A12E2, and then for an unknown reason was slightly reduced on the service tanks to 87bhp each, along with new fuel injection pumps, fuel filters and heater plugs. The design of the mud chutes and side plates was also amended to reduce the number of apertures and modify the access hatches required to allow certain components to be reached for servicing.

The first contract for the new tank in its service form (later to be labelled as the Mk I) was awarded to Vulcan on 11 June 1938, with production starting on 29 September. Some 13 months after the first contract was placed, on 11 July 1939, a report noted that by then the number of A12s *on order* totalled 671. But these were paper tanks only; the reality was that deliveries of actual tanks by 31 October 1939 totalled only 6 A12s, alongside the 84 A11s in service.

As an infantry support tank, at first glance the choice of weapons for the Matilda appears to be somewhat strange. The tank was armed with the 40mm 2pdr Mk IX or X gun, an excellent weapon which was the best anti-tank gun in the world until late 1940; its use – rather than a larger general-purpose gun designed for firing HE – was specified because one of the roles of I-Tanks was to protect the infantry from counter-attacks made by enemy tanks. But because it was incapable of firing effective HE ammunition (made in limited numbers but its explosive content was very small and in any case it was not issued to tank units) it was therefore not capable of providing the necessary fire support to infantry attacking a well-dug-in enemy. Some tanks were designated as CS (close-support) tanks, where the 2pdr was replaced with the 3in howitzer Mk 1 or 1A specifically designed to fit in the same mounting. This did in theory give a very useful HE capability, although two-thirds of the bomb load carried on CS tanks was smoke ammunition, as the ability to produce a local smokescreen rapidly without relying on the artillery featured prominently in British tactical doctrine; such guns were only found in squadron headquarters tanks, not within the 'sabre' troops.

The tank in its Mk 1 guise was also provided with a water-cooled Vickers co-axial machine gun, and although the authorities would have preferred a second MG to be mounted in the hull front, there was no space in which to fit one. This was because Vulcan had been provided with the ROF Woolwich design for the front of the hull, which was similar to the pointed nose of the much-admired Christie medium tank (and indeed similar to the A11), and this necessitated placing the driver in the centre, which had the benefit of prohibiting placing a second crewman operating as the hull machine gunner alongside him. The turret shell was a conical casting with a front plate bolted on and making up the gun mantlet, and was home to three crewmen – commander,

THIS PAGE Internal views of the Vulcan Foundry Matilda production line. Over 18 tanks are in different stages of construction, with a number of turret castings in the rear awaiting completion. *(TM3859A6)*

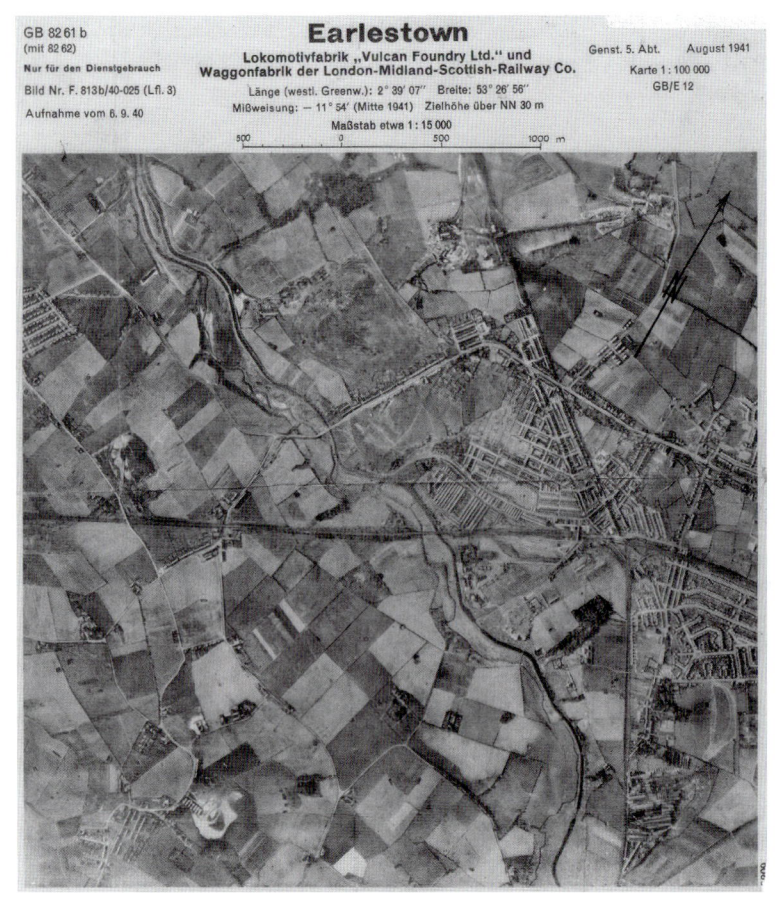

ABOVE **A German target map of August 1941 showing the factories of Vulcan and the London, Midland & Scottish Railway; Vulcan suffered disruption because of air raids but was never seriously damaged.**

BELOW **Airflow through the tank: note how the air was drawn through the toolbox louvres on the hull front, before passing through the fighting compartment into the engine space – this drew large amounts of dust into the tank.**

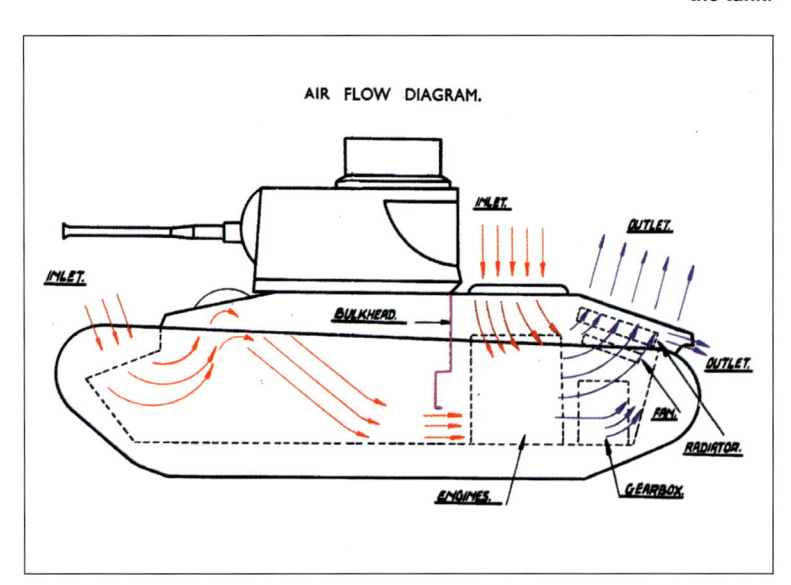

gunner and loader/radio operator. While a three-man turret was a sensible decision in that it shared the tasks between the crew and thus allowed the commander more time to actually control the tank, the space allocated was deliberately minimal[4] and it was a cramped environment to work in for any period of time.[5] It also condemned the tank to obsolescence in the future, as it would prove too small to mount the 6pdr gun. All the tanks were designed to take a bulky No 11 wireless set (later replaced by the smaller and much more efficient No 19), which further reduced the available space in the fighting compartment.

Gunnery trials at Lulworth conducted on the A12E1 in early August 1938 stated that the Matilda provided a good gun platform when moving at low speeds – this tied in nicely with the perceived use of an I-Tank as a slow-moving beast, as well as the RTC doctrine of shooting on the move. However, the 'fighting chamber' (compartment) in its original design was adjudged to be inefficient and impaired the crew. No commander's seat was provided; he simply stood on a metal platform which, it will be recalled, was standard on just about every design of British medium tank in the 1920s and '30s. This meant that a short commander could not use the cupola and an adjustable seat was demanded. The crew positions were described as being 'dangerous', with turret crewmen likely to be struck by the recoiling main gun, and it was found that the driver could easily lean back into the path of the traversing turret. Following an overhaul by Vulcan to rectify these failings, more Lulworth trials followed between May and July 1939. It was then noticed that firing at targets head-on was difficult, caused by the suspension pitching up and down. Another problem was that the cooling fan systems dragged dust inside the tank, so that within ten minutes the crew and equipment were all coated in grime. It was recorded that in Europe this was a nuisance, whereas 'in Egypt this will be unbearable'.

As previously noted, in searching for an engine to power the Matilda II (as it would become known) there was no chance of designing a bespoke powerplant, as Vulcan Foundry was really a locomotive builder and had no experience in internal combustion engine design. In order to deliver sufficient power for a tank which would weigh over 25 tons, 14 tons of which were armour, a fairly novel solution was suggested: use two commercially available engines and bolt them together to give a doubled power output. (A similarly complicated and difficult-to-steer solution had been used at the end of the First World War in the Whippet tank.) Initially the engines chosen were AEC diesels – another novelty for an army wedded to petrol – which had been originally designed to be a bus engine with each delivering 95bhp. To avoid the steering difficulties experienced with Whippet, the power outputs passed into a common transverse gear train, from the centre gear of which a propeller shaft transferred the drive rearwards to the transversely mounted Wilson gearbox. (The initial proposal was to use a Scammell dog-change gearbox which had no synchromesh and required a great deal of skill from the driver to make rapid gear changes, and so the idea was quickly discarded.) Compressed-air assistance for changing gear was provided by a Reavell TBC4 compressor, that allowed the driver to exert enough force on a foot pedal to overcome the very strong springs used in the gearbox. Although this twin-engine solution generated just about enough power to drive what was a heavy tank at a maximum speed of about 15mph, some of the maintenance tasks were exceptionally difficult as certain components were almost impossible to reach, and of course there were two engines to service rather than just one. Different engine combinations were used later and these, with armament changes, defined the five main mark designations.

As well as being a complex tank to operate and maintain, Matilda was also a complicated tank to produce. Despite the imminence and then the declaration of war, by October 1939 only six service tanks had been built. Even as the development of the prototype was in progress it was apparent that Vulcan would not be able to single-handedly produce sufficient numbers of the tank quickly enough, and five other firms were brought in to build the tank. These were Ruston & Hornsby, the London, Midland & Scottish Railway, John Fowlers, North British Locomotive Co. and Harland & Wolff. In total, these firms built Matildas as follows:

LEFT Female factory workers finishing off the assembly of a commander's cupola by fitting a Vickers Tank Periscope. This is the later low-type of cupola.

ABOVE The tank identification plate for a Matilda Mk V (note how the brass has been engraved over the original designation which was probably IIA*). T7341 was built by Ruston & Hornsby and later converted to a Canal Defence Light.

Vulcan	610 plus 10 mild steel instructional = 620
North British Locomotive Co.	619
Fowlers	580
London, Midland & Scottish Railway	426
Ruston & Hornsby	395 plus 5 mild steel instructional = 400
Harland & Wolff	275
Total	2,905 plus 15 mild steel instructional = 2,920

LEFT A newly completed Vulcan-built Matilda II, sans armament, being driven through Newton-le-Willows in 1941. Judging by the indifference of the children, having a 28-ton tank driving down their street was a commonplace event.

Because the tank was built around the capacity, expertise, machinery and preferences of Vulcan, it was not suited to mass production and each tank was in effect built by hand – and each one oh-so slowly. Additionally, each manufacturer made slight changes to the design to suit themselves, leading to a number of minor alterations that can be used by an expert to help identify which firm built it, but which were of no concern to anyone at the time. Eventually the Ministry of Supply – probably at some point in 1942 by which time the tank was really showing its age – decided that production of the Matilda II should be halted once 2,900 or thereabouts had been made – one official record summarised the tank as 'clumsy'. A record of cumulative production totals from later in the war show actual deliveries made by certain dates, as follows:

Dec 1941	June 1942	Dec 1942	March 1943	June 1943
1,437	2,217	2,735	2,805	2,805

ABOVE Three nearly completed Matildas destined for Russia. The 2pdr guns and tools have yet to be fitted; this was typical, as the armaments were provided by the Ministry of Supply as 'free issues'.

BELOW The rear of a late Matilda IVCS, complete with auxiliary fuel tank, No 19 radio, later tracks, bottom-hinged access panels and the low cupola. This tank was built by Vulcan in late 1941 or early 1942. The item coiled up on the turret side is the inter-tank starting cable, used to allow a tank to 'slave-start' another with dead batteries.

The fact that apparently no tanks at all were produced during the final three months is recorded without comment or explanation. This is somewhat odd, as it is known that the last one came off the production lines sometime in mid-1943, so the most likely explanation is that the last figure is a simple typo and should read 2,905 and which thus represents the total number built.[6] However, as always, different documents produced by different parts of the Ministry of Supply tend to muddy the waters rather than provide clarity, and one such record notes that the final tank was produced in the week ending 21 August 1943, with a total of eight tanks, all built for Russian use, being completed between 12 June and that date. You do your research and you take your choice! As soon as the Matildas were no longer required, even in a training role, they were broken up and scrapped, as they were worth more as recyclable materials that could

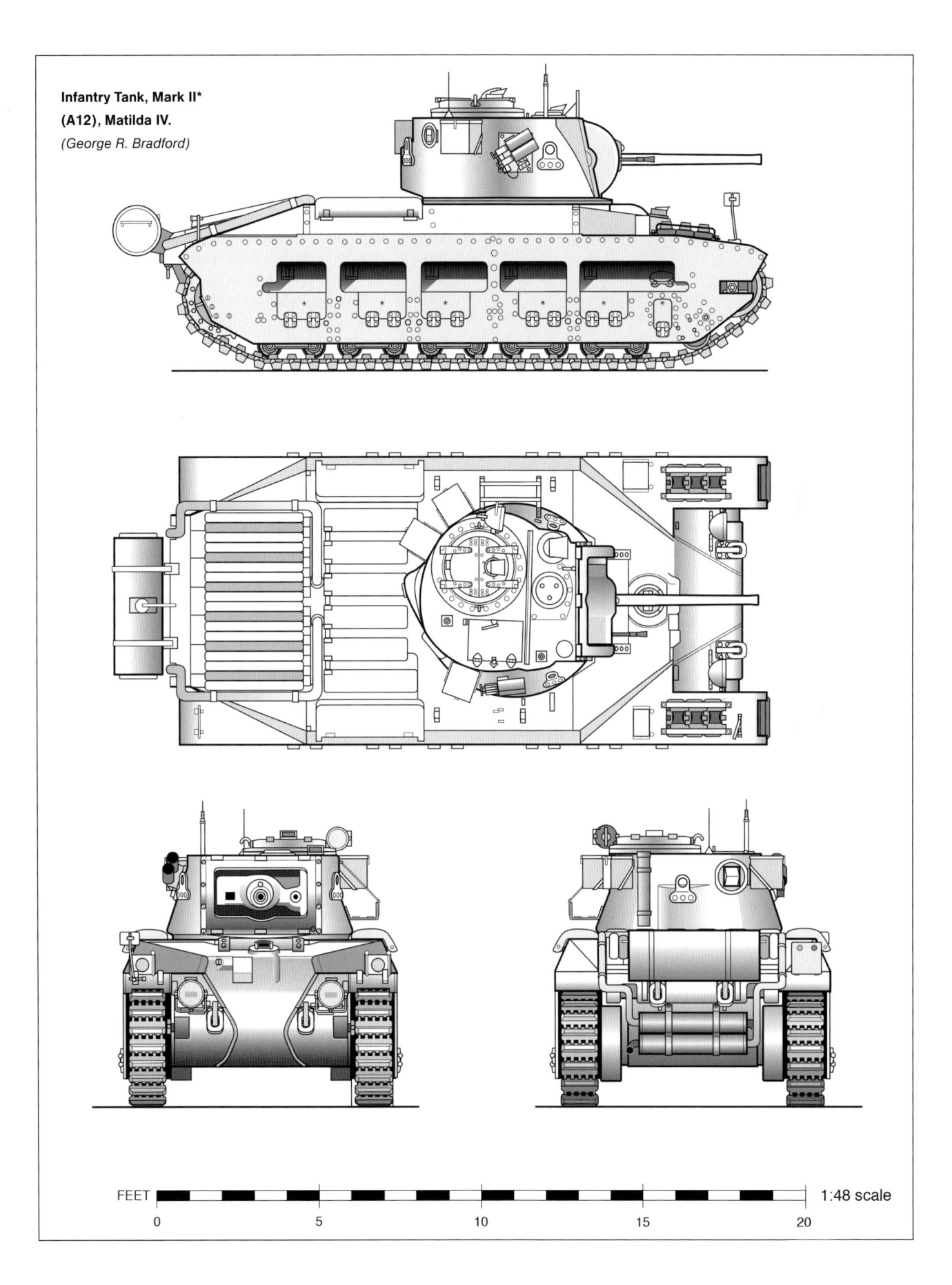

Infantry Tank, Mark II*
(A12), Matilda IV.
(George R. Bradford)

FEET 1:48 scale

LEFT T10159 in Canadian use in the UK, probably in 1941. The Canadians used Matildas as a stop-gap until the Infantry Tank Mk IV Churchill became available, and with which the Dieppe Raid of 1942 was conducted. *(Libraries & Archives Canada)*

be used again in war production; this appears to have started as early as 1943.

Who used the Matilda? Prior to the war starting it was assumed by the WO that many more I-Tanks would be required than cruisers, and so approximately two I-Tanks were ordered to be made for each cruiser. The dramatic armoured manoeuvre conducted by the Germans in France 1940 demonstrated clearly that this assumption was false and so the ratios were reversed, but while changing the priorities of production could be done at the stroke of a pen it took a lot longer for the changes to be implemented in the factories. This led to a situation in which Britain was forming a large number of new armoured brigades and divisions at home but without the cruiser tanks to equip them. The reality was that most of the cruisers produced were being sent straight out to Egypt. And so the Matilda found itself pressed into service as a cruiser tank in some of these UK-based formations, where it would at least allow crew and unit training, even

ABOVE More Canadian Matildas in England, conducting somewhat old-fashioned close manoeuvres using hand signals. Note the different types of track in use. *(Libraries & Archives Canada)*

BELOW T6909 'Greenock', also of 7RTR, complete with the modified suspension. Like so many of her contemporaries, the tank appears to be largely undamaged, so presumably either broke down or ran out of fuel, and was captured before her crew were able to destroy her by fire.

BELOW Another 7RTR tank, this time one of those knocked out during the famous Arras counter-attack. There is no obvious damage to the armour, so she may have been abandoned after losing her track. Her name is possibly 'Golden Miller'. *(Merlin Robinson)*

if its top speed of 15mph hardly matched its new role. As more Valentines became available the Matildas were replaced,[7] but records listing the tanks on the strength of various armoured formations in the UK tell us that some Matildas stubbornly remained in the order of battle within armoured divisions (in the close-support role) as late as September 1942.

The Matilda was of course mainly used in ATBs, the organisations designed around the infantry tank concept. From 1941 in the UK Matilda IIs seem to have mainly been operated by the 25th, 31st, 33rd, 34th Army Tank Brigades and the 1st Canadian Army Tank Brigade. On 18 December 1941 there were 284 Matilda IIs in the UK, of which only 131 (46%) were in running order. On 25 March 1943 only 57% of the Matildas in the UK were fit for battle; these figures indicate that the tank was not easy to keep in serviceable condition, although a lack of spare parts may have also played a role. The 34th Army Tank Brigade was the last formation to operate Matilda II in the I-Tank role in the UK, with its last remaining 85 Matilda II Mk IIIs and IVs being replaced (presumably by Churchills) in about November 1942. In late 1942 a table was produced showing the total tank losses (of all types, in British service) from the start of the war until 23 December 1942. For Matilda II, these totalled 241 and were listed as follows:

Mk I	2
Mk II	30
Mk III	186
Mk IIICS	2
Mk IV	10
Mk IVCS	11

If these figures are correct, two interesting points come out of them. Firstly, the majority of the tanks lost in France were Mk II tanks, *eg* those with the BESA MG and the AEC engine, although this is strongly contradicted by most photos from France, which show a lot more than two Mk I tanks with Vickers MGs. Secondly, as no Mk V tanks are noted as being lost, we can assume that there were (on the date of the report at least) few or no Mk V tanks in North Africa.

On 31 December 1942 there were four Matildas listed as being on Malta, and 274 in Australia. Some 285 Matildas had been shipped to the USSR, of which 55 had been lost at sea. As late as December 1943, 283 Matilda IIs were still showing as remaining in some sort of service in the UK, as follows:

21st Army Group	3
Training units	97
Establishments	15
Other units	2
Ordnance depots	166

The same report indicated that at the same time there were 369 Matildas in Australia with another 7 in transit, 33 in New Zealand and 918 in the USSR.

BELOW A view of the tail skid on 'Gamecock', parked behind a German Panzer III. The single exhaust pipe of the AEC-engined Matildas can be seen, as can the bell-push button immediately above it.

BELOW Stowage boxes often replaced the spare track links on the front trackguards, as demonstrated here by this 4th Australian Armoured Brigade CS tank in New Guinea, 1943. *(AWM016100)*

ABOVE The German Army started the war with the 37mm Pak 36 as their standard infantry-operated anti-tank gun, but along with its tank-mounted version, it was unable to defeat the armour of Matilda II.

ABOVE RIGHT A poor-quality photograph of the unfortunate 'Girvan', a 7RTR tank that was used as a target on Nieuwpoort beach in Belgium. The lack of effect by the multiple strikes from their standard 37mm anti-tank gun must have horrified the Germans. Note the tail skid, designed to aid crossing trenches.

RIGHT AND BELOW The ability to withstand punishment was the Matilda's greatest attribute: two images of different mantlets showing multiple gouges, known in the trade as 'scoops'. Hitting the target and seeing no effect must have been very dispiriting for the enemy gunners. *(TM2792C6/D1)*

FAR RIGHT A Caunter-camouflaged 'Gulliver II' of 7RTR at Tobruk in December 1941. Many contemporary photographs of Matilda crews in the Desert campaign are similar to this, with a happy crewman showing off a strike that failed to penetrate. *(TM2792D2)*

Armour performance

With a maximum of 78mm of frontal armour, it is often alleged that only the German 88mm anti-aircraft gun was capable of penetrating the Matilda. This is not quite the whole story, as the 88mm was able to perforate the armour at long ranges, but at closer quarters the standard German 50mm Pak 38 gun could overmatch the frontal armour – though only just. Using the standard PzGr39 ammunition (armour-piercing capped ballistic cap *or* APCBC in British parlance) at 500 yards against vertical plate (0˚), theoretically the gun could penetrate 61–76mm of armour. Therefore, it is reasonable to suppose that at a slightly closer range, a penetration could be achieved if the projectile struck at exactly the right place. However, when using the improved PzGr40 (armour-piercing composite rigid, APCR) ammunition, performance at the same range and angle was enhanced to 77–86mm. Thus, in theory, the 50mm German gun using

ABOVE A 4RTR crewman examines the damage caused to the driver's periscope on his tank – there were three different methods of seeing where he was going, so this would not have been catastrophic.

APCR could defeat the frontal armour of Matilda at up to about 500 yards, but the shot would have to be near-perfect unless the range was much reduced. The introduction of the German Pak 40 75mm gun and the increasing use of the 88mm in the ground role wiped out the advantage that the Matilda's armour had enjoyed and exposed its other flaws and failings, including lack of mobility and firepower.

LEFT For all its thick protection, 78mm of armour was not enough to withstand the German 88mm gun, as this desert Matilda bears witness to. The hit through the right-hand tool locker would probably have disabled the tank due to suspension damage, and the driver would almost certainly have been killed by the shots through the hull front. *(TM2792B4)*

LEFT T10460 was a North British Locomotive-built Mk III, shown here having been hit multiple times along the 1in-thick skirting armour; whether these shots then penetrated the thicker armour behind is not clear. The build-up of mud and sand in the chutes below can also be appreciated. *(TM4868B4)*

MATILDA MARKS – OVERVIEW

Mark	Engine (R/L)	Co-ax	Remarks
A12 Infantry Tank Mk II (Matilda II Mk I)	AEC 183/184 (87bhp)	Vickers .303in	Original service tank
A12 Infantry Tank Mk IIA (Matilda II Mk II)		BESA 7.92mm	Change in MG to BESA
A12 Infantry Tank Mk IIA* (Matilda II Mk III)	Leyland E148/E149 (95bhp) or Leyland E164/E165		No change in designation regardless of which pair of engines fitted. E148/149 used aluminium crankcases; E164/165 used cast iron
A12 Infantry Tank Mk IIA** (Matilda II Mk IV)	Leyland E170/E171 (95bhp)		Rigid engine mounting. Increased fuel capacity
A12 Infantry Tank Mk II (Matilda II Mk V)			As Mk IV but with Westinghouse air servo for gearbox

Chapter Four

Matilda at war

Although only available in limited numbers, the Matilda acquitted itself well in France during 1940. It really made its name during the early battles in North Africa where only the German 88mm could penetrate its frontal armour. It also saw valuable service with the USSR and with Australian forces in the Far East.

OPPOSITE A painting depicting the action in which Foote won his VC. *(TM11085-002)*

MATILDA AT WAR

Into action – France 1940

By May 1940 it was reported that there were 126 I-Tanks serving with the BEF in France, the vast majority of course being the 97 A11 Matilda Is serving with 4RTR and 7RTR or held by ordnance as spares. At the same time there were 53 I-Tanks in the UK, meaning those on the strength of 8RTR, with only 12 in reserve. The A12 saw limited (in time, not in severity) use in France in 1940, with 4RTR (a Matilda I battalion) possibly operating a solitary example for their Commanding Officer, and 7RTR having 24 of them in addition to the 27 A11s.[1] Owing to lack of transport the tanks had to use up a lot of valuable track miles in a series of road moves, eating up precious fuel and spares and tiring out the crews. They acquitted themselves well once in action, taking part in the Arras counter-attack, and their 2pdr guns confirmed their reputation as the finest anti-tank gun of the day. In order to improve their mobility by increasing the ground clearance, tanks serving with the BEF had their suspension units raised by around 6in, but as this caused other problems it was not widely adopted elsewhere. Although all 29 of the BEF Matilda IIs were lost, they had started to gain a justified reputation for being almost impossible to penetrate by the standard German 37mm anti-tank gun, which to a large degree offset the indifferent mechanical reliability that they exhibited.

After the Arras counter-attack described in Chapter 2, the remnants of the infantry tank force were withdrawn to Vimy, where it was engaged in a morning attack on 23 May 1940 by German tanks and infantry, the former losing seven of their numbers to accurate defensive fire from the depleted force. A composite battalion, known as 4/7RTR, was formed later on that day from the remnants of the two regiments, with 18 Matilda Is and only two Matilda IIs left operational, and all of them desperately in need of maintenance, with their tracks in particularly poor state and with very little ammunition. Engaging the enemy again at Givenchy as it moved north towards the Channel, eight tanks were lost and by the time it reached Dunkirk on the 27th, due mainly to breakdowns, only two tanks remained.

By late June 1940 the only substantial numbers of Matildas that were still owned by the British Army were in the hands of 8RTR, the third unit in 1st Army Tank Brigade, which did not deploy to France as they were still receiving their equipment when the German invasion began. As we have heard, a pre-war production policy decision was in place to build I-Tanks at the expense of cruisers. As an invasion of Britain was expected and the heavily armoured Matildas were judged to be better defensive tanks than the lighter cruisers, this policy seemed sensible to continue with for a while – it was also unthinkable to upset production schedules as building tanks of any type was frustratingly slow. This led to many armoured brigades and divisions which should have been equipped with cruisers in 1941 and 1942 having to be equipped with Matilda IIs, but at least they could train on them, and in fact they were also better in reliability terms than many of the early cruisers, particularly the dreadful Covenanter. In the second half of 1940 the newly formed 8th Armoured Division in the UK (consisting of 1st and 21st Army Tank Brigades) was issued with Mk IIA and IIA* Matildas in lieu of the cruisers that an armoured division, with its fast-moving exploitation role, should have been using. Similarly, once 1st Army Tank Brigade (now comprising 8, 42 and 44RTRs) and 21st Army Tank Brigade (12 and 48RTRs) were fully equipped, Mk IIA* tanks were issued to 25th Army Tank Brigade (43, 49 and 51RTRs) and also sent to the North Africa theatre where they were having great success. The Canadian Army Tank Brigade arrived in the UK at the end of June 1941, and comprised the Ontario Regiment, the Three Rivers Regiment and the Calgary Regiment (from 27 March 1941 these were respectively also known as the 11th, 12th and 14th Canadian Army Tank Battalions). Stationed at West Lavington Down on Salisbury Plain, training began in mid-July 1941. Initially 18 Matilda IIAs were issued as training tanks, along with four Churchills, the type that the brigade would eventually be fully equipped with, but the Matildas served a useful purpose in allowing training in infantry support operations to be commenced. Matilda CS tanks were also issued to Valentine-equipped units in order to give them a close-support howitzer in squadron headquarters, as UK Valentines did not mount a CS gun.

Back into action – North Africa

The next place that the Matilda II saw action was in North Africa. After their harrowing experiences in France, the reconstituted 4RTR was sent to Egypt with its new Matilda II tanks in February 1941,[2] with its partners from the BEF, 7RTR, joining in September, also with its complement of new Matilda IIs. When the British Army went on to the offensive by attacking the Italian forces in Libya, the tank rapidly earned the nickname 'Queen of the Battlefield' as its 78mm of frontal armour made it impervious to Italian anti-tank gunners,[3] and the still-excellent 2pdr was easily able to deal with the thinly armoured Italian light and medium tanks. However, with the arrival of the Panzer IIIs and IVs of the Afrika Korps starting in February 1941 the Matilda's days were numbered. The newly introduced German 50mm anti-tank gun was much more likely to penetrate the armour than the Italian guns or the earlier German 37mm, and with the later introduction of the long 75mm and of course the use of the 88mm anti-aircraft gun in the anti-tank role, the advantage bestowed by the Matilda's armour was negated, and in all other respects the tank had passed its use-by date against a first-class enemy. In a similar way to the Matilda I at Arras, it was often used in a quasi-cruiser role, not supporting infantry directly in the way that it was designed for, but operating in a more mobile and free-ranging style, although its slow speed did not really suit that. However, the inability of the design to be upgunned by mounting the 6pdr doomed it to obsolescence. Again, quotations from memoirs of soldiers who fought in the tank during the Desert campaign provide us with interesting insights into the tank, its capabilities and the type of warfare it was used in:

> During this attack he took on a battery of 105mm guns, one of which scored a hit on his cupola, blowing in the episcope, wounding him and killing his gunner. In spite of further track damage, he was able to withdraw to the rally point. ...

The appearance of the Matildas proved decisive, and by 1700 hours all fighting in Bardia had ceased. ... The Australians were delighted with the support they received from 7RTR, and Waltzing Matilda took on a new meaning. ...

Although 7RTR had managed to get 8 tanks as far as Mechili, the battle was now going too fast for them. ... The Italians were learning. As the Matildas reared up over the walls and other obstacles, the artillerymen chose their aiming-points on the vehicles' thin belly plates, and scored seven kills....

The Mark II does not even shake itself when the first shots go ricocheting off its thick hide. ...

The inability to fire an HE round proved fatal. ...

ABOVE No 4RTR crews in the area around Tobruk in 1941; only a few Matilda IIs of 4RTR and 7RTR were available to help defend the port, where the thick armour was more important than the lack of mobility, and where they were less likely to fall prey to the German 88mm.

LEFT Soldiers can be very sentimental and superstitious; this crew have adopted a panda as their lucky charm.

RIGHT A hull-down Matilda, probably outside Tobruk where the battles were less about manoeuvre and more about defence in depth. The tank would not fight from this position, but emerge when necessary to ward off enemy penetrations. *(TM10104-001)*

BELOW T6875 of 2 Troop A Sqn 4RTR. She is wearing the white-red-white recognition stripes adopted for Operation Crusader. Note also the aerial mast for the No 11 radio set in its lowered position behind the turret.

BELOW RIGHT Matildas supporting the infantry – exactly the role the tank was built for, although it often found itself misemployed on other tasks.

These last two comments deserve explanation. The effectiveness of the armour on Matilda II needs little emphasis; it was the tank's single greatest quality. However, the inability of (all) British tanks of the time to fire an HE shell rather than solid armour-piercing rounds was a constant source of complaint. In large part, this was due to the flawed British doctrine that stated that the machine gun was the most effective killer of infantry, hence the insistence on multiple MGs in designs of the 1930s, including in the use of ergonomically horrendous sub-turrets, on tanks such as the Medium III, the A6, the A9 and even the Crusader Mk I. (It will be recalled that originally the Matilda II was to have carried such a turret, and that the requirement for one was only dropped when it was found to be completely impractical to mount one.) Another feature of over-reliance on machine guns was their limited range; an effective range of about 1,000 yards might have been totally adequate for Europe but would be found wanting when confronted by anti-tank guns in the open spaces of the Western Desert and indeed on the Russian steppe.

The doctrine of 'machine guns first' meant that the main gun mounted in the turret of such designs was viewed not as a support weapon with the function of killing infantry or other non-armoured targets, but merely as a mobile anti-tank weapon to protect infantry from counter-attacks. This did not mean that the tanks mounting such guns were primarily meant to proactively engage enemy tanks, but only that they would be able to ward off enemy tanks if they appeared during an infantry operation. In other words, they were seen only as a secondary defensive weapon rather than the primary offensive weapon. It followed therefore that there was no need for the 2pdr to be able to fire HE ammunition. In fact, a 2pdr HE round was developed, based on a Royal Navy 40mm design, but this does not seem to have ever been issued to tank crews (other than in the Red Army!) Although this TNT-filled nature would have only had about the same fragmentation effect as a hand grenade, it would have proved to have been extremely useful when engaging enemy anti-tank guns which were so effective in North Africa. Hitting such targets with 2pdr solid shot might disable the gun, but more often than not would simply punch a hole in the gun shield, leaving the weapon operational. Skilful use of dug-in anti-tank screens by the Germans completely nullified the effectiveness of the 2pdr and the co-axial MG, leaving the tank crews no option but to try to close the range and hope that they would not be knocked out before they did so. By the autumn of 1942 the Matilda II had had its day as a battle tank and was only to see service in the Second Battle of El Alamein that October in a modified role as a specialist mine-clearing tank, more on which can be found in Chapter 6.

The main units that used the Matilda in North Africa were: 4RTR, 7RTR (which also used the tanks in Crete), 42RTR and 44RTR; and, in addition, the units that operated Valentines tended to have a few Matilda CS tanks in the close-support role within the squadron headquarters. During the campaign two Victoria Crosses were won by RTR officers commanding Matildas:

Captain Philip John Gardner, 4th Royal Tank Regiment

On the morning of 23 November 1941, Captain Gardner was ordered to take two tanks to the assistance of two armoured cars of the King's Dragoon Guards which were out of action and under fire in close proximity to the enemy, southeast of Tobruk.

He found the two cars halted two hundred yards apart, being heavily fired on at close range and gradually smashed to pieces. Ordering the other tank to give him covering fire, Captain Gardner manoeuvred his own close up to the foremost car: he then dismounted in the face of intense anti-tank and machine gun fire and secured a tow rope to the car. Seeing an officer lying beside it with his legs blown off, he lifted him into the car and gave the order to tow. The tow rope, however, broke, and Captain Gardner returned to the armoured car, being immediately wounded in the arm and leg: despite his wounds he lifted the other officer out of the car and carried him back to the tank, placing him on the back engine louvres and climbing alongside to hold him on. While the tank was being driven back to safety it was subjected to heavy shellfire and the loader killed.

ABOVE A Matilda II in Tobruk, possibly 'Grimsby' of 7RTR. (TM1767C4)

LEFT Captain Philip 'Pip' Gardner RTR, who left the safety of his Matilda to rescue the crews of two disabled armoured cars belonging to the King's Dragoon Guards. (TM11085-001)

ABOVE A colourised print of the 'Queen of the Desert' in Caunter camouflage scheme in 1941. The officer with his hands in his pockets is Captain 'Pip' Gardner, who went on to win a VC. *(George Bradford)*

The courage, determination and complete disregard for his own safety displayed by Captain Gardner enabled him, despite his own wounds, and in the face of intense fire at close range, to save the life of his fellow officer, in circumstances fraught with great difficulty and danger.

Lieutenant Colonel Henry Robert Bowreman Foote, DSO, 7th Royal Tank Regiment

For outstanding gallantry during the period 27 May to 15 June 1942. On 6 June, Lieutenant-Colonel Foote led his Battalion, which had been subjected to very heavy artillery fire, in pursuit of a superior force of the enemy. While changing to another tank after his own had been knocked out, Lieutenant-Colonel Foote was wounded in the neck. In spite of this he continued to lead his Battalion from an exposed position on the outside of a tank. The enemy, who were holding a strongly entrenched position with anti-tank guns, attacked his flank. As a further tank had been disabled, he continued on foot under intense fire encouraging his men by his splendid example. By dusk, Lieutenant Colonel Foote by his brilliant leadership had defeated the enemy's attempt to encircle two of our Divisions.

On 13 June, when ordered to delay the enemy tanks so that the Guards Brigade could be withdrawn from the Knightsbridge escarpment and when the first wave of our tanks had been destroyed, Lieutenant Colonel Foote re-organised the remaining tanks, going on foot from one tank to another to encourage the crews under intense artillery and anti-tank fire. As it was of vital importance that his Battalion should not give ground, Lieutenant Colonel Foote placed his tank, which he had then entered, in front of the others so that he could be plainly visible in the turret as an encouragement to the other crews, in spite of the tank being badly damaged by shell fire and all its guns rendered useless. By his magnificent example the corridor was kept open and the Brigade was able to march through.

Lieutenant-Colonel Foote was always at the crucial point at the right moment, and over a period of several days gave an example of outstanding courage and leadership which it would have been difficult to surpass. His name was a by-word for bravery and leadership throughout the Brigade.

RIGHT Lieutenant Colonel Foote won his Victoria Cross commanding a Matilda regiment in the Western Desert, for outstanding acts of gallantry over a period of days, described here as deliberately exposing himself in the turret in order to encourage his crews.

Foote's VC, won while mounted in a Matilda, came at the end of the tank's useful life as a front-line vehicle. As early as Operation Battleaxe a year earlier, the cracks were starting to appear, and as Kenneth Macksey reported:

The first great shock of Battleaxe was the humbling of the Matildas when they ran, unsupported by infantry or artillery, straight into the muzzles of the 88s at Halfaya.

The cry of a tank squadron commander, a moment before he was killed 'They are tearing my tanks to pieces' announced a change in tactical balance. From now on the 88 would dominate and the Matilda was no longer Queen of the Battlefield.

It also marked the beginning of the end for the Matilda in British service, as better tanks were coming off the production line, including the latest British infantry tank, the Churchill.

More action – USSR

In total, out of over 4,500 tanks of various types supplied by Britain, nearly 1,200 Matilda IIs were sent as part of the Lend-Lease support to the USSR – which of course was neither lend nor lease, as no payments back were ever made by Stalin. Britain had to do all it could to keep the USSR in the war, and the Soviet position for all of 1941 was terribly precarious. Under the provisions of the Moscow Protocol, Britain initially agreed to supply quantities of Matilda II, Valentine and Tetrarch tanks to the Soviets, along with ammunition (apparently most if not all tanks were shipped fully bombed-up with ammunition) and spare parts. Because of their doctrine based on weight of armour rather than on firepower, the Matilda was classed by the Soviets as a heavy tank. (The Valentine was a medium in Russian parlance, and the Tetrarch a light, despite all carrying the same 2pdr gun.) The supply of British tanks was possibly more crucial than some assume, as the vast majority of the Soviet tank force in late 1941 was made up of either light or obsolete types that were no match for the Germans. The fêted T-34 was not to become significant until 1942 – Factory 112 at Gorky, manufacturing the tank, had only been ordered to be converted from making submarines to producing T-34s in July 1941.

Shipments of British tanks, along with other weapons and materiel of war, were sent starting in the autumn of 1941, many on the hazardous northern convoy routes. The Matildas were all Mks III, IV and IVCS; in Soviet service they seem to have all been referred to simply as the 'British Mark Two'. By the end of 1941 Soviet figures indicate that 361 Matildas and Valentines had reached the Red Army. Although this list is probably incomplete, the following Soviet Independent Tank Battalions were known to be operating Matildas by November 1941: 132nd (with 19 Valentines and 2 Matildas); 136th (3 Matildas and 9 Valentines); and 138th (15 Matildas and 6 Valentines). By the end of that year, one report indicated that 8 Matildas and 38 Valentines were the only survivors of the nearly 200 British tanks thrown straight into action in northern Russia, in an attempt to stem the German advance on Moscow. Beginning in November 1941, at least some instructional staff were sent with the tanks to train the Soviets on the technical aspects of what was, after all, a very complicated design; it is not clear if all of these personnel were military. By summer 1942, many more Matildas had arrived, and two battalions of the

BELOW Matildas and Valentines being loaded for the hazardous convoy that would take them to the USSR; some tanks went direct from the manufacturers, while others had been in the hands of British units before being sent overseas.

ABOVE AND ABOVE RIGHT T6886 was a Matilda II Mk III built by Vulcan in late 1940 and subsequently shipped to the USSR. She is now in the Russian Tank Museum at Kubinka.

BELOW AND BELOW RIGHT The same tank photographed during snow trials; it can be seen how the snow would pack into the mud chutes. The tracks also struggled to gain purchase and so steel bars were sometimes welded on to them to assist with grip and traction.

Soviet 10th Corps were equipped solely with Matilda II, along with four battalions in the 11th Corps. The 5th Mechanised Corps, formed in autumn 1942, was the only Soviet unit equipped exclusively with British tanks, using both Matilda and Valentine, and Red Army formations continued to use the Matilda until they were able to be retired from active service during 1943. By the end of 1942 230 Matildas had arrived in the Soviet Union, with another 55 lost at sea. Of the total of 1,185 Matilda II tanks shipped from the UK, it appears that 932 were actually received by the Red Army, the remainder being sunk en route, as follows:

Mk III	Sent 113, received 113
Mk IV	Sent 915, received 694, sunk 221
Mk IV CS	Sent 157, received 125, sunk 32

Overall, therefore, the Soviets were allocated just over 40% of all Matilda IIs produced.

The Russian Matildas (and Valentines) did receive something that their British counterparts did not, the 2pdr HE round, over 53,000 of which were sent to the USSR. The Soviets also demanded – and received – many more HE than smoke rounds for the 3in CS howitzer, approximately $4/5$ HE to $1/5$ smoke, showing that they used the weapon more effectively and offensively than the British, who tended to carry only $1/3$ HE to $2/3$ smoke. As an experiment in upgunning the tank, as well as standardising ammunition, one Matilda (the H&W-built T10157) was modified to mount the standard Russian ZIS-5 76mm F96 gun as used on the T-34 and KV-1. The tank was tested from early 1942 in the Moscow area, but the modification was not proceeded with as the breech took up too much space in the small turret, and no service examples were used.

The Matilda was also not suited for use in winter conditions of snow and ice, and only 5–6in of snow was enough to stop the tank moving; unditching logs were therefore often carried along the sides of the tank to assist with getting it moving again by giving the tracks something to grip on to. Of course, the Matilda, as originally conceived, was never designed for such harsh conditions, but snow and ice would pack behind the side armour and block the suspension units, and even the later TD5910 spudded tracks provided poor grip on ice; Russian crews sometimes welded bars across the track plates to improve the grip. The pneumatic elements of the transmission were not liked as they caused problems in low temperatures, and it seems that a 'mechanical alternative' was used, although there are no details of how this was done. Overall, Russian tank crews judged the tank as strong in terms of protection, but slow

ABOVE LEFT Germans involved in their fascinating hobby of examining captured Matildas. This tank appears to be T35163, which was assigned to the Soviet 183 Tank Brigade, and still bears its old British A Sqn triangle marking.

ABOVE Two Soviet Matilda III or IV CS tanks – the one on the right appears to have suffered a 'premature' in the barrel, usually caused by an obstruction, which has burst the barrel into the characteristic banana shape.

LEFT Another Soviet CS tank, again with damage to the barrel, this time from being struck externally. It has also suffered miscellaneous hits on the hull and turret.

FAR LEFT The German 88mm anti-aircraft gun was used in all theatres as a makeshift anti-tank weapon as it could penetrate the armour of all known tanks at long ranges, including that on the Matilda. This led to the Germans developing specialised versions in a specific anti-tank configuration.

LEFT A Soviet drawing showing one of their methods of giving Matilda track better grip – the welded blocks of steel on to the outside edge.

MATILDA AT WAR

and under-armed, much the same opinion that experienced British crews had formed as early as May 1940. One report speaks of a single tank receiving no fewer than 87 hits, none of which penetrated, but this must surely be either an exaggeration or refer to the use of very low-calibre weapons.

Final action – the Far East

Australia was another recipient of large numbers of Matildas, with 409 being supplied directly between 1942 and 1944. In total 442 were operated, as in 1944 an additional 33 Mk IVCS versions were supplied from New Zealand stocks, 18 of them without their armament, as their 3in howitzers had been removed for use in Valentines. Some of these tanks were then refitted with 3in howitzers in Australia while others were converted into Frog flamethrowers.[4] Just over 15% of all Matildas therefore were used by the Australian Army. Although obsolete in other theatres of war, the Matilda proved to be an excellent tank when used in the Far East in exactly the role that it was originally conceived for – supporting the infantry. Its slow speed was not a handicap in the jungle, and its armour was more than capable of resisting the low-calibre anti-tank guns used by the Japanese. Nevertheless, the Australians made a number of modifications to the tank to address some specific vulnerabilities.

In addition to modifying their gun tanks, and despite the lack of anything resembling

TOP An Australian Matilda, belonging to 13 Troop, C Sqn, 2/9 Armoured Regiment. This tank has not yet been fitted with the typical Aussie modifications and improvements. *(AWM081707)*

CENTRE Another 1st Tank Battalion Matilda in January 1944, with a wooden plank wedged behind the headlamps to secure even more stowage. *(AWM016490)*

LEFT Mantlet covers have been added to these wading – as opposed to waltzing – Matildas. Note how the exhaust pipes have been angled upwards. *(AWM108956)*

ABOVE An Australian tank commander operating the No 19 wireless set from his low cupola.

tank designers pre-war, the Australians also modified a number of their Matildas into specialist roles, their equivalent of the famous British 'Funnies'. In this group were the Matilda Frog, a flamethrower tank known officially as the Flamethrower Transportable (Aust) No 2 Mk 1 Frog; the Projector Hedgehog No 1 Mk 1, capable of throwing seven[5] 63lb bombs from a raised box mounted on the engine decks; and a bulldozer tank which used a D7 blade operated hydraulically from a power take-off. The Australian Army Tank Museum at Puckapunyal has examples of these tanks on display.

ABOVE The Australian Matilda Bulldozer No 3 Mk 1, another Puckapunyal survivor. Two hydraulic control pipes feed out of the driver's compartment through the visor to the blade.

BELOW LEFT The Frog flamethrower in action, clearing stubborn Japanese resistance. This tank has British-style smoke grenade dischargers fitted to the hull rear. *(AWM109024)*

BELOW The Pucka Frog, complete with armoured collars and trackguards.

RIGHT **The Matilda Hedgehog, with the projectile box raised into the firing position; when not in use it was lowered on to the engine decks. An example bomb lies on the decks.**

BELOW **A close-up of the Frog muzzle and counterweight.**

Matilda seemed to have been quite a popular tank for its Australian crews – and supported infantry. Its first deployment to eastern New Guinea at Milne Bay in late August 1942 was kept secret, but the opportunity to use the two squadrons of tanks did not present itself for some time. A report from the first use of it in action, on 17 November 1943, over a year after the British had ceased using it as a gun tank, gives us a glimpse of the types of warfare it was used in:

> *The first tank was unable to see [the target, an MG post] because of the dense jungle, but after some jungle had been blown away by 3" howitzers and 2 pounders,[6] the third tank put the gun out of action. Actually, most of the tanks' firing was more or less blind. The infantry platoon commander would give the order 'Rake the BESA between this tree and that'. The attack continued in a series of short bounds with the tanks firing rapidly on both sides of the road at enemy defences, mainly pill-boxes and foxholes, all with strong overhead cover and sited in depth. . . . Morale in the squadron was*

LEFT **T35357 was a North British Locomotive-built Mk IV, subsequently converted to Hedgehog.** *(AWM133687)*

LEFT An Australian crewman takes a break; the BESA MG on this CS tank has its muzzle cover in place. *(NIMH)*

high. All were happy about the Matildas which had proved to be powerful and successful weapons, and undoubtedly saved the infantry many casualties . . . the performance of the tanks had amazed even their own crews.[7]

After the end of the war, the 1st Armoured Brigade was resurrected in April 1948 with two regiments, the 1st Armoured and the 12th/6th, and both were equipped with reconditioned Matilda tanks which, although recognised as completely obsolete, were at least available and allowed training to take place. By 1955 all of the Matildas had been completely withdrawn from active service and many were sold as farm vehicles, this marking the end of the road for a tank which had been in service for over 15 years.[8]

CENTRE End of the road. This Australian Matilda has suffered a terminal engine explosion, most likely caused either by a Japanese sticky bomb or a direct hit from an HE shell. *(NIMH)*

RIGHT The A20 project was to lead to the A22 Churchill, or Infantry Tank Mk IV, the successor to the Matilda. The A20 could have featured a Matilda-style turret, which would have seriously limited the main armament options.

MATILDA REGISTRATIONS & CONTRACT DETAILS

REGISTRATIONS (QTY)	MARKS (AS NOTED OR INFERRED ON CONTRACT CARDS)	MAKER	CONTRACT (DATE)
T6729–T6868 (140)	II (55) & IIA* (85)	Vulcan	T5115 (11 June 1938)
T6869–T6908 (40)	III	Vulcan	T6929 (19 April 1939)
T6909–T7029 (121)	II (50) & IIA* (71)	London, Midland & Scottish Railway	T5741 (19 April 1939)
T7271–T7350 (80)	II (20) & IIA* (60)	Ruston & Hornsby	T6907 (19 April 1939)
T7351–T7390 (40)	IIA	Ruston & Hornsby	T5694 (25 August 1938)
T7391–T7440 (50)	II (20) & IIA* (30)	North British Locomotive	T6904 (1 July 1939)
T10034–T10073 (40)	II (25) & IIA* (15)	Fowler	T5693 (24 October 1938)
T10074–T10203 (130)	II (10) & III (120)	H&W	T6905 (19 April 1939)
T10204–TT10283 (80)	III & IV	Fowler	T6906 (19 April 1939)
T10284–T10293 (10)	II MS Instructional	Vulcan	T7711 (26 September 1939)
T10294–T10303 (10)	II (1) III (9)	Fowler	T7712 (26 September 1939)
T10304–T10308 (5)	II MS Instructional	Ruston	T9959 (12 June 1940)
T10309 – T10313 (5)	IIA* or III	North British Locomotive	T9958 (12 June 1940)
T10422–T10471 (50)	III	North British Locomotive	T7717 (September 1939)
T17685–T17784 (100)	III & IV	North British Locomotive	T9958 (12 June 1940)
T18761–T18885 (125)	III & IV	Ruston & Hornsby	T9959 (12 June 1940)
T18886–T18935 (50)	III (16) & IIICS (34)	London, Midland & Scottish Railway	T9862 (12 June 1940)
T18936–T18985 (145)	IIA* (44) & III (6), IV (95)	London, Midland & Scottish Railway	T302 (25 July 1940)
T27721–T27870 (150)	III & IV	Ruston & Hornsby	T1267 (12 December 1940)
T27871–T27940 (70)	III (9) & IV (61)	Harland & Wolff	T310 (26 July 1940)
T29791–T29860 (70)	IIICS & IVCS	Vulcan	T311 (26 July 1940)
T29861–T29970 (110)	IVCS	Vulcan	T1244 (16 December 1940)
T35148–T35277 (130)	IV	North British Locomotive	T1243 (18 December 1940)
T35278–T35377 (100)	IV	North British Locomotive	T2043 (15 March 1941)
T37121–T37230 (110)	III (41) & IVCS (69)	London, Midland & Scottish Railway	T1242 (13 December 1940)
T45964–T46033 (70)	III & IV	Fowler	T312 (26 July 1940)
T46034–T46108 (75)	III & IV	Fowler	T2045 (4 April 1941)
T72704–T72753 (50)	IV & IVCS	Vulcan	T2044 (15 March 1941)
T72754–T72953 (200)	V	Vulcan	TM5618 (15 September 1941)
T82088–T82162 (75)	III & IV	Harland & Wolff	T1268 (13 December 1940)
T88064–T88243 (180)	IV & V	Fowler	T5590 (9 September 1941)
T88244–T88427 (184)	IV	North British Locomotive	TM5617 (12 December 1941)
T130770–T130844 (75)	III or V	Fowler	T2042 (15 March 1942)
T131126–T131175 (50)	III	Fowler	TM10605 (15 December 1941)

MANUFACTURE DATES	SERVICE USE	REMARKS
29 September 1939–April 1940	Majority of first 40 to BEF, majority of rest to North Africa	IIA* from T6784. Civilian registrations PMV85–224
May 1940–November 1940	Majority of first 20 to North Africa, majority of rest to USSR, some to Australia	Civilian registrations PMV225–264. Tanks sent abroad probably as 'second-hand'
November 1939–August 1940	Majority to UK or North Africa	IIA* from T6959. Civilian registrations PMV265–385
November 1939–August 1941	Majority to North Africa, some to UK and Australia	IIA* from T7291. Civilian registrations PMV747–796
March 1939–October 1939?	Majority to North Africa, some to UK and Australia	Civilian registrations PMV707–746
May 1940–January 1941	Majority to UK or North Africa	IIA* from T7411
1 June 1939–24 March 1940	Majority to UK or North Africa, some to Australia	IIA* from T10060
June 1940–?	Majority to North Africa, some to UK, Australia and USSR	Original order for 70, increased to 130
March 1940–late 1940?	Most to North Africa, some to Australia	First few completed as Mk III, remainder either III or IV
13 June 1940–14 August 1940		Mild steel instructional, aka A12M
Late 1940–early 1941?	Majority to North Africa, Australia and USSR	
?		Contract marked as transferred to Contract T9959
?	USSR?	Marked as cancelled but probably to USSR
February 1941–June 1941?	Majority to North Africa	
June 1941–October 1941	Majority to USSR and Australia	Last 55 built as Mk IV?
12 August 1940–February 1942?	All to USSR?	Original order was 75. Last 56 built as Mk IV?
March 1941–August 1941?	All to North Africa?	Original order was 100 (to T18985) – probable that last 50 were not built under this contract but were transferred to T302
4 August 1940–March 1941?	North Africa, USSR and Australia	
2 March 1942–early 1943?	Majority to USSR and Australia	All built as Mk IV?
18 September 1940–?	All to USSR?	
20 June 1941–18 October 1941	Some to UK and North Africa, majority of second half of contract to USSR	Majority (all?) Mk IIICS
November 1941–cApril 1942	Most of first half to USSR, rest to Australia and North Africa	
November 1941–March 1942?	Majority to USSR, some to Australia	
2 April 1942–July 1942?	Most of first half to USSR, rest to Australia	
?	To UK, Australia and USSR	
October 1941–December 1941	All to USSR from new	
January 1942–February 1942	Majority to USSR, some to Australia	Cost each £5,600 ex-works
17 April 1942–June 1942	To North Africa, USSR and Australia	All built as Mk IVCS?
23 June 1942–May 1943	To North Africa, USSR and Australia	Contract card says Mk III but other indications show all built as Mk V. Final Matilda built probably T72953
19 March 1942–December 1942	First half or so to USSR, remainder to Australia	
February 1942–August 1942	To USSR and Australia	
August 1942–mid-1943?	To USSR and Australia	Original order for 234, reduced by 50
October 1942–December 1942	Some to Australia and USSR	Original London, Midland & Scottish Railway contract T11972 (7 March 1942) transferred to Fowler. Due to date possibly built as Mk V
August 1942–September 1942	To USSR and Australia	Majority (all?) built as Mk IV

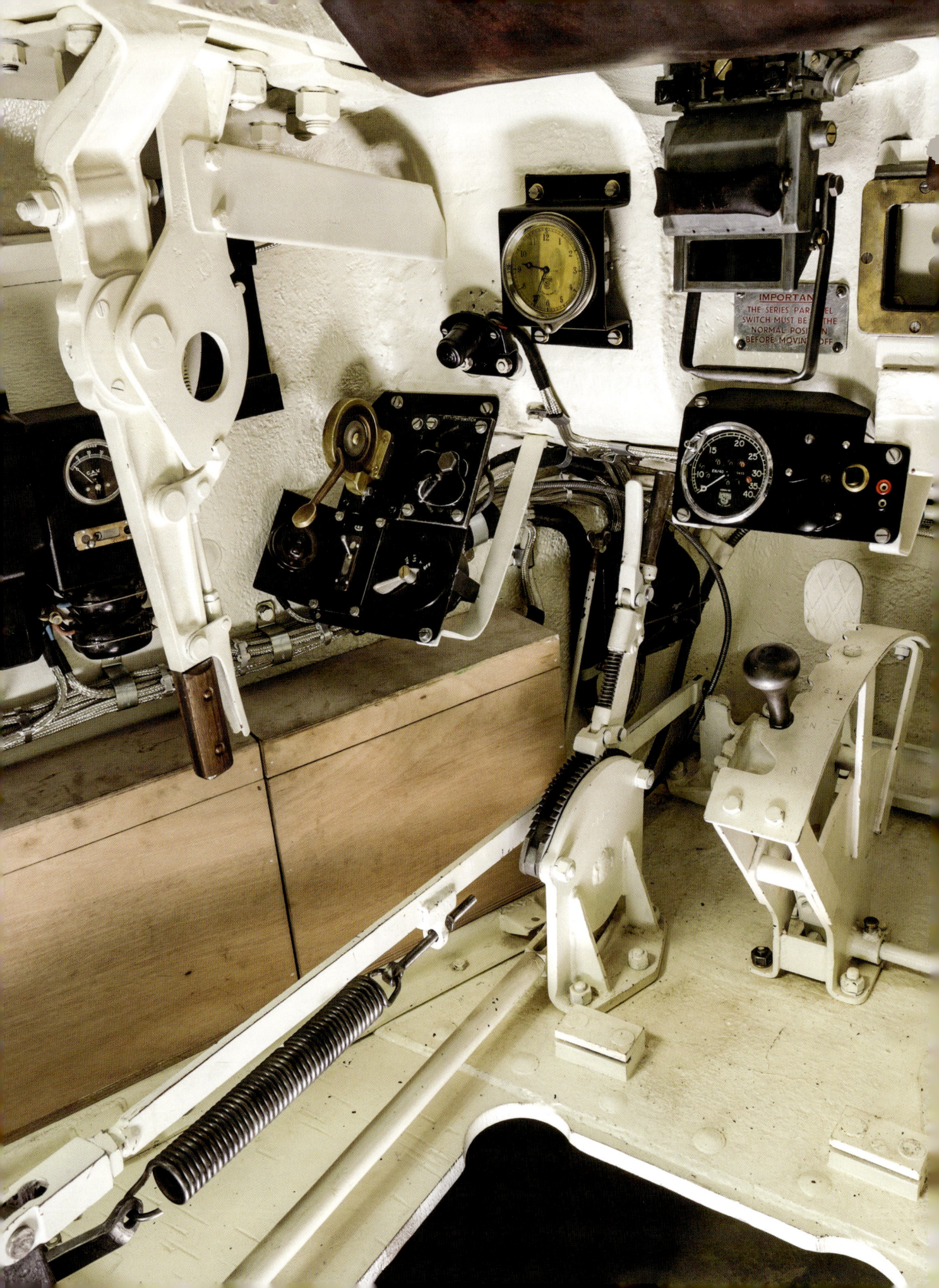

IMPORTANT
THE SERIES PARALLEL
SWITCH MUST BE IN THE
NORMAL POSITION
BEFORE MOVING OFF

Chapter Five

Anatomy of Matilda

The Matilda was a complex tank that featured many unusual features, including the linking together of two engines to give the required power output. It was also cursed with a complex layout of pipes and wiring, which made it difficult to service and repair.

OPPOSITE The driver's compartment, with the gear selector lever in the centre, and steering levers (or tillers) either side. The brown boxes contain the hull batteries. *(TM)*

General layout

The description used here is generic, and while reference is made to differences between the marks, the detailed descriptions contained in Chapter 6 should also be consulted.

The Matilda is laid out in a manner similar to that used on many modern tanks, but which was quite unusual for the time: it had a three-man turret crew (commander, loader/radio operator and gunner) with only one other man, the driver, in the front centre of the hull. There was no fifth crewman employed as the hull machine-gunner as was frequently the practice across most nations at the time. The engines, gearbox and final drives were situated in the rear of the hull, with the tracks and suspension protected by armoured side skirts with prominent mud chutes, the latter being a distinguishing feature of the tank and giving it a somewhat old-fashioned look.

Unlike almost all large British tanks built before it, the Matilda did not utilise a metal frame or skeleton with armour steel plates bolted to it. This method of construction was traditional and easy for the builders as riveting was an established industry in Britain and thus simple to recruit skilled workers, but the

THIS PAGE T6781 'Grampus II', a Mk II made by Vulcan, was sent to Aberdeen Proving Ground in the USA in early 1940 for evaluation – it was an ex-7RTR tank and was in less than pristine condition. Why a brand-new example was not sent is not clear. *(TM)*

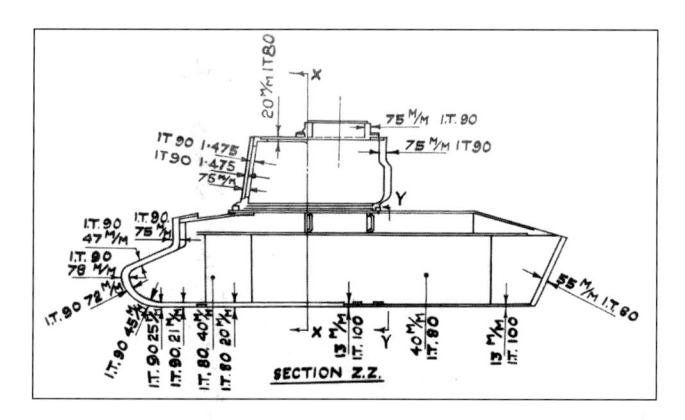

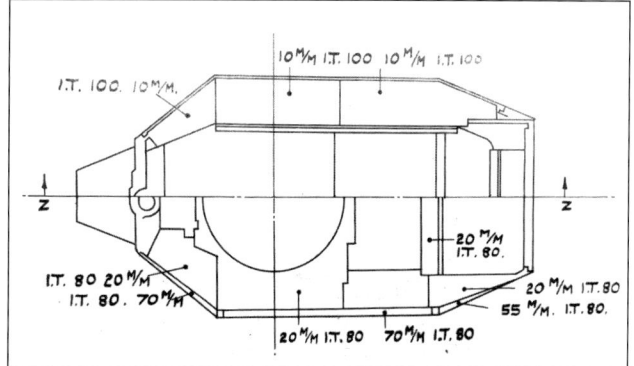

ABOVE AND ABOVE RIGHT Armour thicknesses of the Matilda II: the oft-quoted 78mm represented only the maximum amount carried, but for its day it was reasonably well-armoured elsewhere.

method had serious drawbacks. The frame itself had to be substantial and added a lot of weight, as did the many hundreds of large rivets. Additionally, in action, rivets which were struck from the outside by incoming fire could be driven into the inside of the tank at high speed, damaging components and injuring or killing the crew. Removing the need for the frame was therefore of itself both innovative and added to the protection afforded by the tank's exceptionally thick armour as well as helping to reduce weight and add survivability. In a period when 25mm (1in) of armour would be considered to be a high level of protection, the Matilda fielded a maximum of 78mm, just over 3in, of armour at its thickest point (the extreme front of the hull nose), and elsewhere

ABOVE A Matilda hull under construction in 1941, showing off the side brackets that the hull armour and mud chutes were fixed to.

BELOW LEFT AND BELOW A Mk III in Russian service; this now is preserved in the Russian Tank Museum at Kubinka. It has the later tracks, two-headlamp configuration and modified tool box covers, as well as other detail changes that different manufacturers incorporated. 'ESC' on the armour indicates that the casting was made by the English Steel Company. *(Merlin Robinson)*

A cutaway illustration from an official handbook, showing the layout of an early BESA-armed Matilda fitted with a No 11 radio set. This would be typical of a Matilda II Mk II or III. *(TM)*

1. Instrument Panel
2. Periscope
3. Lever to operate Visor
4. Driver's Hood
5. Lever to operate Driver's Hood
6. Power Traverse
7. Gun Sight
8. Breach of 2-Pounder Gun
9. Signalling Lamp
10. Commander's Cupola
11. Aerial
12. Wireless
13. Telephone
14. 2-Pounder Ammunition Racks
15. Reavell Compressor
16. Stop Control
17. Fuel Oil Filter
18. Fuel Pump
19. Dynamo
20. Dynamo and Water Pump
21. Lubricating Oil Filter
22. Engine Fan
23. Radiator
24. Gear Box
25. Scavenger Oil Pump Outlet
26. Main Oil Pump Inlet
27. Drive
28. Power Traverse Oil Pump
29. Loader's Seat
30. Turntable
31. Recuperator for Power Traverse
32. Gunner's Seat
33. Gunner's Crutch for elevating Gun
34. Trigger for 2-Pounder Gun and Besa Machine Gun
35. Bag for Spent Shells
36. Air Reservoir
37. Driver's Seat
38. Accumulators
39. Steering Lever
40. Gear Selector
41. Gear Change Operating Rod
42. Throttle Control
43. Gear Change Operating Pedal

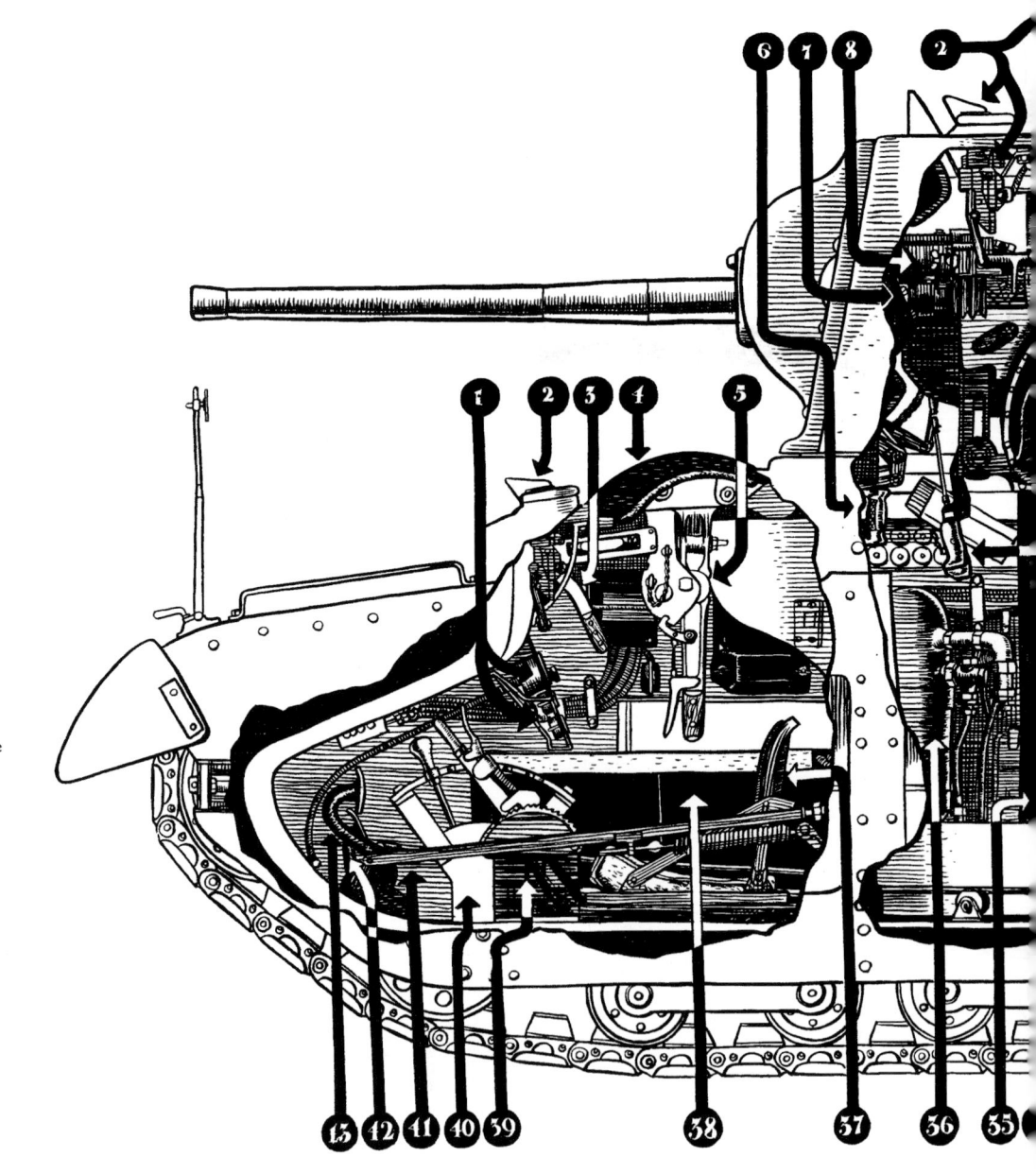

MATILDA INFANTRY TANK MANUAL

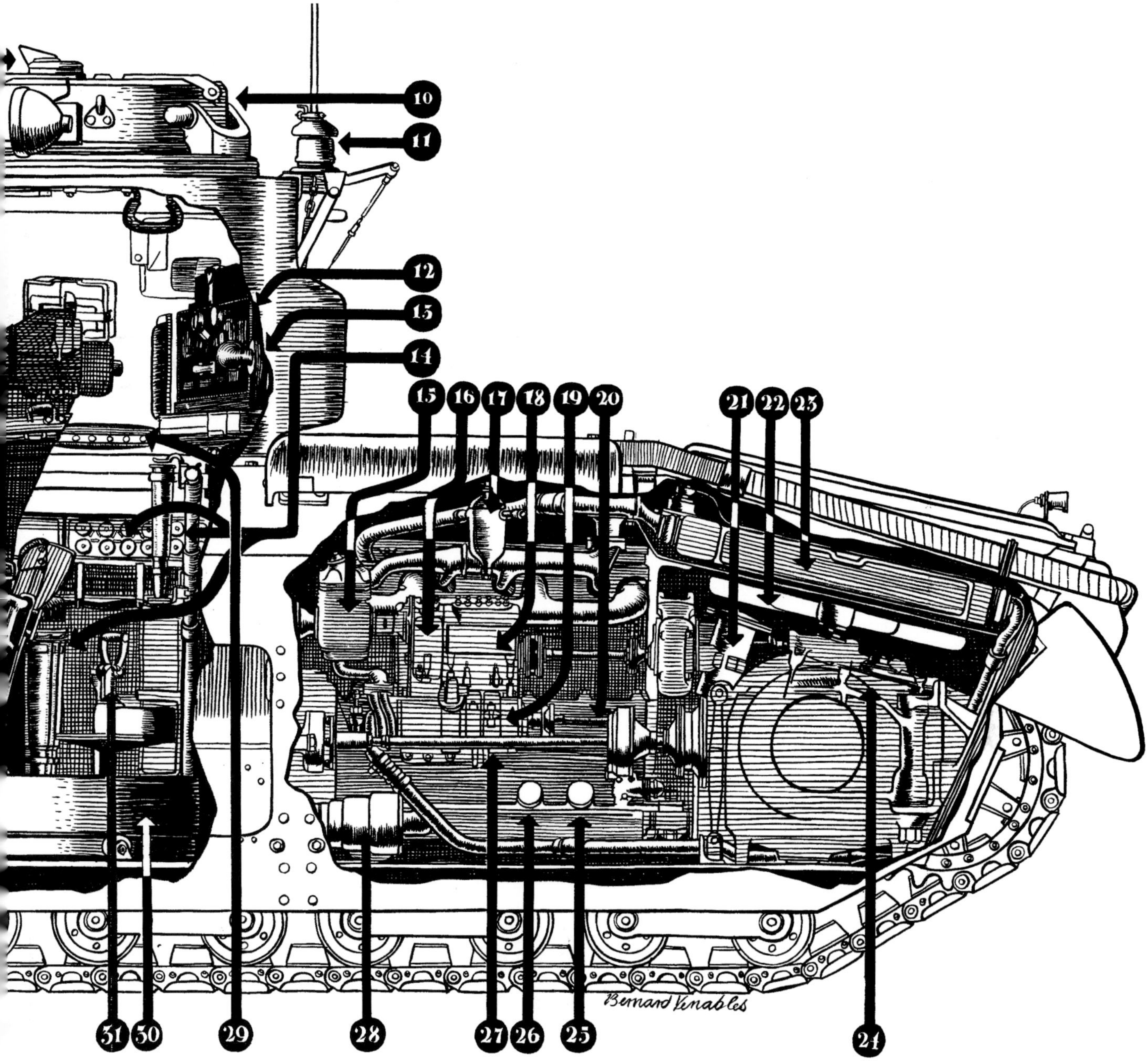
10
11
12
13
14
15
16
17
18
19
20
21
22
23
24
25
26
27
28
29
30
31
Bernard Venables

75mm was the standard around the whole of the turret and much of the hull nose and front. Even the rear plate was an amazing 55mm thick, and the floor plates under the crew compartment 20mm – compare this with the maximum of 14mm on the Medium II, or indeed the 30mm maximum on the contemporary version of the German Panzer III. Producing the nose casting was one of many reasons why building Matildas was a laborious process. The nose came out of the casting thicker than it needed to be, and so to remove excess weight the inside of the armour was ground down by hand to the correct thickness, a slow job known as 'cheese-paring'.

Despite the armour thickness Matilda II was far from perfect. The experiences of the 7RTR crews who fought in Matilda in France during 1940 was analysed, and one of the complaints concerned the design of the stowage bins located either side of the main nose. These castings had been designed with hinged, louvred covers that were part of the secondary air cooling and ventilation system, but it was found that in action shell splinters or tracer bullets frequently penetrated through the gaps and ignited the contents – which being driver's equipment would include oil-soaked rags, tins of servicing oil and the like – that would be quite worrying for the crews, and may have led to unnecessary 'bailouts'. Solving this was simple; a wedge-shaped armour plate was welded over the louvres, and this probably had the added benefit of reducing the amount of dust drawn into the turret – a drawback that had been commented upon in trials; later a simplified lid was introduced as part of production.

Driver's compartment

The Matilda was officially described as being of 'bolted and riveted construction with a cast-nose piece and turret'. To increase overall rigidity and to absorb shocks (whether from cross-country driving or from enemy fire), the hull top and floor plates were rebated into the side armour, allowing the shoulders of the joint to take some of the load off the fixing screws. Additional transverse rigidity was provided at the front by the one-piece nose casting braced either side by the toolbox castings, in the centre by the bulkhead at the rear of the fighting compartment, and at the rear by the hull rear plate. The central section of the hull, behind the driver and forward of the engine bulkhead, formed the lower part of the fighting compartment (sometimes referred to archaically as the fighting chamber), with the fully rotating turret above it forming the upper part. A rectangular driver's escape hatch was fitted under the vertically adjustable driver's seat, which, with the limited space inside and the low ground clearance below, must have been very difficult to use, although some reports do refer to it being successfully employed in action.

Placing the driver in the centre of the hull front in his own compartment conferred a number of benefits: the driver had a reasonably spacious area in which to work; exiting out of the tank in an emergency through the fighting compartment to the rear of his seat could be made simpler; and judging the width of the tank was very much easier, important when crossing bridges or manoeuvring in confined spaces. The preferred method of driving the tank when out of action was 'head out', with the driver's hood which covered his compartment fully opened, *ie* rotated to the rear and behind him. This was achieved by operating two spring-loaded levers, one either side. When going into action, the driver would 'close down' – drop his seat

BELOW T10291 was an AEC-engined example, as evidenced by the single exhaust pipe on the hull top – the other ran under the hull and was prone to damage. Despite this, the rear hull casting is typical of the twin-exhaust Leyland engine. The gong button can be seen in the centre of the hull between the two lifting eyes.

LEFT Straight out of the factory and still lacking its main gun and tools, this Matilda shows the early layout of the hull front, with single headlamp, the early detail around the driver's visor and mysterious square blocks on the front of the nose. It is not clear why they exist, but the author's opinion is that they are there to assist with the lifting of the tank by dockside cranes.

to the lowest position, and then shut the hood by operating the levers until the curved armour hood closed off the area over his head. He would then use the Vickers Tank Periscope as his primary means of viewing the outside world, or, if this was damaged, could use a lever on the right-hand side to open up the armoured block to his front and use the 'lookout', which was the name given to the series of horizontal slits drilled through the armour plate. In this case, to further protect him from splinters, the rear (inside) of the slits was covered by a thick toughened glass Triplex block, with a number of spare blocks carried in his compartment. Driving using the periscope was difficult enough, but using the slits and glass blocks would have made it even worse; it does, however, indicate the British requirement to design-in emergency and backup systems to reflect the realities of combat and the likelihood of damage.

Controls were reasonably conventional, with a steering lever either side of the driver; these operated on a ratchet and the two together were used as the parking brake. The gear selector lever in a gate was to be found immediately in front of the driver, between his knees, but there were only two, rather than three, foot pedals. The left one was the gear-change pedal (and was *not* a clutch in the conventional sense), and the right one the accelerator. A separate footbrake pedal was not required as braking was done by pulling on both steering levers.

On all tanks up to and including the Mk III there were three instrument panels for use by the driver. The left-hand one mounted the starter switch, with positions for each engine, the engine heater switches (on AEC-engined vehicles only), the all-lights switch (with positions for all on, side and tail only, tail only and all off), and a two-way tail light switch; on Leyland-engined Matildas an engine stop control switch/lever was also provided. In the centre panel was the illuminated speedometer,

BELOW A close-up of the later hull armour around the driver's cab, in which an extra chunk of armour steel was added below the driver's lookout block, presumably to remedy a perceived weakness. *(John Bryce)*

RIGHT The driver's position with seat removed and the emergency escape hatch clearly visible. The two levers for opening and closing the curved driver's roof are in the down (open) position. *(TM)*

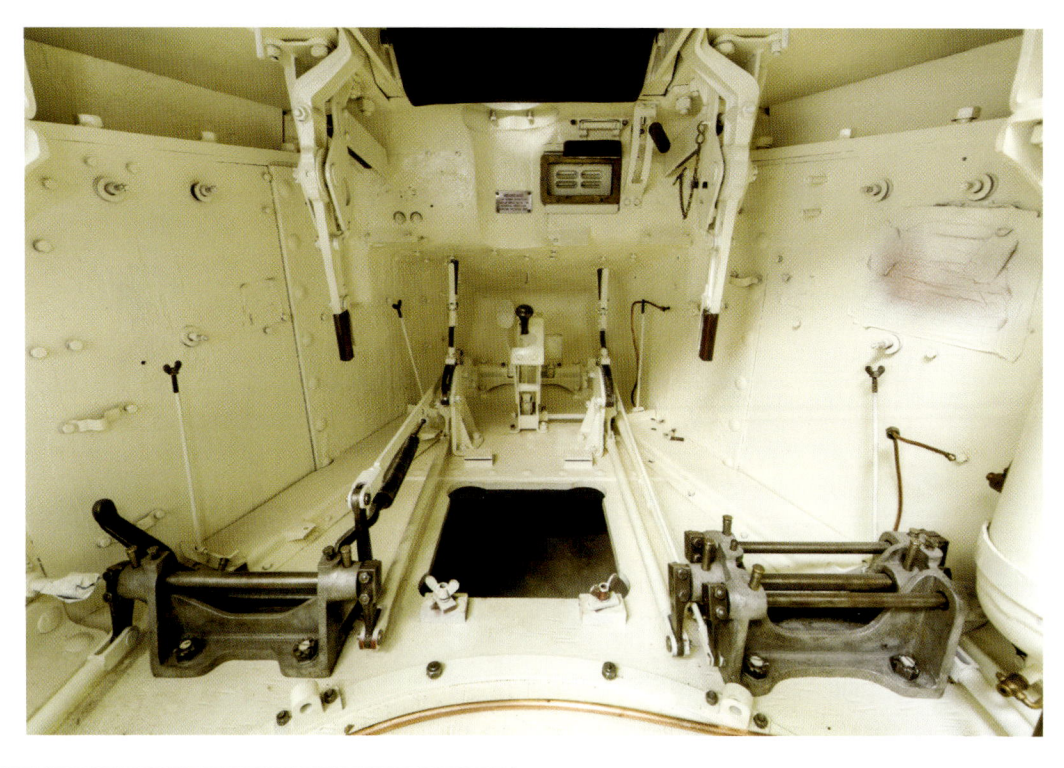

BELOW The gauge and switch layout on the three driver's instrument panels – later tanks only had two.

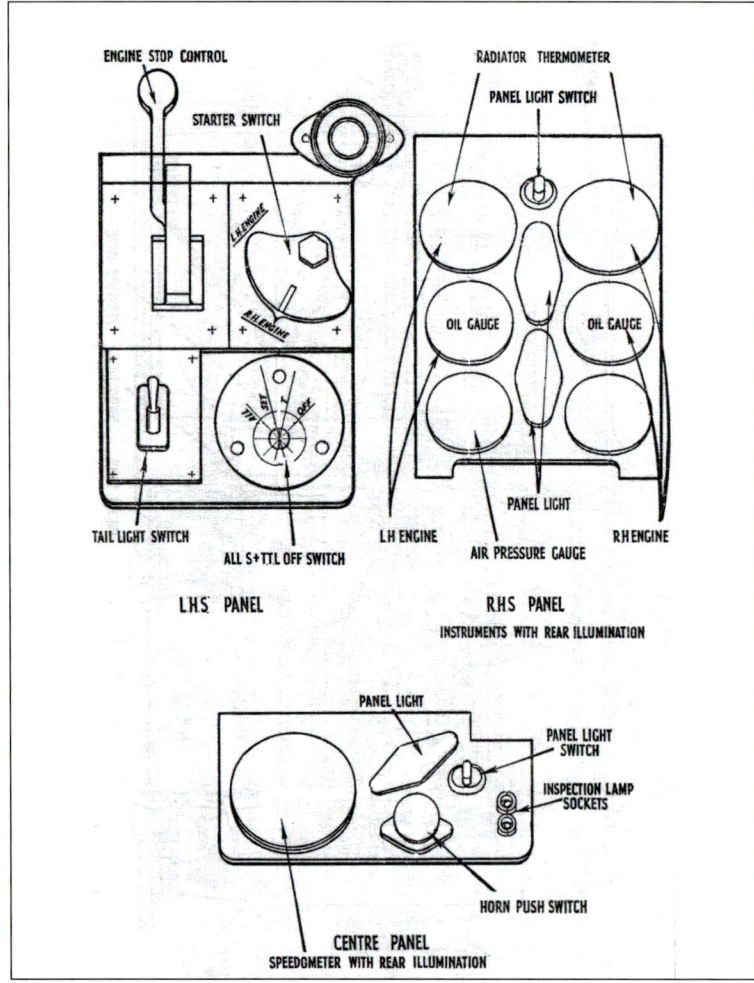

the horn button, a panel lights switch and light and a twin-core inspection lamp socket. On the right were to be found two radiator temperature gauges, an oil pressure gauge for each engine, the air pressure gauge and the fuel gauge. Between the left and centre panels was mounted a luminous eight-day clock, clearly something no self-respecting driver could do without. On the Mks IV and V the switchgear was revised and only two instrument panels were used.

BELOW The left-hand panel, incorporating the brass engine cut-off switch/lever. On AEC-engined tanks the driver 'killed' the engine by lifting up the accelerator panel with his toe! *(TM)*

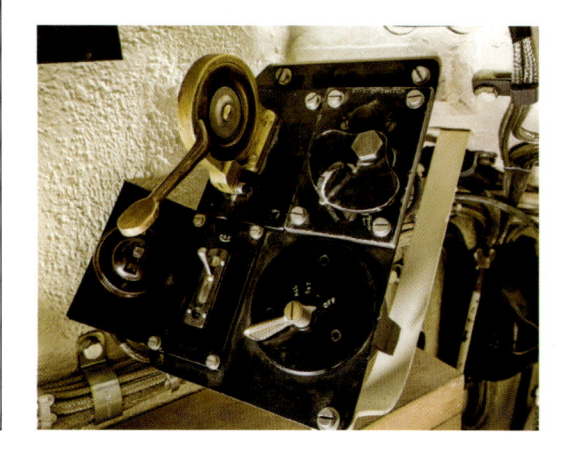

Engine and transmission

The engine on the Matilda was in fact a pair of engines linked together. This was necessary because there was no suitable single off-the-shelf powerplant available that was compact enough to fit in the hull and produced the necessary power for the tank, which was originally set at 220hp (for a tank whose weight was specified to be 20 tons only), giving a power-to-weight ratio of 11:1, but which was never achieved despite the tank being re-engined a number of times. The first engine types used were a pair of AEC diesel engines called the A183/184. With Matilda engine designations, the first number always refers to the right-hand engine (as viewed from the rear facing forwards), and the second number the left-hand. Tanks with the AEC engines were designated Matilda II Mk I if a Vickers MMG was fitted as the co-ax, and Matilda II Mk II if the BESA was used. All engines shared one thing in common, the use of diesel fuel. Originally, Vulcan specified that the fuel that should be used was either Light Diesoleum or Shell Dieseline, but of course during the war any grade of diesel available was utilised. The use of diesel was groundbreaking – Rudolf Diesel had demonstrated his first compression-ignition engine using the fuel that took his name in 1900, but it was only in 1923 (in Germany) that diesel engines started to be used in lorries, and the first British trucks did not use these engines until 1927, with garages selling the fuel few and far between, requiring special maps to be printed for UK hauliers.

One of the untold stories about the AEC engines was that the specification, in terms of output, was changed at some point after the tank entered service. Publications from the time refer to a 94.1bhp at 2,000rpm (often rounded up to 95bhp) engine as the 'original' specification, but which was then reduced to 87bhp on what were termed as 'modified' engines. The method of doing this and the reasons for this slight reduction in power are not clear; the difference is only about 8% but on a tank with such a low power-to-weight ratio every horsepower counted, and as it

ABOVE T6934 'Horace' was a C Sqn 8RTR tank that was built as a Mk II. It is pictured here in the MG works in Abingdon, presumably in the middle of a re-engine operation. The gearbox is at the bottom right, with the paired AEC engines on the trestle alongside it, identifiable by the triple belt fan drives. A new Leyland E148/149 is on the floor behind it. Once the modification is complete, 'Horace' would become a Mk III. *(TM1766C1)*

BELOW A more organised-looking workshop scene, with 'Shocker', probably of 43RTR, nearest in the line; at least another dozen Matildas are having work done on them. The early-pattern side-access hatches can be seen, hinged at the top and the cause of many unnecessary hand injuries.

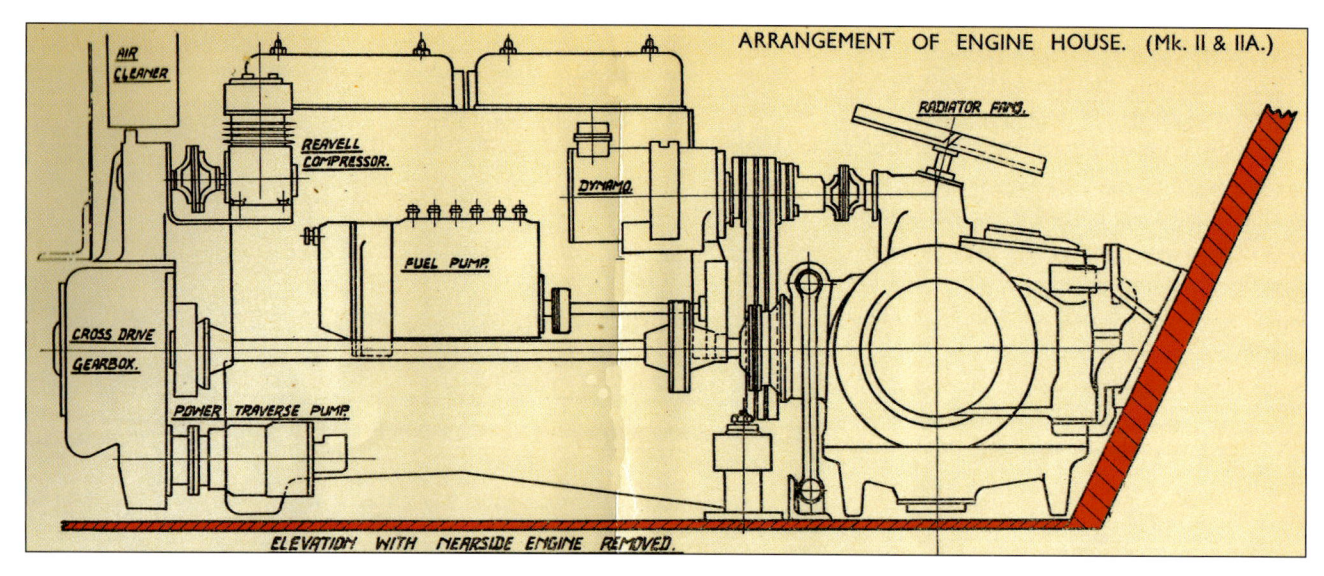

ABOVE AND BELOW Schematic layouts of the engine and rear hull with the early AEC engines fitted. *(TM)*

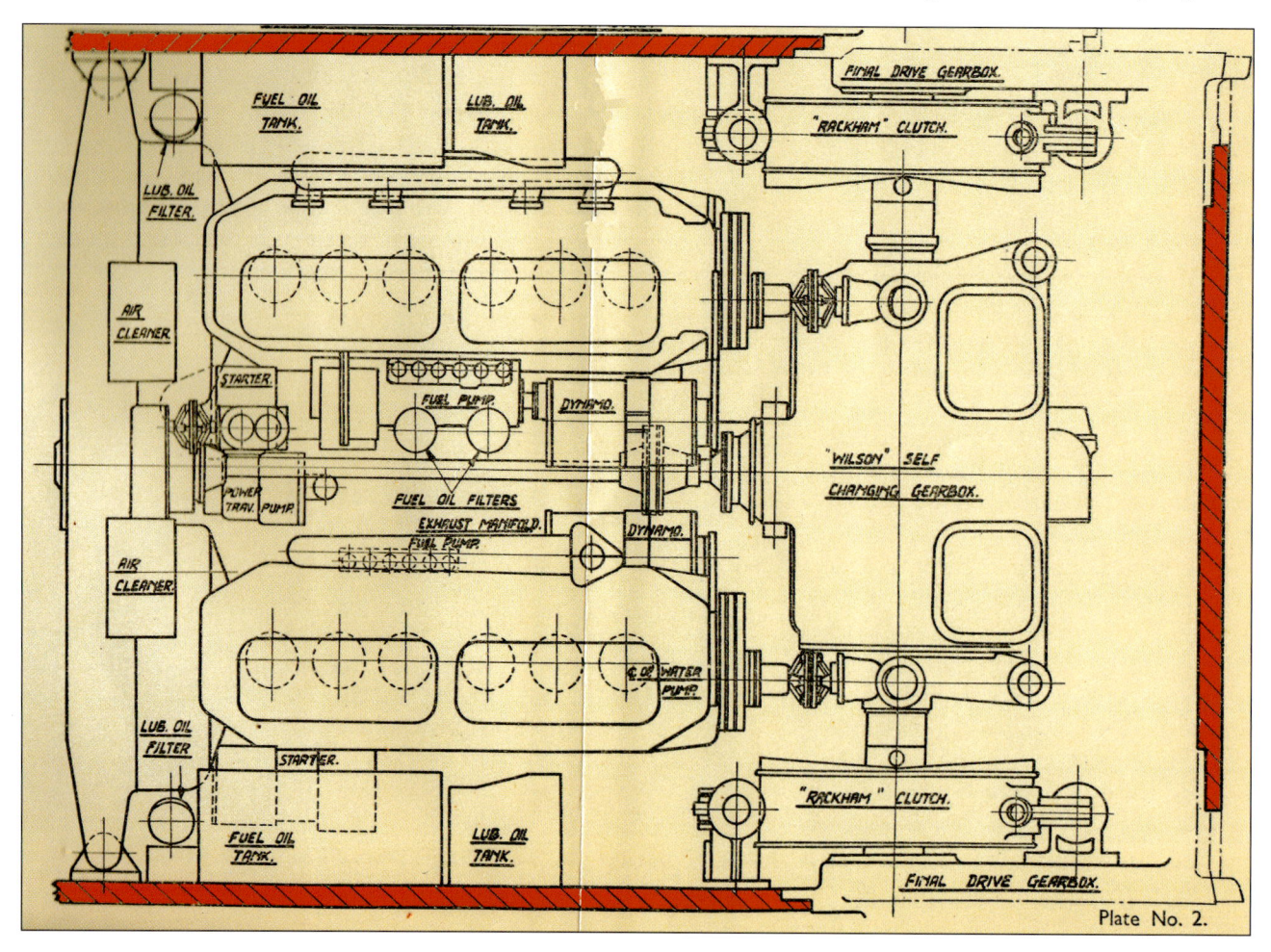

was a negative move it must be assumed that the reduction was meant to solve some unspecified problem, probably to do with reliability. When the AEC engines were first suggested for the A12 it was assumed, or thought, or hoped, that each engine would be capable of around 110bhp, but 95bhp was the best it would ever get, condemning the tank to a maximum speed of only about 15mph, and much less on any sort of uphill slope. This, plus the cramped turret on a too-small turret ring, were more than anything else the factors that led to the tank going out of front-line service in 1942.

The AEC engine was never going to be the optimum solution, merely the only one that was readily available when the tank was originally designed. It was decided subsequently that it would be an improvement to replace the AECs with a pair of Leyland engines, designated the E148/149 and giving the tank the new designation of Mk III.[1] The two Leyland engines used some identical components, the remainder being specific as they were mirror images of the other. The common components to both were the clutch, crankshaft, fuel injectors, the pistons and con rods and the sump. The new engines each developed 95bhp, taking the output back up to where it had been with the original AEC engines, but still short of the desired 110bhp. However, the torque was increased, from 6,240lb/in on the AEC to 7,000, a useful improvement of some 12%. Another Leyland-designed pair of engines were later introduced, the E164/165; tanks with these engines were also designated Mk IIIs. The mark designation stayed the same because the only real change was that the new pair used cast-iron crankcases, whereas the 148/149 had used aluminium. Whether this change of material was for efficiency reasons or merely reflected the general difficulties of obtaining scarce aluminium for army projects (at this time the RAF was operating a near-monopoly on the metal) is not clear, but for all practical purposes the old and new engine pairs were entirely interchangeable and both could be found on the Mk III.

The final iteration was when (probably in the autumn of 1941) the Leyland team developed the design to produce the E170/171 for the Mk IV, and which was retained in the final version, the Mk V; once again one was the mirror image of the other. This design, sometimes obliquely referred to in official publications as 'improved Leyland machinery', used two cylinder heads. This was thought to

BELOW The first type of engine pair fitted to the Matilda was the AEC 183/184; the exposed pulley-driven fans at the rear end are a recognition feature of this type. Note the three-point mounting system.

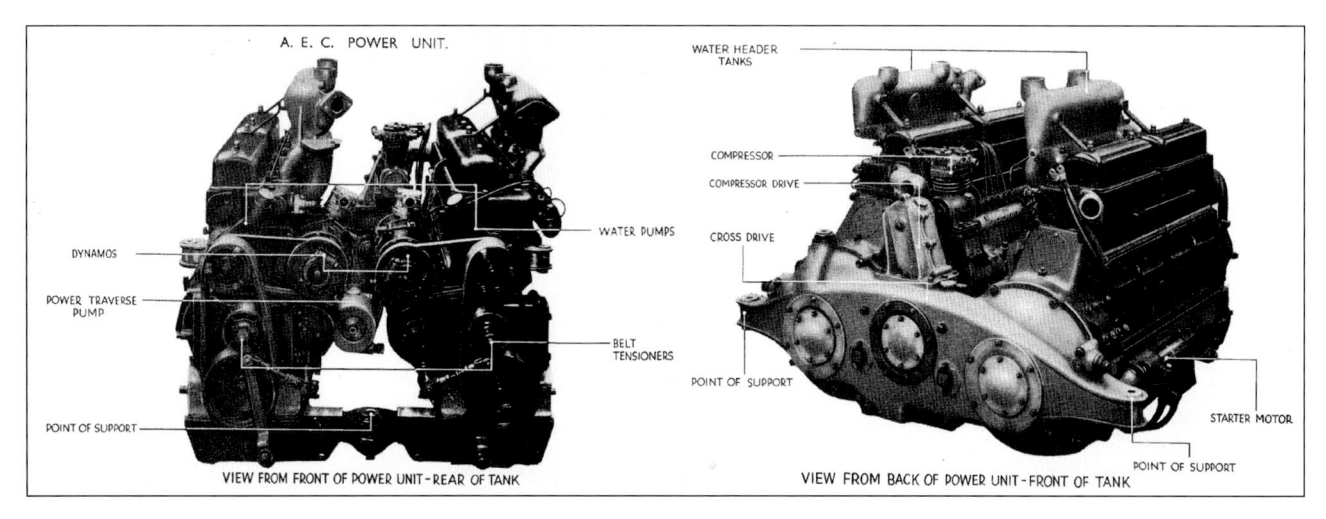

A. E. C. POWER UNIT.

VIEW FROM FRONT OF POWER UNIT – REAR OF TANK

VIEW FROM BACK OF POWER UNIT – FRONT OF TANK

MARK II & IIA.
A. E. C. POWER UNIT.

VIEW OF POWER UNIT FROM RIGHT REAR OF TANK

VIEW OF POWER UNIT FROM FRONT OF TANK

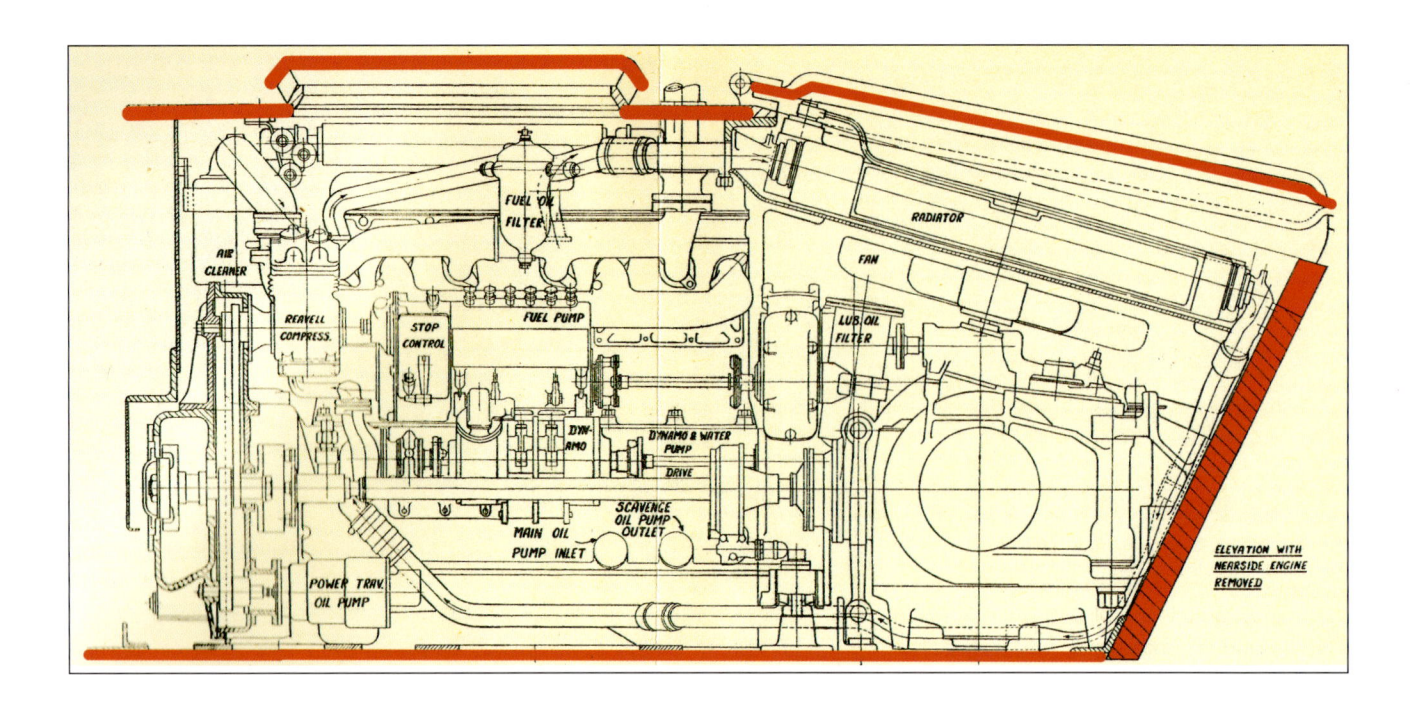

ABOVE AND BELOW Schematics of the improved Leyland engines used; as well as being fitted during production, earlier tanks were re-engined in RAOC workshops with the Leylands.

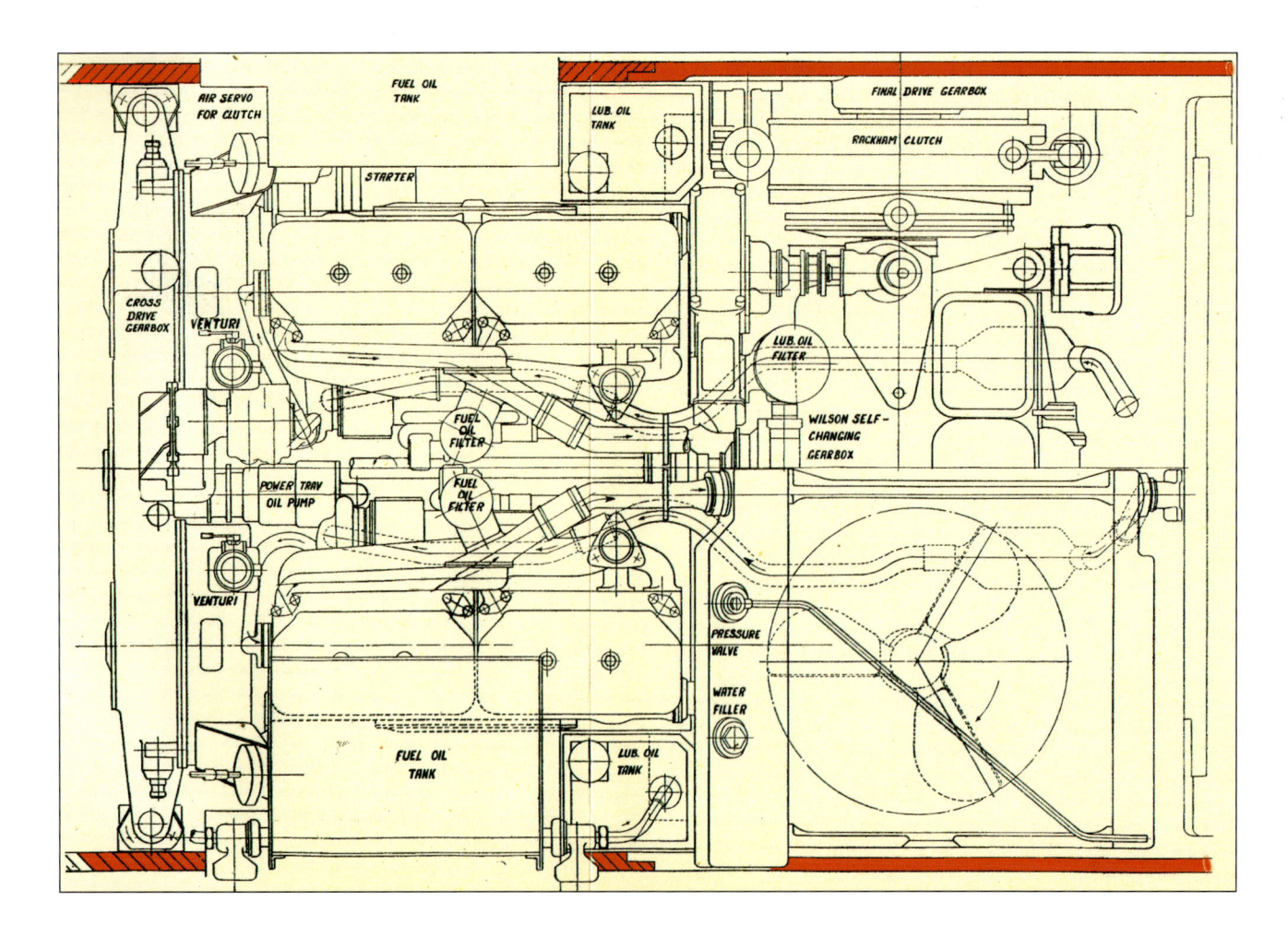

be a big improvement and led to the terrible pun circulating in Leyland circles that 'Two heads are better than one!' A scavenge pump was used to draw the M160 lubricating oil from the sump, meaning that the oil level could only be checked with the engine running; this arrangement was specifically designed to give better lubrication when the tank was operating on sloping ground. After the war many of the surplus E170/171 engines were sold and used as stationary engines linked to dynamos, often to provide the power for fairgrounds, where by all accounts they gave great service.

As well as engine improvements, at the time that the E170/171 was fitted on the Mk IV the opportunity was taken to improve and reroute the terribly complicated 'plumbing' that had resulted from the tank being designed and brought into service so quickly by a manufacturer unfamiliar with the needs of tank crews and maintenance teams in the field. Some components were moved in order to aid accessibility and to reduce the number of pipes and connections. This mainly affected the lubrication oil system, the air compressor system, the air inter-cooler, as well as the introduction of an ether cold-start device. The engine was also now mounted rigidly, unlike the previous Silentbloc HE 12524 mounting used on the Mk III and earlier marks; this was a three-point system designed to absorb vibration. In itself this was a sensible idea, but when applied to a pair of engines working together through the cross-drive, led to too much flexing within the whole system, which caused problems, and so replacing it with a three-point rigid mounting

BELOW The Leyland E148/149 as fitted to the Matilda Mk IIA*, otherwise known as the Mk III version. Although this only gave an 8bhp power increase, the engine was altogether a better design.

BOTTOM The final engine pair fitted to Matilda II was the Leyland E170/171. This was only used on the Mks IV and V tanks. The lubricating oil tanks are mounted on the starter motor brackets on each side.

MARK IIA*.
LEYLAND POWER UNIT

VIEW OF POWER UNIT FROM REAR OF TANK

VIEW OF POWER UNIT FROM FRONT OF TANK

MATILDA IV, IVC.S. & V.
LEYLAND POWER UNIT E170/171.

VIEW OF POWER UNIT FROM REAR OF TANK.

VIEW OF POWER UNIT FROM FRONT OF TANK.

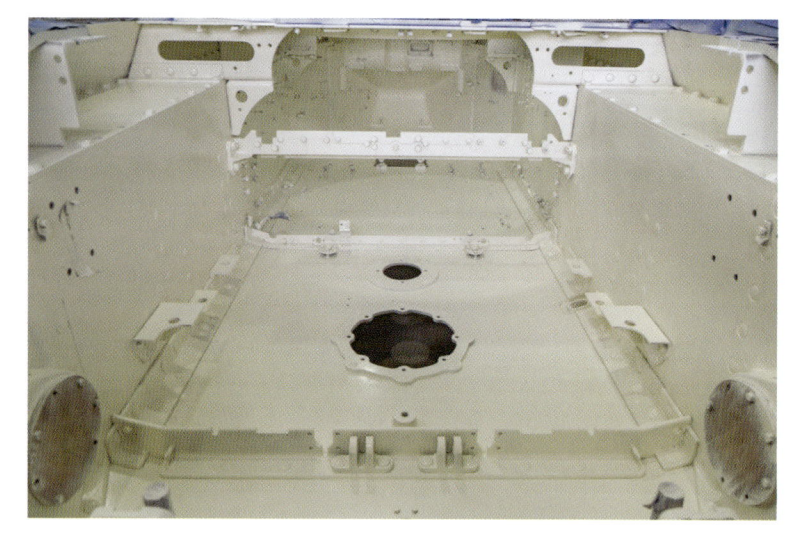

LEFT Inside the Tank Museum's restoration Matilda, showing the engine compartment ready to receive the very complex 'plumbing' that bedevilled Matilda and made maintenance such a hard task for the crews. The circular access hatch underneath the engines was referred to as the 'manhole cover'. *(TM)*

RIGHT AND BELOW Australian crews lifting and servicing a Leyland E170/171 in Queensland in 1944. *(AWM084898, AWM016611)*

removed one of the causes of malfunctions. Clearly the type of engine fitted was one of the biggest factors in deciding the mark of the tank, but externally they were almost identical, with only the Mk I being readily identifiable. The workshop instructions even tell the crew how to differentiate the Mk III from the Mk IV. The crewman was instructed to lift one of the hinged air inlet louvres; if there was a fuel evacuating pump visible on the top of the fuel tank it was a Mk IV, if no pump was there it was a Mk III.

The Mk V was the final Matilda mark. Very similar to the Mk IV, the biggest difference was that the original Clayton Dewandre air servo (mounted inline and located next to the cross-drive) was replaced by a Westinghouse unit, mounted on to the gearbox. Very little can be found in the way of information on the Mk V, and it is not at all clear from the production records which tanks from the final production runs were built as Mks IV or V. Although the new servo – and its location – were clearly intended to confer a tangible benefit, in terms of performance there was nothing notable and externally the two marks were identical. Manufacturers were often instructed by the Ministry of Supply to change the mark of the tanks they were building in mid-production run, and there is no indication that this caused them any technical difficulties. Some Australian records refer to Mk IV tanks being converted to Mk V, and so we can reasonably assume that the modification was relatively straightforward and able to be completed in a competent workshop. No clear records have been found of the Mk V in British service, and it seems probable that most were sent overseas for Australian use, which may be an indication that the modification was intended to improve performance in tropical conditions.

Whatever the mark, running a pair of engines together caused problems that a single engine would not present. In particular, the output of the two engines had to be synchronised. Ideally this was achieved on a specially designed rig, but in the field it could just about be done, although clearly not as well, by conducting a road run which would indicate to the crew whether 'the engines were reasonably synchronised or badly out'. If the latter, the crew and fitters were advised to improve matters as best they could by cleaning the whole fuel system, paying particular attention to the injectors. The fuel used was diesel, variously described in pamphlets as diesel oil (distillate type), gas oil, solar oil or by the trade names of Light Diesoleum and Shell Dieseline. Diesel oil was specified as it was thought to lower the risk of fires when compared to petrol, although once diesel is ignited it burns just as fiercely as petrol. The use of the fuel did cause logistic problems in an army that mostly ran its vehicles on petrol, but the crews of Matildas would at least benefit from increased range and economy. This could be taken too far: one wildly optimistic early pamphlet suggested that a full tank of diesel would be enough for one week's running.

Engine cooling was separate for each engine, with a water pump mounted on the engine, and a fan and radiator mounted at a slight angle to the horizontal above the gearbox; each fan had three blades or, when used in tropical conditions including the Australian variants, six. Early AEC-engined tanks had a fan drive taken off the crankshaft pulley turning three V-section belts, whereas Leyland-engined marks had a direct drive coming from a small gearbox on the engine timing case. The fans were correctly adjusted if they could just be turned by hand. When fitted, the coolant could be drained by the use of drain taps, one per engine, fitted either side of the engine bulkhead inside the fighting compartment, hardly the best place from the crew's perspective, and another example of poor design which failed to consider the servicing of the tank in real conditions. Air was drawn by the fans through the inlet louvres where it passed over the engine blocks and was blown out to atmosphere through the outlet louvres. A secondary air-cooling route drew air in through the front toolbox louvres where it passed through the driver's and fighting compartments before being pulled under the bulkhead and across the engine sumps, dragging lots of dust in as it did so.

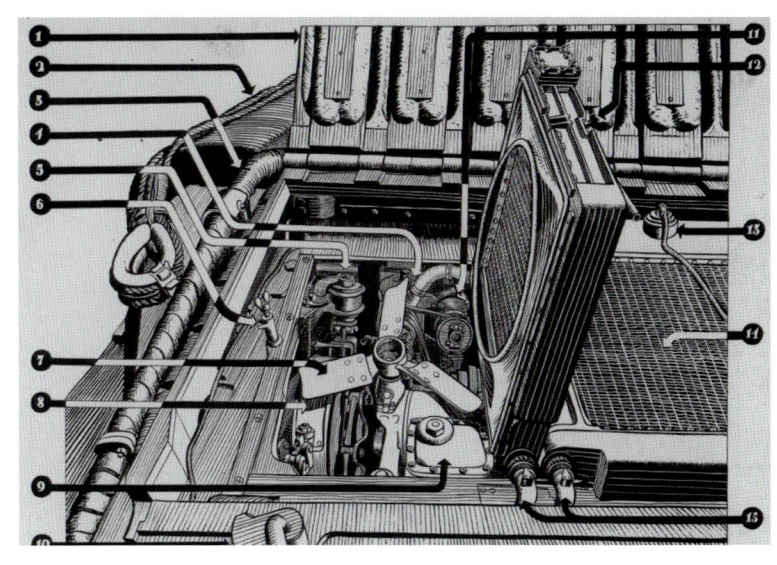

ABOVE An image taken from a Russian handbook, showing the transmission louvres raised and the left-hand radiator up, with the three-bladed fan below.

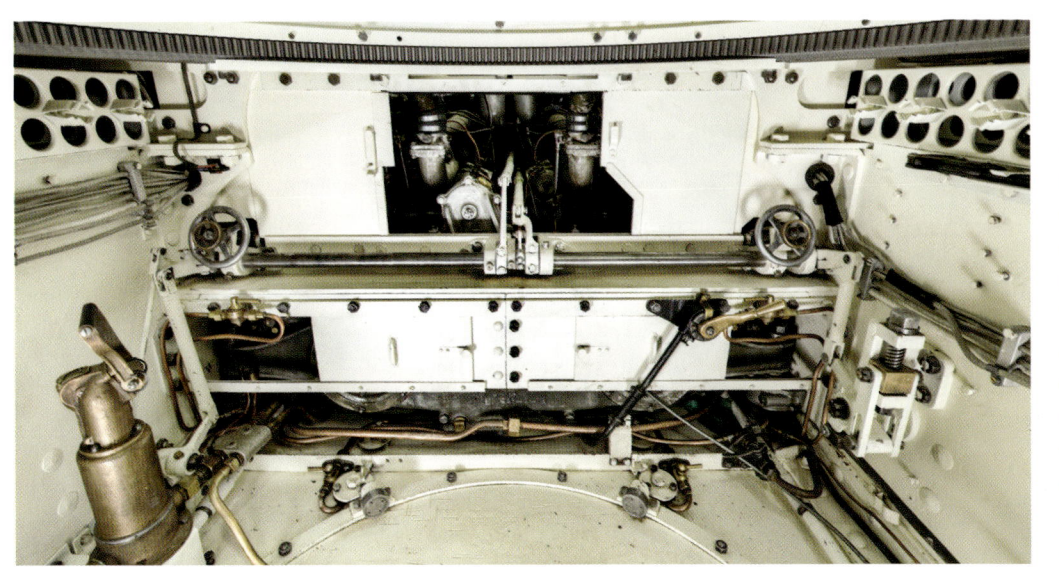

LEFT The rear of the fighting compartment showing the bulkhead separating the crew from the engine etc. The handwheels either side are used to operate the engine clutches when starting. Once again the complexity of the plumbing is painfully apparent. *(TM)*

RIGHT In addition to the diesel tanks mounted either side of the engine within the hull, a 36-gallon auxiliary fuel tank was often fitted externally on the hull rear.

BELOW The terribly complicated but totally necessary cross-drive, used to link the outputs of two separate engines and pass the power to the gearbox at the rear.

A constant pressure fuel pump drew fuel from each fuel tank (through a pre-filter on AEC engines only) to the main high-efficiency filter located above the engine. From here it was fed into a fuel gallery in the injection pump, where it could be distributed to the injectors. To clean the air before it was mixed with the fuel, an oil bath air cleaner fitted above the cross-drive was employed, which used a steel wool pre-filter mounted above the main oil bath to remove gross contamination – airborne particles such as sand and dust. A secondary take-off from the air filter provided clean air for use in the air compressor. The Reavell air compressor was a two-stage unit driven from the engine. High-pressure air from the compressor was produced when an engine was running with the clutch engaged, and stored in a reservoir in the right front of the fighting compartment; from the Mk III onwards the capacity of the reservoir was doubled, which allowed more gear changes to be made if the charging system became disabled. The stored air was required to allow the driver to change gear, by operating a pedal which in turn activated a master gear-change servo located on the nearside (left) of the fighting compartment. When fitted, auxiliary clutch servos were also operated using this high-pressure air, with the controls mounted to the front right of the driver; this meant that starting the engines could now be a one-man job requiring only the driver.

The gearbox received the drive from the two engines by way of the connecting cross-drive, with the centre pinion of the drive coupled to the input shaft of the gearbox via a prop shaft with rubber bush 'Layrub' couplings at either

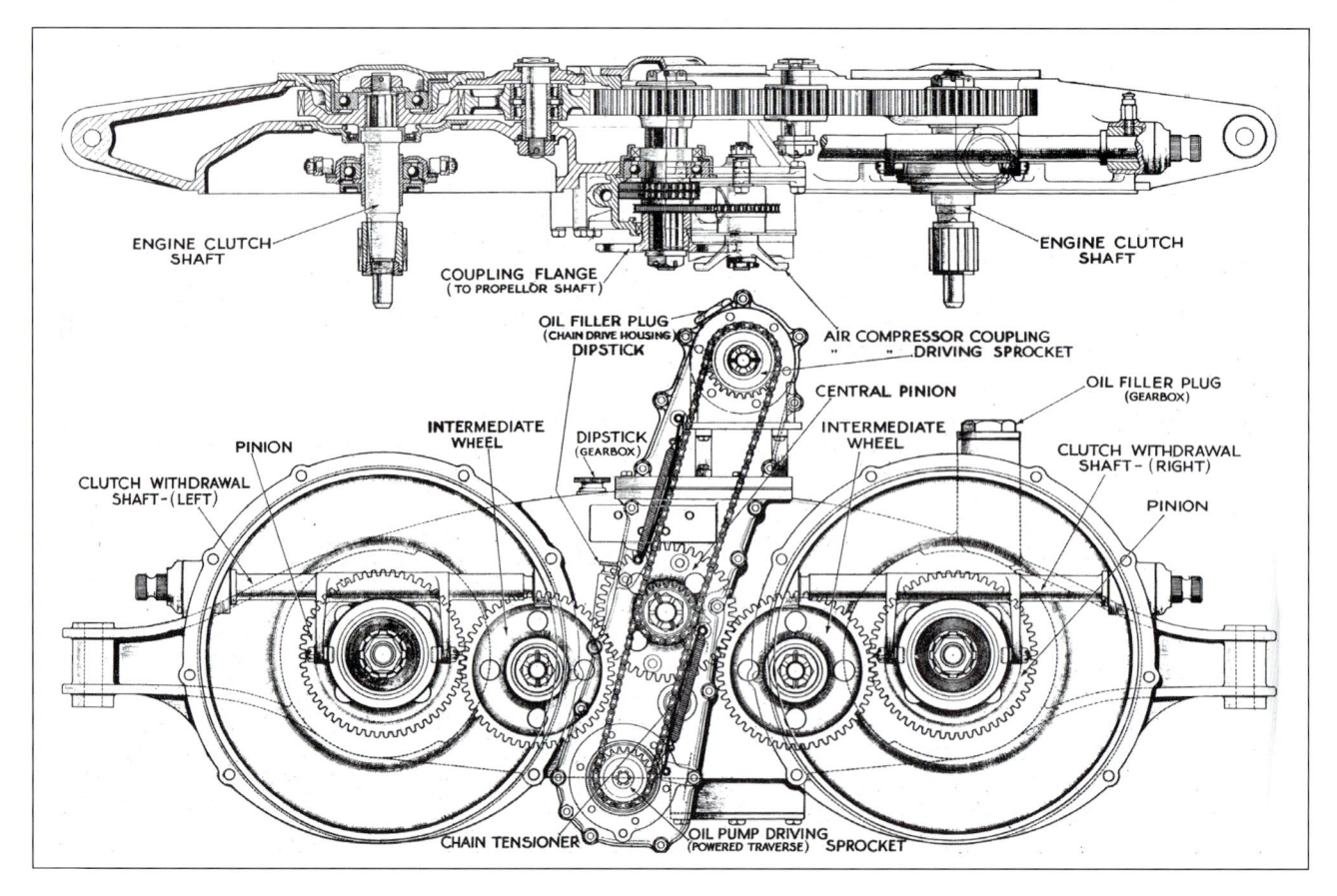

ABOVE A gearbox as taken from a hard-worked Matilda, showing all the typical accumulated grease and grime. The connection at the left corner is for the coupling coming forward from the cross-drive unit that linked the two engines together.
(George Moore)

RIGHT Gearbox details; the same type was used on all Matilda marks.

end. The cross-drive unit mounted between the rear of the engines and the gearbox was a complication necessitated by having two engines and contained a single dry plate 15in clutch for each engine which was engaged and disengaged using a transverse rod operated by handwheels in the inside of the fighting compartment.

The Armstrong Siddeley-built gearbox was a sophisticated and therefore complicated Walter Wilson-designed epicyclic pre-selector box, with five normal forward gears, an emergency low forward gear and a single-speed reverse. Drivers were taught that when changing up or down they must never miss out a gear (which could be done on other, more conventional gearbox types). The output from the gearbox was connected to a Rackham steering clutch on either side via a splined coupling, and thence to the drive sprockets.

RIGHT The drive train from a Mk III. The engines are in light green, the cross-drive in buff, the driveshaft in purple, the gearbox in dark green, the clutch in yellow and final drive and sprocket in pink and blue respectively. The three-bladed radiator fans are indicated by the red discs.

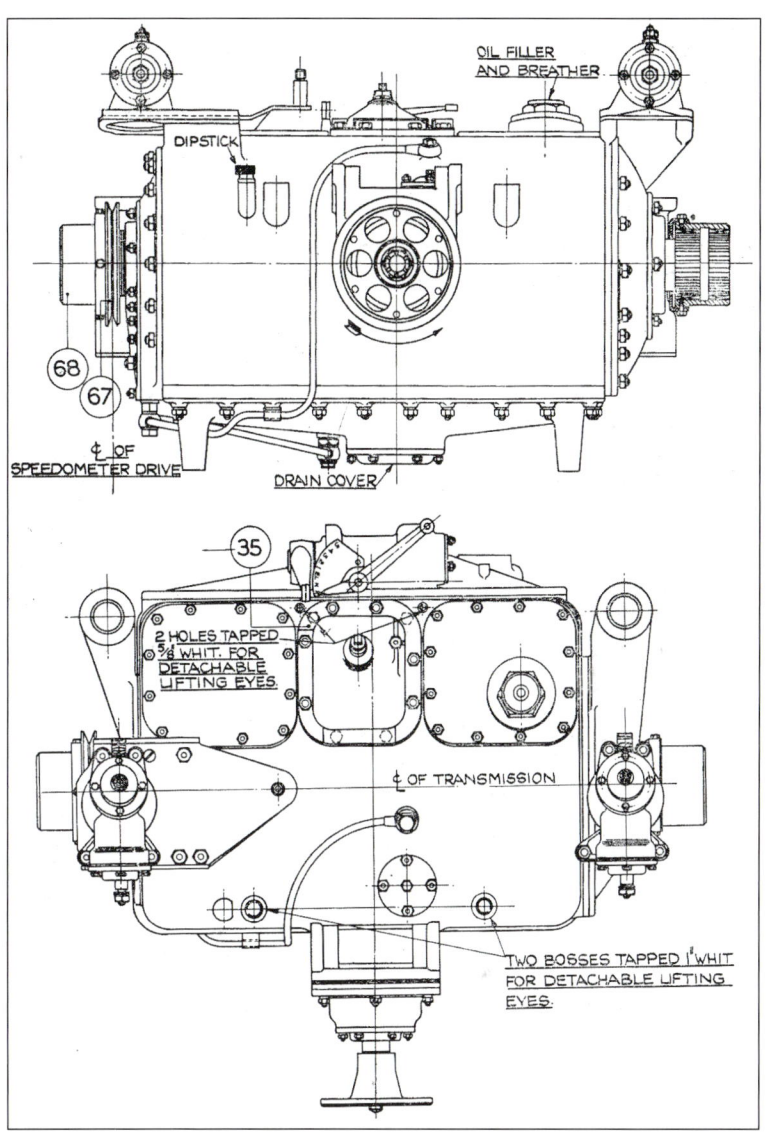

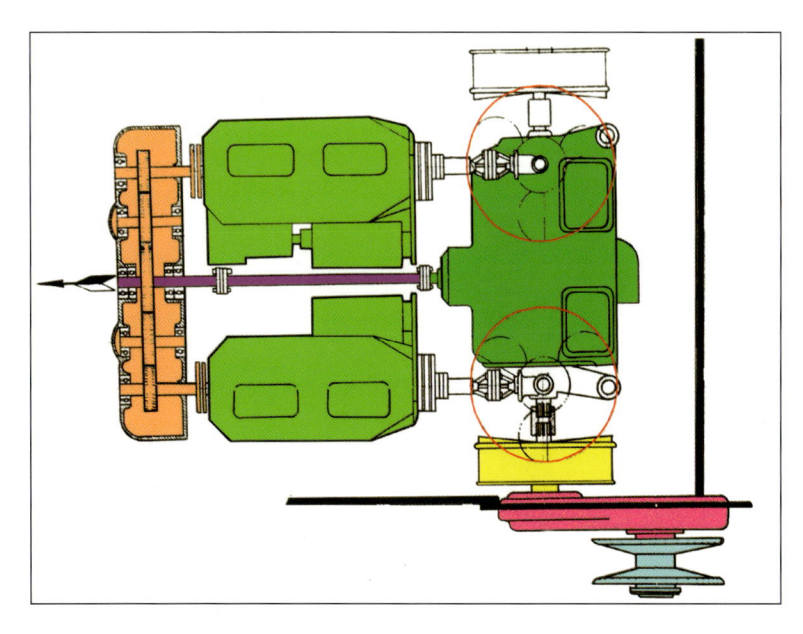

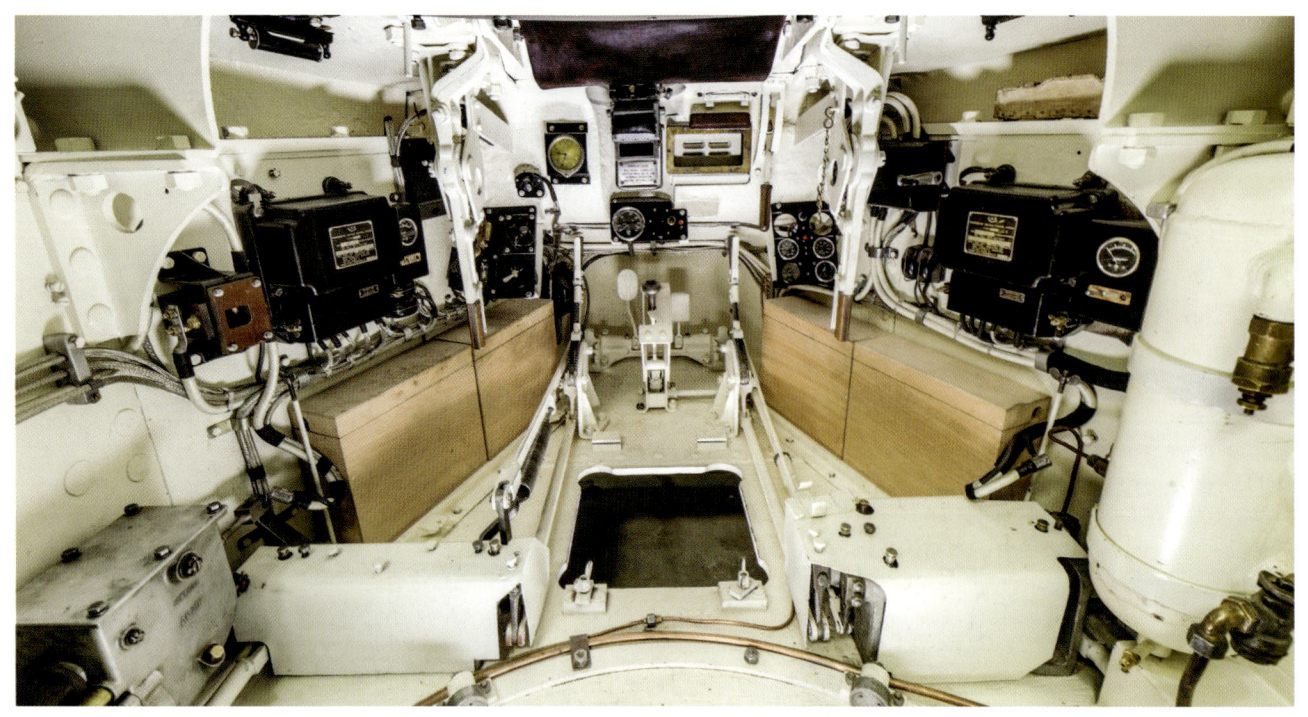

ABOVE **A fantastic overview of the driver's compartment, showing the extremely high-quality restoration work carried out at Bovington.**

Starting-up procedure (cold engine)

Starting the engine was a fairly lengthy and complicated procedure, made necessary by the way that the tank was designed.

- Check the power traverse recuperator is full
- Set the master control lever to OFF
- Check fuel, oil, coolant levels, top-up if required
- Turn fuel taps ON
- Prime the fuel pump (if engine has not been started for some time)
- Disengage both engine clutches
- Switch batteries to 'series' (up)
- Select which engine to start first using the appropriate starter button
- (On AEC engines only) Depress the fuel injector plug heater button for 20–30 seconds
- Depress the accelerator pedal fully
- Press the starter button, and release as soon as the engine starts
- Release the accelerator pedal, let engine warm up and settle to an idle
- Check oil pressure
- Select the other engine
- Start the other engine, note that the first engine revs will surge as the accelerator pedal is depressed
- Check oil pressure
- Engage both clutches and lock the handwheels
- Switch batteries to 'parallel' (down)[2]
- Check air pressure.

A hot start was similar, save that it was unnecessary on AEC-engined tanks to warm the plugs up using the heater button. Starting a warm tank would always be quicker and more importantly would allow the tank to be driven almost immediately. Drivers were taught that starting up both engines together from a single starter with the clutches engaged should only be done in emergencies, and then only when the engines and gearbox were already warm. If one of the two 24V CAV starter motors was unserviceable, that engine could still be started by running the other engine first, and then engaging the clutch progressively to start the second engine.

One of the unusual features of the gearbox design was that it required something called 'pedalling up'. This was carried out to prevent brake band slippage and was done by driving the tank forward, preferably on a slight downhill gradient, while keeping the engine speeds at 2,000rpm. While doing this each gear was selected in turn, and the gear-change pedal operated six times in succession in each gear.

If in use the driver sensed that a gear was slipping, he could repeat this procedure to tighten the bands up.

Driving the tank off was best achieved on a level or slightly downhill start. First gear should be engaged, with emergency low only used if in a bog or similar difficult ground, or if the ground in front was rising, although a well-trained crew would always try to halt their tank facing downhill. To change gear the gear selector lever was placed into the required gear, ensuring that it was the next higher (or lower) – as we have seen, it was stressed that missing out an intermediate gear was never to be done. To action the gear change, the gear-change pedal was operated smoothly in and out, and again it was emphasised was that it was not to be 'ridden' in an interim position like a conventional clutch pedal. When changing up, the driver was to momentarily release pressure on the accelerator in order to effect a smooth change; however, when changing down, the reverse was true: the driver kept the accelerator depressed throughout the change. Another point that was highlighted during tuition was that the tank must be brought to a complete standstill before changing from forward to reverse or vice versa, in order to move off in the opposite direction.

To switch off the engines, the driver would halt the tank, apply the ratchet handbrake by pulling the two steering levers backwards, and then select neutral. With the Leyland engines, the stop control lever on the left-hand instrument panel was used to kill the engines. On earlier AEC-engined Matildas, it was necessary for the driver to pull up and back on the accelerator pedal with either the hand or the toe of the boot until the engines stopped. In either case, the driver would then immediately select 'series', not only to place the switch in the correct position for a subsequent start, but more importantly to prevent the batteries being slowly drained due to the fuel gauge still being operative if 'parallel' was left selected.Servicing, repairs and maintenance on the Matilda were much more difficult, time-consuming and complicated when compared to most other contemporary tanks. This was due not only to the two-engine design, but also because of the routing of the various cables and pipes which were not in the best places for the crew to get to, as well as the difficult-to-access suspension and some of the ancillary systems like the compressed air required for gear changing. Along with the standard 'before use', 'halt parade' and 'after use' daily checks, the crews had maintenance tasks based on time or mileage, including specified servicing at the weekly, 500- and 1,000-mile points. A monthly inspection for functionality was completed using the G865 form.

Suspension and tracks

The suspension was based on the so-called Japanese suspension (apparently nicknamed as such because it was intended to be used on Vickers-built tanks destined for sales to that country) and first trialled on

BELOW The suspension – the side armour is the red outline, and the track is in yellow. The diagram at the bottom shows the shock absorbers (or bogie springs), used between the paired suspension levers.

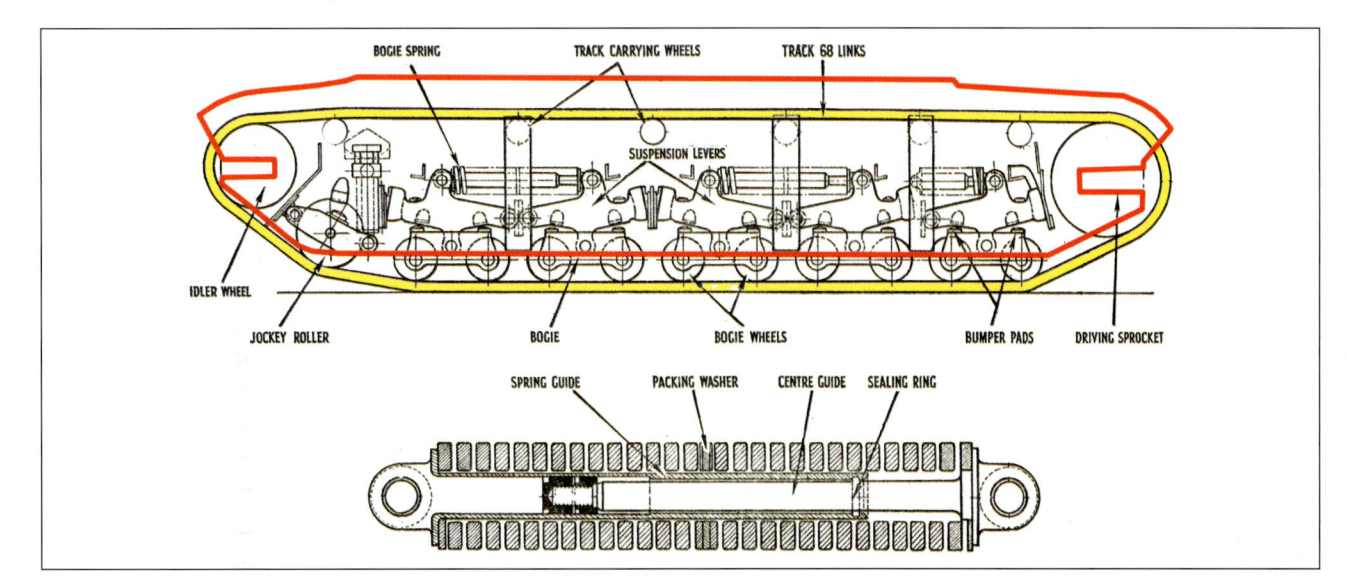

RIGHT AND BELOW One pair of bogies, with the bogie spring in between. Note the lockwire securing the wheel nuts and the rubber bump pad.

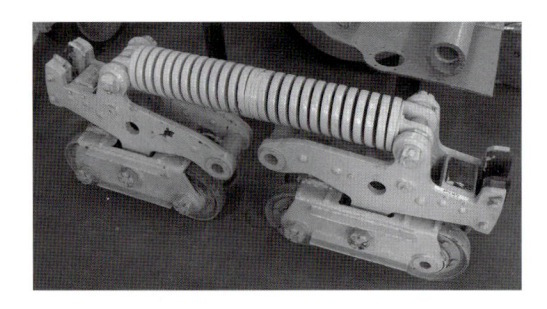

RIGHT Bogie units, sans roadwheels, having been removed from the Bovington Matilda prior to restoration. *(TM)*

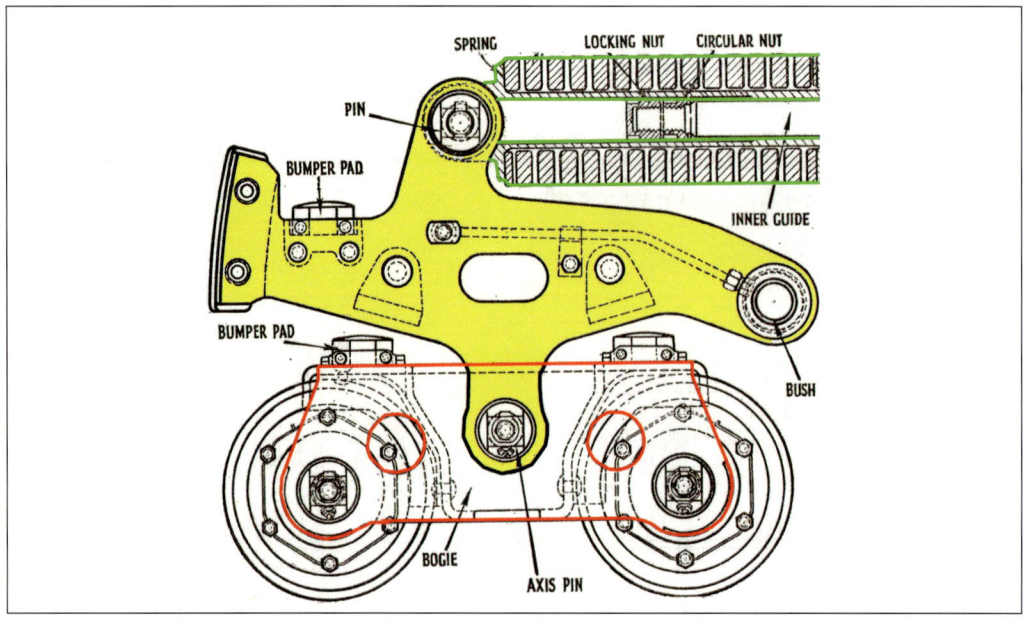

RIGHT The so-called Japanese suspension with its bell crank design. This allowed the crank (in yellow) to pivot around the top axis pin, with the roadwheels mounted on a bogie frame (the red outline) and pivoting about a lower axis pin.

T15, a Medium I tank, in 1924. This type of suspension was designed for vehicles which did not require high speeds, hence the choice of it for use on the Matilda. The suspension consisted of ten pairs of small steel roadwheels either side. Two pairs of these wheels were mounted on to each bogie frame, which was able to pivot around a central pin at the bottom of a bell crank unit. The bell crank units (or suspension levers) worked in opposition to a (nearly) mirror-image opposite number, with a horizontal bogie spring joining the two cranks at the topmost point. The first eight pairs of roadwheels shared this arrangement, and the final two pairs were mounted on a half unit, comprising only one bell crank, similar in design to the rearmost in a pair, and a half-length spring. Supporting the tracks at the top were five steel return rollers, sometimes called track-supporting wheels. On later marks these were replaced by simpler track-carrying skids. As a deliberate policy to reduce weight, the suspension units were welded. At the very front of the tank was an idler wheel, adjustable by the crew to maintain the correct track tension, as track links stretched when in use. Between the idler and the front roadwheel was an intermediate vertically sprung wheel, known as the jockey roller. At the very rear was a toothed sprocket, transmitting the drive from the gearbox via the final drive units to the tracks.

FAR LEFT AND LEFT Inside the mud chutes on the Matilda at Saumur. This has the later simple skids that replaced the earlier top roller wheels. *(John Bryce)*

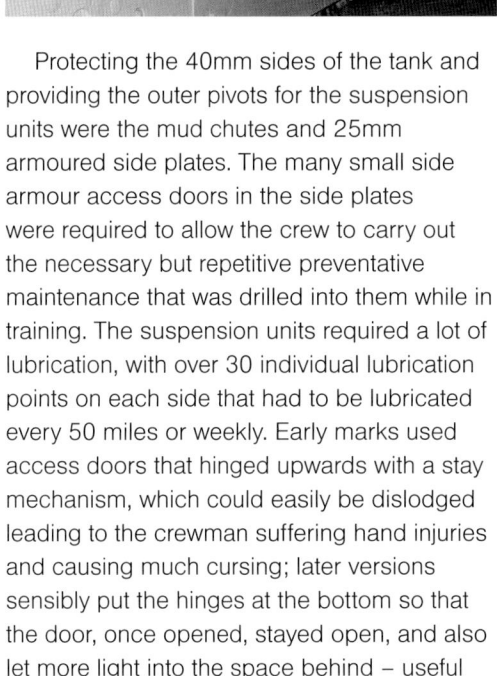

Protecting the 40mm sides of the tank and providing the outer pivots for the suspension units were the mud chutes and 25mm armoured side plates. The many small side armour access doors in the side plates were required to allow the crew to carry out the necessary but repetitive preventative maintenance that was drilled into them while in training. The suspension units required a lot of lubrication, with over 30 individual lubrication points on each side that had to be lubricated every 50 miles or weekly. Early marks used access doors that hinged upwards with a stay mechanism, which could easily be dislodged leading to the crewman suffering hand injuries and causing much cursing; later versions sensibly put the hinges at the bottom so that the door, once opened, stayed open, and also let more light into the space behind – useful when servicing.

The original 14in tracks were a direct copy of the design used on the Medium III. These tended to collect mud within the H-shaped indentations designed to increase grip, and over its life the tank used a number of different track designs and materials in order to find a better design; at least five different types were used in service, and others were trialled and rejected. Some 68 links were used either side. The first design used hollow track pins, but these were described as 'useless' in a post-BEF report of late 1940 and we can assume that solid pins were employed thereafter. Track tension was adjusted using the front idler wheel; it was correctly adjusted when there was a slight sag between the top rollers, although how this was to be set when the top rollers were replaced with skids on later marks is not clear.

FAR LEFT The original 14in stamped tracks, with the distinctive H shape, and very much based on designs from the 1920s. They proved to be good at collecting mud, but not much else.

LEFT One of the later track designs was this 14in Ford-designed cast track, an improvement on the earlier type as mud could not pack into the shoe, which had the effect of reducing grip.

RIGHT AND BELOW A section of six links, and a single link with track pin. During operations with the BEF in 1940 it was found that the hollow pins were next to useless, so a stronger solid type was introduced.

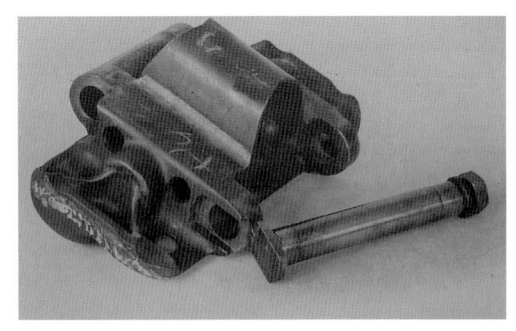

RIGHT Another variant, this one coming from the Vulcan Foundry handbook.

BELOW Spudded tracks. The track adjuster mechanism in its fully rearward position for a new track, and the early track supporting rollers, can both be seen.

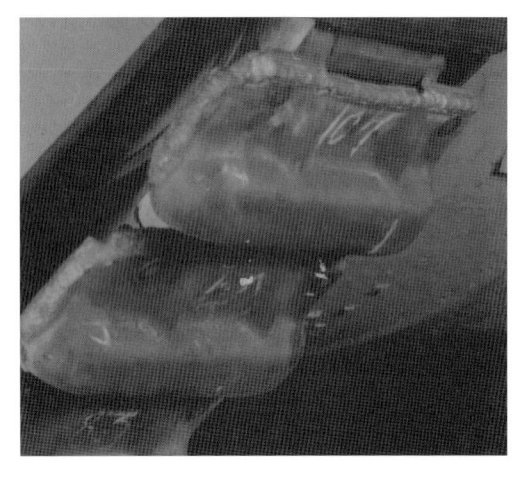

As another example of how the tank was designed for ease of production at Vulcan, rather than ease of maintenance for the crews in the field, the design of the sprockets is worthy of attention. Looking at the rear end of the side armour, it is quickly apparent that over half of the sprocket rings are hidden behind the armour. This was meant to give them protection but made changing them in the field extremely difficult, and every time an old track was changed for a new one, new sprockets would also be fitted. To get around this, the crews would cut the new sprocket rings in half. Although this weakened them structurally, for the crews this was a price worth paying as it allowed the rings to be changed much more quickly.

BELOW A different type of problem – coral mud packing between the sprocket rings on the Solomon Islands. *(AWM079163)*

Electrical supply and equipment

Three different electrical cabling layouts were used, known as Schemes A, B and C. Scheme A is not well documented other than to say it was only used on the earliest tanks; it may have been the scheme used with No 11 radio sets only, but this is not confirmed. Scheme A must logically have been the one used on the tanks armed with the Vickers MMG in the co-axial position; these used a take-off from the turret electrical circuit to run the Vickers MMG cooling pump. When the BESA MG was mounted on later marks, this take-off was used to run the ventilator fan fitted into the turret roof.

Schemes B and C were broadly similar to each other but differed in the type of cable used and the location of some of the components. Scheme B used screened cable whereas C had the cables in steel conduits. The easiest method to determine which scheme is used is by the number of driver's instrument panels: A and B both had three panels, but C rationalised the location of some of the most important controls and switches and grouped them in a more ergonomic way on two panels. It is likely that all Mk IV and V tanks used Scheme C, although exactly when the scheme was introduced is, like so many other details, unclear. It is probable that in many cases it was introduced midway through production runs, and so Mk IIIs were the types most likely to be found with either Scheme B or C. The batteries were two pairs of 6V lead acid CAV 6MMW17 130Ah batteries wired in series to provide 12V with one pair mounted in a box, one either side of the driver's seat; each engine had a CAV No 2 12V dynamo for charging. Early tanks featured lower-capacity batteries, but these were found to be inadequate and higher-capacity units replaced them.

The 12V headlamps (36W originally, 60W later) were mounted in shock-absorbing brackets on the nose and were generally covered by 'Standard ARP[3] masks', which reduced the light to a small half-moon. Sidelamps were fitted on either trackguard. A Klaxet 12V horn was mounted behind the left-hand 6W sidelamp, which is why the protective box on that side is slightly larger. An alarm gong was mounted inside the fighting compartment with the push-button operating it mounted on the centre of the hull rear, allowing an infantryman to attract the crew's attention in the days before infantry tank telephones. On early tanks a retractable day signalling lamp was fitted to the loader's side, which used a Morse key to illuminate the lamp, but this was found to be impractical and of little use and so it was deleted.

Radio

The No 11 radio set was introduced into British service just before the war to replace the older Set No 1 as used on the medium tanks. This became the first radio set to be used in the Matilda; it was only fitted to the early Matildas until it was replaced from 1941 onwards. The main set was positioned in accordance with British doctrine, in the

ABOVE Inside the driver's compartment. The pairs of brown battery boxes can be seen either side of the driver, and a main CAV distributor panel above the right rear box. Note the clock, something no self-respecting driver could do without. ... *(TM)*

BELOW The original No 11 wireless set, as used on early Matilda marks.

turret right rear where it was readily accessible to the crew, particularly the loader who was also the radio operator. The No 11 set was a crystal combined transceiver operating in the 4.5–7.1MHz range, with a theoretical operating range of up to 20 miles, although 8 miles for voice and double that for Morse were more likely. The antenna base was mounted on a cage fitted to the turret rear externally, with a cable-operated mechanism which allowed the antenna to be lowered nearly to the horizontal from within the tank for tactical reasons. The antenna rod was either 6ft or 9ft high and of a fairly thick cross-section, so it was something of a giveaway which could be easily seen over a horizon – it is also useful as an identifying feature of tanks fitted with that type of set. Most antenna bases had a metal dome fitted over them to protect the vulnerable rubber base from damage or even being ripped off if the antenna caught on a low branch or similar obstruction. Some tanks in the command role could be fitted with a second No 11 set to allow them to operate on two radio nets, but information on this option is scanty and where the second set was mounted is not clear, though almost certainly not in the turret.

BELOW The antenna base for the No 11 mounted on the turret rear; this could be lowered from within the turret in order to reduce the tank's signature, particularly when occupying ridgelines.

The much improved Pye-designed No 19 radio set was developed from an earlier type, the No 9, and introduced as the replacement for the No 11 in Matildas produced from 1941; it could also be retrofitted to the earlier models. It was a great step forward in providing British AFV crews with reliable communications over a greater range. The two main components were the (power) Supply Unit No 1, mounted separately but connected to the Wireless Set No 19 by a 12-point (core) cable connector. The No 19 was in fact two radio sets in one: a longer-range high frequency (HF) A set used at squadron or regimental level, and the lower-power and thus shorter-range very high frequency (VHF) B set, usually used for troop nets. The division into two sets meant that two different antenna bases were required, the No 8 for A set on the right rear of the turret roof behind the loader's hatch, and the No 9 for the B set on the right front of the roof. Antenna lengths also differed, 8ft (two 'F' antenna sections, the standard option) or 12ft (three sections to increase the range) were used for the A set and a 20in 'G' rod antenna for the B. The absence of the No 11 antenna base and bracket on the turret rear, with or without the dome, and/or the presence of two thinner, rather than one thick, antenna, are the key recognition features in deciding whether a Matilda has the earlier or later radio set.

With the No 19 set, the commander and gunner both plugged their headsets into the same Control Unit No 1 on the left-hand side of the turret, and the loader (radio operator) used his own Control Unit No 2. The driver had a Junction Distribution Box No 3 in the cab to plug into. An inbuilt audio amplifier allowed the crew to use the intercommunication (IC) system, again a huge improvement over the outdated voice tubes of only a few years previously.

Weapons

The main gun was officially known as the 'Ordnance Quick-Firing 2 Pounder Mk IX, IXA, X or XA, in the Mounting 2 Pounder & BESA MMG Mk I–III'. The quick-firing or QF part of the designation meant that the gun used cartridge case obturation – gas sealing of the breech when firing – and that the gun

ABOVE Fitting the mantlet to a Matilda. In this Ministry of Supply image it can be seen that a wooden barrel has been used to allow the mantlet to be manoeuvred into position.

ABOVE RIGHT The mantlet and 2pdr gun. For almost the whole of 1940 this was the best tank gun anywhere in the world, despite its lack of an HE capability.

ABOVE Matilda II Mk I tanks were the only marks equipped with the Vickers MMG as the co-ax. The steam aperture for this gun is outlined in red.

BELOW An RTR corporal instructor supervises a crew of trainees in July 1941. They are learning the operation and handling of the Vickers MMG, including its use on the tripod.

would eject the spent case as the gun 'ran forward into battery', the technical way of saying that after full recoil, the recoil system pushed the gun forward into the fully run-out position, opening the breech block as it did so, known as semi-automatic operation. The main differences in Matilda armament was when the earlier Mk I tanks fitted with Vickers MMGs were superseded by the BESA MG, which was specified as the standard MG for use in all tanks from 1940 onwards.

The other option was found in CS tanks. These used the 'Ordnance Quick-Firing 3in Howitzer Mk I or IA, in the Mounting 3in Howitzer & BESA MMG No 3 Mk I', and this gun only appears to have been fitted to Mk III and IV Matildas. The installation of the 3in howitzer in Matilda was not part of the original design, although the 3in mounting had been used on other tanks including the A10 and was easily interchangeable to fit in the same space envelope as the 2pdr mounting. Records exist of trials conducted in

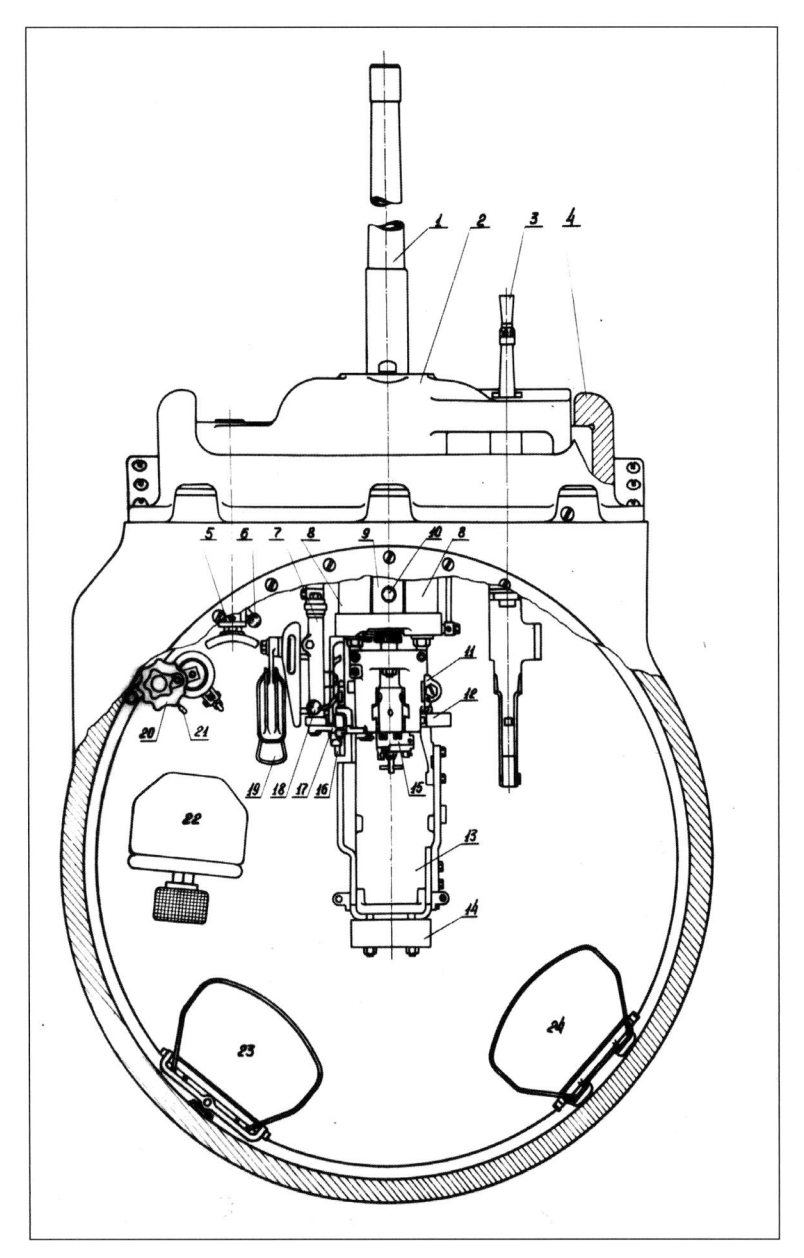

Farnborough in January 1941 to optimise the ammunition stowage of a Mk IIA as a CS tank, and this probably followed earlier gunnery trials to confirm that the tank/gun combination was technically feasible. Apart from modified ammunition stowage CS tanks were technically much the same as 2pdr gun tanks. This weapon was an L23, meaning that the barrel length was 23 times the calibre, in this case 76.2mm, making the barrel 1.75m long overall. The 3in gun was designed in the mid-1930s, primarily to fill a requirement to fire smoke ammunition, although an HE round was also manufactured. The gun was used not only in Matilda CS tanks, but also in early Churchills, as well as the close-support versions of the Tetrarch light tank, and also in the Covenanter and Crusader cruiser tanks.

LEFT A diagram from a Russian handbook, showing the turret layout, with the BESA MG (3) to the right of the 2pdr breech (12) and the gunner's controls and sight to the left. The gunner's, commander's and loader's seats are 22, 23 and 24 respectively.

BELOW LEFT Inside the fighting compartment, this time from a British handbook. Note the next-to-useless signalling lamp shown as No 10.

BELOW A posed photograph (as the recoil guard has been removed) of the gunner (left) and loader (right) in position. Notice that they are wearing their respirator haversacks on the chest in the ready position, something not often done in action after 1940. *(TM2835C5)*

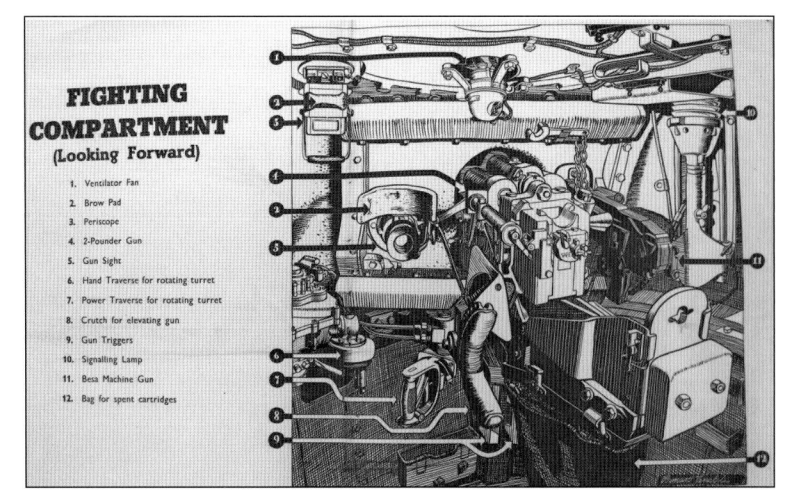

ABOVE A Matilda CS. The thicker barrel of the 3in howitzer also lacks the distinctive taper of the 2pdr barrel. Matilda CS tanks were used in the squadron headquarters of Valentine-equipped units.

BELOW Australian crews replenish with 3in howitzer ammunition – this is the HE variety, which proved to be very useful in the jungle when artillery support was difficult to rely on. *(AWM090293)*

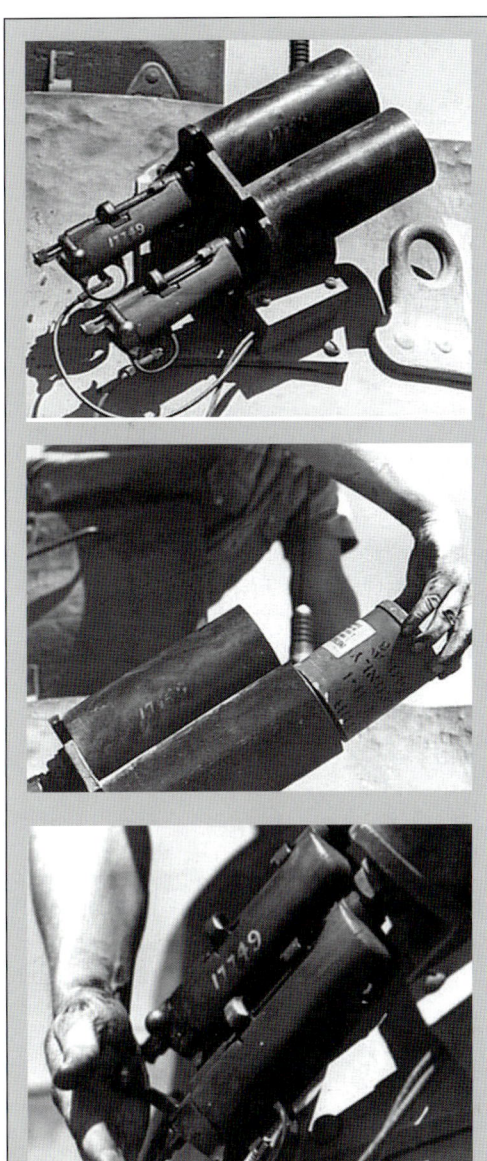

ABOVE The twin 4in smoke grenade dischargers on T17749 in the Western Desert. A crewman demonstrates how to load the smoke cylinder and then the .303in blank cartridge used to fire them. *(AWM028515 series)*

LEFT Inside the Tank Museum Matilda's turret. The two bicycle brake levers used to fire the smoke dischargers are on the right-hand turret wall, complete with safety chains and pins.

RIGHT The rear turret lookout. Note how agricultural the welding around the mounting plate is.

BELOW With the turret removed, inside the hull centre, with the RBJ in the middle and the ammunition stowage arrangements clearly visible. This tank does not have the later 26-round ammunition bin fitted on the floor.

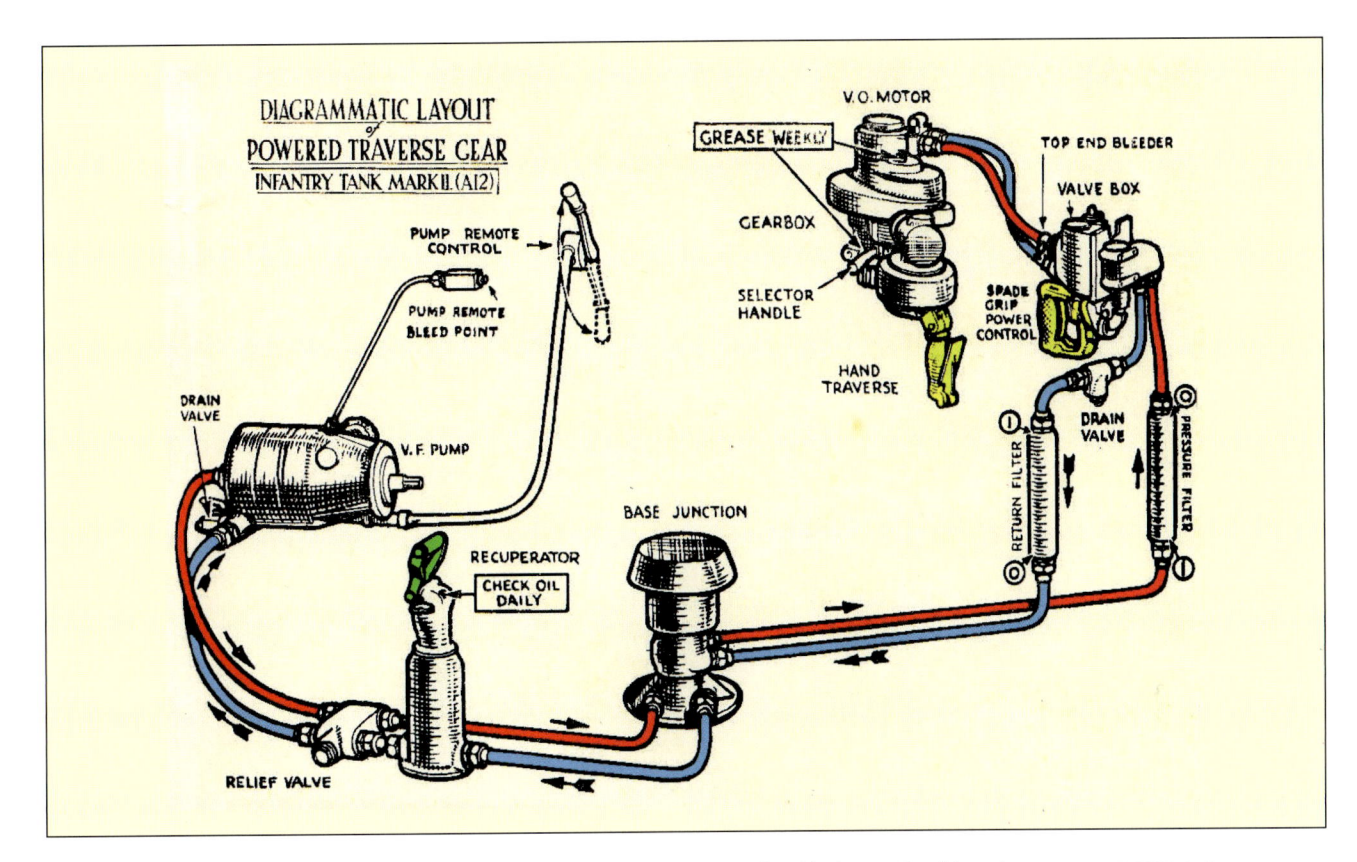

ABOVE A diagram showing the layout of the hydraulic power traverse system. Note the recuperator handle in green, and the gunner's power and manual controls in yellow.

Turret layout

The turret was provided with a floorplate for the crewmen to stand on, which was supported on rollers and traversed with the turret. In the centre of the floor was the Rotary Base Junction or RBJ, which allowed electrical signals to pass between the hull and turret. Unusually for the period, the Matilda was equipped with a hydraulic power traverse system, designed to allow the crew to make rapid line switches between widely spaced targets. Although a useful feature, hydraulic power traverse was to go out of favour in Britain by the end of the war, as experience showed that ruptured hydraulic pipes in action were the cause of many crew casualties, and with other tanks (Churchill, Valentine, etc) electrical systems were specified, but that was in the future. In 1938, the system was a great leap forward in fire control and helped the crew in 'quickest on the draw'-type engagements.

For normal (non-powered) traverse, usually used when the arc to be traversed was not great, the gunner was provided with a manual hand traverse handle. This was mounted directly underneath the traverse gearbox which was in mesh with the toothed turret rack. In order to traverse, the gunner would take hold of the grip switch on the handle to engage the gearing, and turn the handle in the required direction – the faster he rotated the handle, the faster the turret moved; for fine laying on to a target, delicate movements were required. The powered traverse system used a valve box connected by pipes to the power traverse motor situated on top of the traverse gearbox; underneath the valve box was the spade grip for controlling the speed and direction of traverse. A recuperator cylinder was mounted in the right rear of the fighting compartment, with a handle on the top which was used to pressurise the system. When the gunner wanted to use power, he would grasp the spade grip and twist the whole grip in the direction he wanted the turret to move; the more he deflected the controller, the faster the turret moved. The minimum deflection of the spade grip for fine laying (if he chose not to use hand traverse) was 5°, with 45° deflection giving maximum speed. At full rate the turret could traverse through 20° of arc per second, allowing the turret to move through a complete half circle, 180° (the theoretical worst-case line switch), in only 9 seconds. For safety, a cut-off switch in the gearbox prevented the manual traverse handle from spinning around when power was used. Another clever feature was a cam which lifted the barrel up automatically over the engine louvres when the gun was traversed towards the rear if it had been depressed below the horizontal.

The vision cupola was designed to allow the commander to exercise efficient control of his tank while remaining closed-down under armour. A Vickers Tank Periscope was fitted in the front hatch, and although space was tight, gave the commander all-round vision. When aligned to the front, the blade vane sight mounted on the turret roof in front of the cupola allowed the commander to align the gunner with a distant target to a fair degree of accuracy. For engaging targets the gunner was provided with a Telescope Sighting No 30 or 33 mounted into the mantlet; a spare was carried in case of damage, but if this had to

LEFT The recuperator mounted in the rear right of the fighting compartment, with the handle used to pressurise the system. At the risk of sounding like a stuck record, notice again all the plumbing. *(TM)*

BELOW The two firing grips in the Tank Museum's Matilda (before restoration); the left one fired the main armament, the right one the co-axial MG – the Bowden cable on the top of the grip was linked to the MG firing mechanism. *(TM)*

RIGHT Two types of cupola were used in the Matilda. This is the early higher type, with a Lulworth Gunnery School instructor demonstrating the use of the Bren LMG with drum magazine on the Lakeman mounting.

be fitted midway through an engagement this would be inaccurate as it would have not been aligned with the gun or, better still, 'shot in' to ensure the very best chance of a first-round hit. For reasons that are not fully understood, later marks of Matildas were built with a lower cupola, effectively a simple hatch system; almost all of the Australian tanks used the low version. For navigation purposes a compass in a cylindrical binnacle was mounted on the turret floor.

RIGHT The simplified low-cupola design, here used on the three nearest Aussie Matildas, although the fourth tank retains the earlier dustbin cupola. *(AWM027499)*

BELOW A closer view of the low cupola, again in Australian use. Note that the spotlight is still deemed essential equipment. *(AWM095833)*

BELOW RIGHT Inside the cupola hatches on a preserved Matilda. The wire loop across the top is pulled by the commander to release two spring-loaded plungers and allow the hatch to be opened from inside. *(George Moore)*

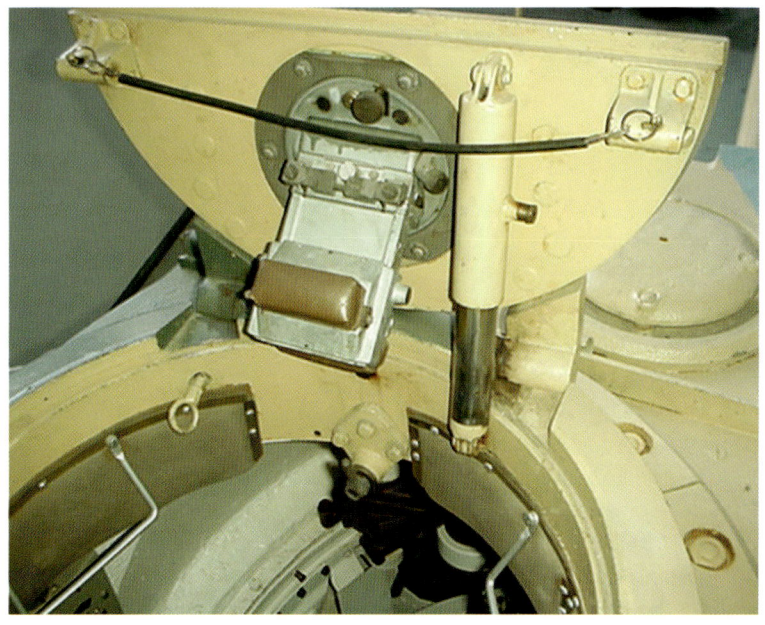

Ammunition, stowage and tools

Ninety-three rounds of 2pdr ammunition were carried. Of these, 52 rounds were stowed in the hull, 26 in boxes in each sponson in a 14 + 12 configuration, but the rest of the ammunition (41 rounds) was stored in easier-to-reach spring-loaded clips or bins in the rotating turret floor. Eight were in a horseshoe around the RBJ in the centre of the turret floor, 7 in a rack under the radio set, and 26 in an open-topped bin on the turntable floor. Early marks *may* have carried less 2pdr ammunition than this: on 10 June 1941 an official visit to Vulcan Foundry took place in order to view a suggested ammunition stowage amendment to increase the number of rounds carried by 26, so it may be that the early tanks only carried 67. The lack of a very early stowage diagram makes this difficult to prove, but it does seem unlikely that it would be possible to put an additional 26 rounds in over and above the 93 carried, in what was an already very cramped fighting compartment. As 26 was the number carried in each sponson as well as in the bin on the turret floor, it may be that very early Matildas featured a different stowage arrangement in which either only one sponson carried 2pdr ammunition or the floor bin was not used; the latter is more likely.

Some 13 boxes each holding 225 rounds of BESA 7.92mm ammunition for the co-ax were stowed, including the one in use on the feed tray, giving a total of 2,925 rounds. When tanks were provided with a Bren LMG for use as a local and air defence weapon (the latter using the Lakeman mounting[4]), six drum magazines of 100 rounds were stored in the three boxes on the turret rear, two drums in each. Six No 36M hand grenades or Mills Bombs were stowed inside the turret. Ten smoke grenades for the 4in smoke dischargers were carried, two loaded and eight spares, again within the turret. Also carried as stowage were:

- 3 × flags distinguishing (on 2ft 6in poles)
- 3 × yellow flags (on 3ft poles)
- 1 × camouflage net 35ft × 15ft
- 1 × crowbar 3ft 6in
- 1 × towing hawser 2¼in × 30ft

Tools were carried both internally and externally. Although the layout of these changed slightly over the service life of the tank, and of course was often modified by the crews, the units, and because of the theatre of

RIGHT An RTR-operated Matilda II in the UK on exercise, *c*1941. This tank has the UK-style trackguard extensions and a full stowage layout, including towrope and the various canvas items on the turret shelf. Note that the engine decks have been raised.

operations, the basic stowage remained fairly constant. In broad terms, a typical stowage layout was as follows:

Turret external
- Lakeman AA mount for Bren LMG
- 3 × stowage boxes each holding 2 × 100-round Bren LMG drums
- Camouflage net, cover turret, cover engine, cover tank and bivouac plus poles bivouac, 4 × groundsheets, 4 × blankets on rack on left-hand side
- 4 × distinguishing (signal) flags in canvas tube
- Inter-tank starting cable (coiled and stowed under turret rear right lookout)

Hull rear
- Auxiliary fuel tank

Hull external right-hand side
- 3 spare track links
- Crowbar 3ft 6in
- Pickaxe helve (handle)
- Shovel GS
- 3 × POW cans on rack (desert use)

Hull external left-hand side
- 3 spare track links
- Case aerial with mast and spare sections
- 30ft towing hawser
- 3 × POW cans on rack (desert use)

Tool locker left-hand side
- 4 × haversacks
- 4 × greatcoats
- 6 × ration boxes (2 men, 1 day)
- Portable cooker in canvas bag
- Canvas bucket
- Air identification discs and strips
- Fuel tank evacuation pipe 9ft

Tool locker right-hand side
- Gun cleaning kit
- Pick head
- 15in machete in sheath
- Junior compressor No 2
- 1-gallon oil can
- 5-ton screw jack and handle
- Wire cutters in sheath
- Tools in tool roll

- Spare track pins
- 11in cleaning brush
- Brush, bass hand
- Bleach powder 2lb

Driver's compartment
- 2 or 3 boxes BESA
- Anti-gas equipment 4-man (capes and gloves)
- 2 × spare periscope prisms
- Handbook
- Water bottle
- Signals satchel
- Oil can
- Pyrene fire extinguisher
- 2 × spare Triplex screens

Turret floor
- 26 × 2pdr (in bins)
- 8 × 2pdr (horseshoe)
- 1 box BESA
- Bren LMG and bipod
- Hellesen lamp

Inside fighting compartment
- 3 × water bottles
- Spares and tools 2pdr or 3in
- Spares, cleaning rod and tools BESA
- Spare periscopes and prisms
- Wireless spares
- Inspection lamp
- Cocking lanyard
- Map case
- MG oil can
- Spare gunner's telescope No 24 in case
- 6 × hand grenades
- Pyrene fire extinguisher
- Wallet Bren LMG
- First-aid kit (underside of turret roof)
- Signals satchel
- Spare smoke grenades and .303in cartridges
- Clutch spanner

Weapon covers carried
- 2pdr or 3in howitzer muzzle cover
- Breech cover
- 2 × rifle breech covers (smoke gen)
- 8 × spare muzzle covers (smoke gen)
- Muzzle cover BESA MG.

DOVER
T 73

Chapter Six

Marks and modifications

Although unable to be upgraded to carry the larger 6pdr gun, the Matilda was developed for use in a number of specialist roles, including carrying a top secret searchlight apparatus, as well as being used as a mine-clearing flail tank and as a flamethrower.

OPPOSITE The Tank Museum's Canal Defence Light Matilda. *(Shutterstock)*

Calling a spade a shovel – the story of the name

Prior to the Second World War, it was not British policy to name tanks. True, there were such vehicles as the Whippet, the Hornets and the Independent, but these were never officially sanctioned names, at best they should be considered as semi-official. As new designs evolved, they were often called, again unofficially, by project names intended for use by the manufacturer pending the allocation of the official type and mark designation when it entered service. The first of these was the A11 (which was simply the General Staff specification serial for the project and again never intended to be used once the tank was in service) also known as the Infantry Tank Mk I, and which was called the Matilda. This was, according to legend, because it apparently resembled a waddling cartoon duck of the period. As research has never found any trace of such a character – although one did exist but only *after* the Second World War and which was probably responsible for the apocryphal story – the real reason is probably simpler: the designer at Vickers, Sir John Carden, who initiated the project allocated a codename from those used by his own family members. This cannot be proven, but as both Matilda and Valentine were Christian names used within the Carden clan, it does make logical sense. What probably happened next was simply that the soldiers involved in early trials and so on heard the name being used by the Vickers team and the name stuck. When the larger Mk II known officially by the GS designator A12 came out, it then inherited the name, initially being called Matilda Senior and then Matilda II. Sometimes noted in records as Waltzing Matilda, this longer name was clunky and unofficial and pre-dated Australian use of the tank – it probably started simply because most people associated the name Matilda with the popular Banjo Paterson song of the same name from the start of the century.

The WO published a list of tanks in service on 11 June 1940 stating that, 'to avoid confusion' the following types of AFV will be designated as listed. This stated that the tank 'previously known as A11 or Matilda I' would now be known as Infantry Tank Mk I, and the tank 'previously known as A12 or Matilda II' would henceforth be referred to as Infantry Tank Mk II. The note went on to explain that the addition of the letter A after the mark signified a difference in armament only, so by way of example Infantry Tank Mk II is equipped with a Vickers-type machine gun, whereas Infantry Tank Mk IIA is equipped with a BESA MG. The addition of an asterisk signifies an alteration in the type of engine; Infantry Tank Mk IIA* is equipped with a Leyland engine, whereas Infantry Tank Mk IIA is driven by an AEC engine.

On 8 August 1940 Sir Edward Bridges (the Cabinet Secretary) was sent a letter at the behest of Churchill:

Dear Bridges, in your minute to the Prime Minister of August 2nd you stated that the War Office were opposed to the proposal to adopt descriptive names for tanks and would prefer to retain the Mark system. On this the PM minuted 'Ask them why?' Peck [Churchill's private secretary] . . . has left a note to the effect that the War Office says that the army as a whole knows and understands the mark system and feels that to make a change now would cause confusion which would take a long time to straighten out. On this the PM has commented 'This is not an answer. Let me see a full list of the various marks.'

By the following year, on 27 June 1941, the issue had still not been resolved and so Churchill, doggedly persistent as ever, again asked that all tanks be named; he struggled to decode the designations and logically realised that he was certainly not alone. In late August, Churchill wrote that:

Some time ago I formed the opinion that it would be far better to give names to the various marks of tanks. These could be kept readily in mind and would avoid the confusing titles by marks and numbers. This idea did not find favour at the time, but it is evident that a real need exists because the 'I' tank, Mk II, is widely known as Matilda, and one of the other Infantry tanks is called Valentine. [. . .] Pray therefore set out a list of the existing official titles of all the

MATILDA MARKS

MATILDA II MARK	I	II	III	IV	V
AKA	A12 Infantry Tank Mk II	A12 Infantry Tank Mk IIA	A12 Infantry Tank Mk IIA*	A12 Infantry Tank Mk IIA**	
Co-ax MG	Vickers	BESA			
Engine type	AEC A183/184		Leyland E148/149 or E164/165	Leyland E170/171	
Engine capacity	6.75 litres			6.98 litres	
Engine power	94.1bhp (original) or 87bhp (modified)			95bhp	
Engine mounting	3-point Silentbloc HE12524			3-point rigid mounting	
Engine crankcases	Aluminium		Aluminium (E148/149) or Cast-iron (E164/165)	Cast-iron	
Cylinder heads	1 per engine			2 per engine	
Cylinder liners	Wet			Dry	
Big-end bearings	Lead bronze			Aluminium alloy	
Oil tanks	Fixed to fuel tanks			Mounted on the starter motor brackets	
Oil filters	Tecalemit OF2445			Bypass type	
Oil cooler	On top of the engine			Mounted on the timing case end of engine	
Air compressor	Reavell type, mounted on to bracket on cross-drive casing with drive from shaft and flexible coupling			Reavell TBC4, directly mounted on cross-drive casing with no drive from shaft and coupling	
Air reservoir	760cu in			1,520cu in	
Air filters	Vokes C7561 oil bath			Leyland EAF16 cylindrical triple-element oil bath	
Fuel injectors	CAV-type			Leyland-type	
Fuel	46.5 gallons. Balance pipe between tanks, drain taps			55 gallons. No balance pipe between tanks, no drain taps. Fuel pump on top of tanks	
Fuel filters	CAV BFJSJI/501 with pre-filter			CAV BFA II, no pre-filter	
Cooling fan drive	V section belts			Direct drive from PTO	
Ether cold-start device	Not fitted			Fitted	
Gearbox servo	Clayton Dewandre air servo. Mounted behind bulkhead in engine compartment				Westinghouse air servo mounted on top of gearbox
Suspension	6 top rollers			6 top rollers (early only) or track skid	
Electrical	2 pairs 12V 100Ah batteries. Scheme A on earliest tanks, Scheme B thereafter	2 pairs 12V 130Ah batteries. Scheme B or C.		2 pairs 12V 130Ah batteries. Scheme C.	
Instrument panels	3			2	
Radio	No 11	No 11 (early) No 19 (later)		No 19	

Note: Exactly when the different marks were first introduced into service is not clear, but the last record of Mk IIA tanks in service units within the UK was in November 1941, all subsequent reports referring only to IIIs and IVs.

tanks by types and marks . . . together with suggested names for them in order that these may be considered and discussed.

The list then produced ignored the A11 as only in-service types were included. Instead it noted that the A12 was otherwise known as the Matilda, and that this unofficial name was now the preferred official name to be adopted in accordance with Churchill's wishes.

Therefore, decoding exactly what each type of Matilda II was referred to in documents of the period depends upon the date as well as the preference of the person involved. The table here gives an overview of the five marks that made up the Matilda II story with their names/designations, but does not include those Mk III and IV tanks fitted with the 3in CS howitzer, ammunition stowage and sighting equipment, as these tanks were indicated by the letters CS after the main designation and in all other respects were the same. However, as is typical in the story of British tanks, things were not quite as simple as that; in some publications CS tanks were referred to using the suffix letter B, as in Matilda II Mk IIIB or Mk IVB. However, there is more to the defining features of the marks than this simplistic overview, and the table here gives much more detail.

Crossing trenches

The specification for Matilda II called for it to be able to cross an 8ft trench; the smaller Matilda I could cross a gap of 6ft 6in. However, as war approached, concerns were raised that the trench-crossing ability of the larger tank fell considerably short of that specified. On 16 September 1939 a report on the performance of the first pilot model, the A12E1, stated that in fact it was incapable of crossing a representative enemy 6ft trench with an 18in-high parapet and parados (the raised lips to the front and rear); the problem was that the tail of the tank tended to drop into the trench. To counter this, the MEE at Farnborough designed an extension tail or skid to increase the effective length. This allowed the tank to cross a 6ft trench (but not 7ft and certainly not the desired 8ft) without markedly degrading its cross-country ability. The tail was 2ft 10in long overall, and the report mentioned the possibility of making an even longer 3ft 9in skid in the future, presumably to try to increase the crossing ability still further. The skid drawings show a curved box extending from the rear hull, made of mild steel and braced by two internal stiffening plates. The skids were used on at least some of the tanks

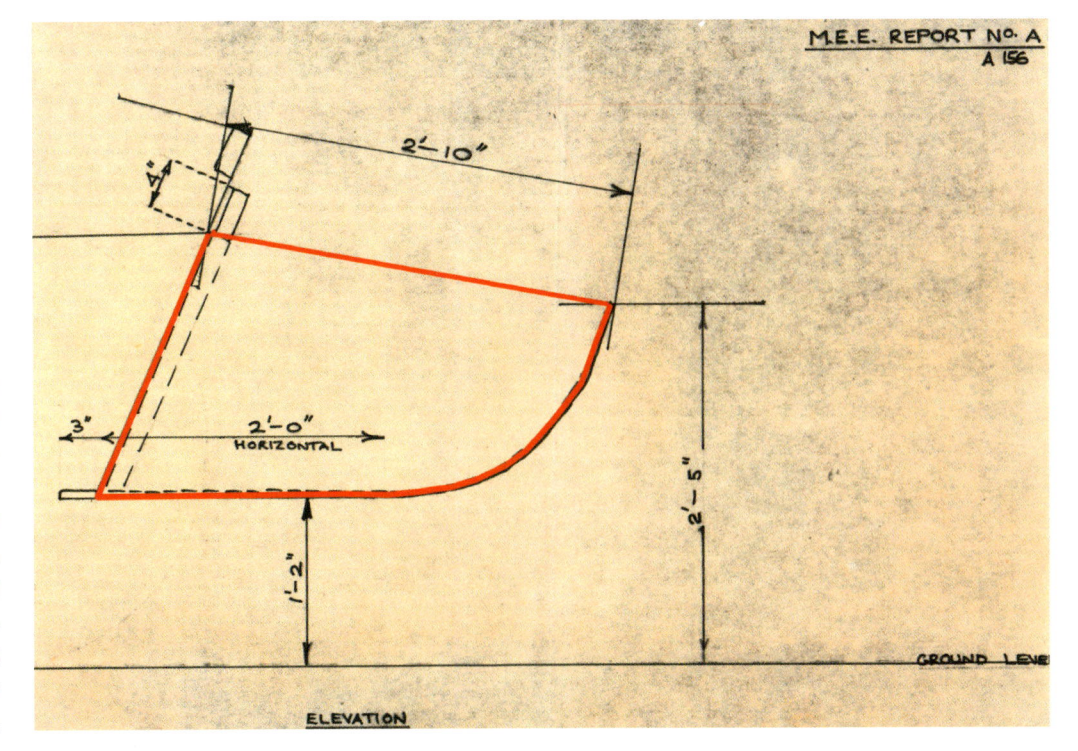

RIGHT The original design of the BEF tail skid, with the profile emphasised in red. Because this size did not allow the Matilda to cross the desired 8ft-wide trench, there was discussion around making an even longer version of the skid.

deployed to France in 1940, with some having the top covered by a thin metal plate, as the boxes thus formed were used as expansion chambers for the exhaust system of the Mk I. However, no trenches had to be crossed in France, and tellingly, one post-action report submitted in summer 1940 by an RAOC[1] staff sergeant observed that the boxes caused 'vibrations'. Although the exact problem this caused was not specified, this appears to have sounded the death knell for the modification as it was not used again.

Increasing the ground clearance

The standard ground clearance of the Matilda was only 13in, but it also was found that the bottom of the side armour tended to come into contact with the ground when the tank was travelling cross-country, which added drag and was undesirable. The exhaust pipe from the AEC engine on the Mk I ran underneath the tank, and this must have been susceptible to damage on rough terrain. The emergency egress of the driver using the floor escape hatch was also very difficult, particularly in action. As a result of one or more of these problems, the suspension of tanks serving with the BEF in France (and some of 8RTR's in the UK) was lowered – or raised if you prefer; the effect was to add about 6in of ground clearance. There are two main theories as to how this might have been done. One is that the pitch of the suspension was altered to force the suspension down; whereas the second suggestion is that a bracket was fitted to lower each bogie unit. The records of the modification do not appear to have survived, but technical investigations carried out since the war indicated that altering the pitch of the suspension through modifying the springs is not feasible, and that the simplest method was to use a bracket; each bracket would be set at an angle slightly off the vertical in order to ensure that the bogie wheels could not contact each other at maximum reach.

One question that remains to be asked is why the modification was not carried out on other tanks after the BEF campaign? One answer could be that the suspension units, thus lowered, were adjudged to be made vulnerable, negating the whole raison d'être of the side armour. However, and possibly more importantly, Staff Sergeant Brown of the RAOC from 1st Army Tank Brigade workshops noted immediately after his experiences with the tank in France that despite them being designed not to do so, the suspension units tended to come into contact with each other, possibly due to the brackets not being robust enough. Another possibility is that it was found that it hindered production and so was cancelled in a period when building tanks as fast as possible was all-important. For what it is worth, this author's preferred suggestion is that with the introduction of Leyland engines the exhaust pipe under the hull was deleted and thus the reason for the modification was removed. Whatever the truth, the modification was discontinued after the summer of 1940.

Sunshield

The received wisdom here is that the original idea for this came from no less a personage than General Wavell, then C-in-C Middle East, who sent a brief handwritten note in blue pencil to his Camouflage Directorate on 23 April 1941: 'Is it a wild idea that a tank could be camouflaged to look like a lorry from air by light canvas screen over top? It would be useful during approach march etc. Please have it considered.' Included in Wavell's own hand in

ABOVE Under new management: the new owners examine 7RTR's 'Goat', which demonstrates the effect of the lowered suspension. As the tank seems unharmed, it may have been abandoned because of the broken track, a common problem due in large part to the poor design of the track pins.

blue pencil was a *very* basic sketch of the idea; he was obviously no draughtsman! All of this is correct – but in actual fact the idea pre-dates Wavell: RTC crews had used similar devices on their light tanks in Egypt in about 1937, so it was probable that Wavell had seen or heard of these and was merely recycling the idea.

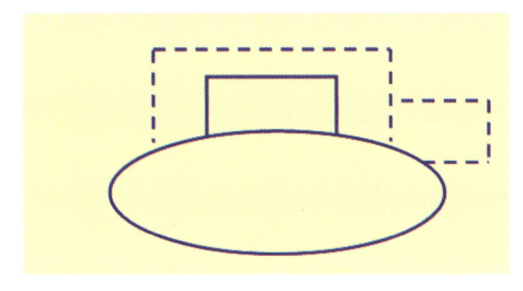

Just three months later, on 21 July 1941, a report was sent to the WO in London, explaining what had happened as a result – and probably because of Wavell's involvement, things had happened quickly! By 29 April, a design sketch had been prepared by the Camouflage Experimental Section, and a mock-up was made and satisfactorily passed initial testing by the MEE. The idea of a frame fitted to a tank and covered with canvas in order to resemble a lorry was now established as feasible. An organisation called Ordnance Services at No 4 Base Ordnance Workshop (the workshop that also built the early Flail mine-clearing vehicles) then produced a pilot model which was tested over 'typical desert going' on 3 May. The frames of the device were deliberately designed in two halves, split down the middle, allowing the device to be discarded when required. Part of this demonstration/test showed that the whole device could be thrown clear of the tank within five seconds by pulling on a lever which allowed both sides to drop away under their own weight, allowing it to remain fitted right up to the point of contact with the enemy if necessary. (Of course, doing this would give the whole trick away; a better idea would be to make the transition out of sight and recover the devices for future use.) From head-on, it was deemed hard to distinguish the device even at 50 yards, and side-on only the tracks gave the game away, but these became less apparent as distance increased. It was also noted that real wheeled vehicles tended to weave on soft sand to aid momentum and avoid bad going, whereas tanks drove in straight lines. From the air view the deception was adjudged to be 'strikingly successful', only the track marks spoiling the effect. It was also advised to fit a rear canvas flap so that an air observer could not see into the device from the rear. A final note from the test estimated that up to 16 men could be hidden inside the device, an unexpected bonus for the Poor Bloody Infantry who were used to marching everywhere!

Some 400 sets of Sunshield – as the device was codenamed – were immediately ordered from Ordnance Services, 200 each for infantry tanks and for cruisers. The designs for each type of tank were different, and the WO file includes some of the blueprints for the different types. The first batch was successfully used by 7th Armoured Division; unfortunately the date was not stated, but we can confidently assume it was around June 1941, and not, as is sometimes claimed, solely for El Alamein in October 1942. The frames of this first batch were made mainly of 3in × 1in timber, and this was found to break too easily and prevented them being stacked when not in use, meaning they had to be dismantled for transportation and reuse. The divisions operating the Sunshield-equipped tanks also had no integral transport capable of moving them once discarded – a 10-ton lorry or larger was required – not because of the weight, but due mainly to their volume. Enter the Royal Engineers! In July 1941 they designed an improved version with a tubular metal frame made from ½in gas tubing which solved the durability and stacking problems, and this version, known as the 'E' device, replaced the original 'OS' version. No 143 Field Park Company/Squadron RE, part of 7th Armoured Division, were involved in the production of the devices, but it is not clear if they were the RE unit that had designed the tubular-framed version. The accompanying photographs show Matilda II T6947 being fitted with the 'E' version of a Sunshield. This tank was built by the London, Midland & Scottish Railway in mid-1940 and was originally with 4RTR as it is named 'Dangerous II' and bears painted 'Chinese Eyes' on the top of the turret sides.

THIS PAGE A sequence of images showing the Sunshield device, starting with it in fully 'lorry' mode – quite a convincing arrangement when viewed from the air at a distance. The 4RTR crew then open it up to reveal 'Dangerous II' underneath.

117

MARKS AND MODIFICATIONS

These 'E' versions seem to have used a simpler method for attaching and discarding the frames than that previously employed. Each side had four or five metal prongs that slotted downwards into corresponding special brackets welded to the tank mud chute armour. The photographs seem to show that each bracket was made up of two short sections of tube or pipe, with sheet metal wrapped around and with a keyway cut into the top. The prongs on the frame had a semicircular bottom section. The device was assembled by laying the frame on the floor and locating these semicircular sections on to the outer tube of each bracket. Two crewmen on the ground then raised and rotated the complete half frame upwards and inwards while one or two others standing on the hull took over halfway; in doing this, the semicircular prongs rotated around the bracket pipe and locked into the keyway. To lock this half of the entire device in an upright position, an L-shaped metal bracket located itself over the gun barrel. The same procedure was repeated for the other side. In order to discard the device, the gun barrel was simply depressed a little, freeing the two L-shaped brackets from the gun, and thus causing both side frames to rotate outwards and downwards under their own weight and literally jumping the prongs out of the keyways – apparently this can be called a 'tumbling hinge'. The fabric shields over the frames were made of double-thickness hessian (to ensure opaqueness), painted or preferably dyed dark green over light green, using a substance called 'Green Paste for Tents'. In those areas where the hessian could potentially come into contact with hot exhausts and so on, it was to be treated with a fireproof solution such as 'Faspos', made by ICI and apparently obtainable in Cairo. The hessian was secured to the frame with lots of wire ties, windlassed tight. (As an aside, the obvious question here is why did they choose two shades of green as the colour for the canvas? The only reasonable answer is that a significant proportion of the lorries in use in the desert at that time employed this camouflage scheme.)

In order to remove the very clear and telltale tank track marks that Sunshield-equipped vehicles would leave, as noted in the trials, a 'Smoother' device was designed in June 1941. This consisted of a metal bracket welded behind the extreme rear of each track and standing approximately 16in above the ground, trailing a section of old unserviceable track behind, which removed the tell-tale ridges left in soft sand. A photograph caption showing the device attached to Valentine T16399 noted that it was 'Unnecessary for whole of the "smoother" to be made of U/S [meaning unserviceable, not United States] track. The upper portion could be either cable or chain and hauling portion in links.' Thus, two short lengths of either cable hawser or chain could be used to pull only one or two track links and have the same effect.

Vehicle camouflage was sometimes altered to assist with the deception. At least one Matilda had a *tromp l'œil* effect painted on the side armour attempting to portray wheels, and many Crusaders and other Christie-suspensioned cruisers had the second, third and sometimes fourth roadwheels painted black to try to disguise the suspension into looking like a 4×4 or 4×6 truck. The hessian itself usually had a two-colour scheme of broad stripes; it was essential to copy the prevalent scheme then being used on real trucks as noted above. It is probable that the rear flap of hessian was sometimes painted or dyed black or a dark shade, to attempt to replicate the deep shadow cast within the 'canopy'.

By 1942 Sunshield fittings had become commonplace on many if not most tanks, and it appears that the design had been altered by this stage so that the whole frame and canvas was in one piece, and that it was no longer possible to discard the device quickly by pulling a lever; rather, the whole device had to be lifted in and out of the frame by hand. This later design consisted of a long rail on each side of the vehicle, with up to six slotted brackets on each side for the frame uprights to drop into. These side rails were complemented by another rail along the front of the vehicle; these proved to be ideal for stowing any number of items on. Even after Matilda had ceased front-line service the Sunshield and later similar Houseboat device remained in service, which was a testimony to the usefulness of the design.

Canal Defence Lights – CDL

Experiments into the use of tanks at night led to an appreciation that light could be used not only as an aid to driving, navigation and gunnery, but also to disorientate the enemy.[2]

Captain Douglas Browne MC, Tank Corps, a First World War tank officer with G Battalion, wondered why the Germans had never thought of bringing strong searchlights up to their forward positions, in order to light up the British forward areas if they thought that an attack was imminent; this would have exposed every single tank attack as they had to approach the trenches at night before launching attacks at first light. After the war, in 1927 a series of night exercises conducted by 2 Battalion RTC against infantry in Oxfordshire showed that the blinding effects of white light upon infantry were both disorientating and potentially terror-inducing, and so a seed of thought was sown. General Hobart came to the same conclusion seven years later. His report on the tank exercises of 1934 included a comment that:

a strong headlight . . . should be provided on a sufficient number of tanks to enable an experiment to be carried out next year. If such a headlight not only dazzled the enemy but enabled tank gunners to shoot more accurately it might be possible to reduce or even abolish the star shells which are at present our only means of lighting an attack at night.

An invention called the De Thoren dazzle device had been submitted to the WO for consideration as early as 1920 to be mounted on what was described as a light tank, possibly a Whippet. Despite the rights to it being obtained by the WO, its potential was initially dismissed by many and ignored by most, leading to yet another good idea being placed into the 'too difficult' tray, like so many others.

In a separate experiment, in 1936 the RTC had begun to conduct night-firing from tanks using MGs aided by spotlights. It was found that when firing at an 8ft square white target from a range of 300 yards, nearly half of the bullets found their mark. Dark targets representing men could be picked out at about the same range. It was realised that the more powerful the searchlight, the greater the range and accuracy. Whether this led to, or merely confirmed, a policy of mounting a commander-operated spotlight on each tank turret is not clear, but white light was a feature on almost all British tanks during the Second World War. The use of very powerful tank-mounted spotlights (also known as searchlights or light

LEFT The Matilda CDL. The turret shown here is slightly different from the (incorrect) one at Bovington, which carries the CDL turret more typical of an M3 Grant.

RIGHT How to remove a Matilda gun turret and replace it with the CDL type.

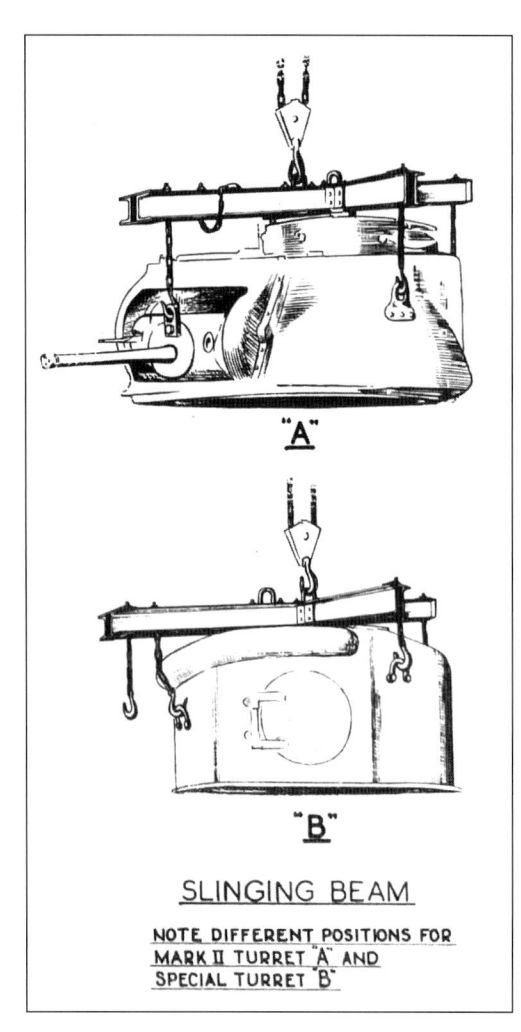

BELOW Some Matildas in CDL units were fitted with this crane device to allow turret removal, necessary if a Matilda hull had to go to a workshop, for example.

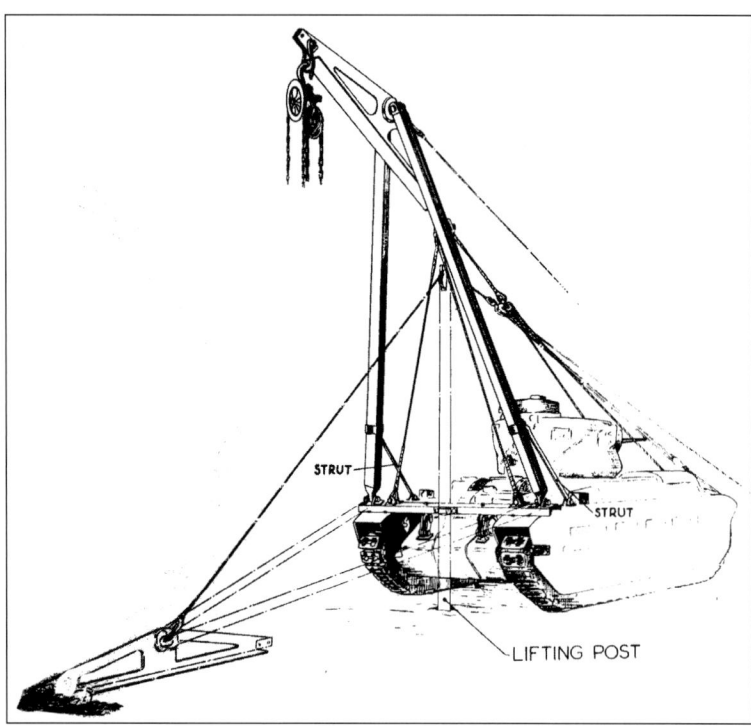

projectors) as a means of firing accurately at battle ranges at night was not finally realised until the late 1950s on Centurion, and later on Chieftain, but before this happened the idea of using the dazzle effects of light were to be resurrected during the war, where Matilda once again was to play a large part.

In order to produce a battleworthy system employing the dazzling effects of light, the De Thoren device was dusted off in early 1940 and after further trials it was decided to place it in a heavily armoured turret, on a Matilda IIA hull, with 300 turrets ordered in June 1940.[3] The intention was to equip one brigade for use in the UK, and another for deployment overseas, probably to the Middle East. Having about 50 tanks per battalion, and three battalions per brigade, was thought to be sufficient to allow an infantry attack supported by such tanks to take place over a frontage of 7,000–8,000 yards (just under 5 miles, or 7km). Of course, a codename had to be devised for the experimental device, and so the title of Canal Defence Lights or CDL was born – some modern commentators remain fooled by this and continue to insist that it was built purely to defend canals, particularly the Suez, presumably by using its solitary machine gun! In fact, the idea seems to have been to deliberately include the word 'Lights' (originally used in its plural form in documents) in the code name in case the Germans discovered that the vehicles were fitted with special lights, thereby assuming that it was a sort of anti-aircraft searchlight.

Vulcan Foundry was one of the companies involved in the manufacture of the 5-ton turret. A special Matilda tank with a crane device was issued to Matilda CDL units to allow them to change gun turrets for CDL types. The tall and ungainly but well-armoured CDL turret used on the Matilda II was known as the Type A,[4] and was designed around the 15 million candlepower light projector, with a separate dynamo providing the necessary current to power the lamp and its ancillary equipment, which occupied the right-hand side of the structure. In the centre of this light chamber was the carbon arc lamp, with a curved para ellipse mirror in front of it that focused the light on to a reflector in the turret rear, and thence

OPERATOR'S VIEW.

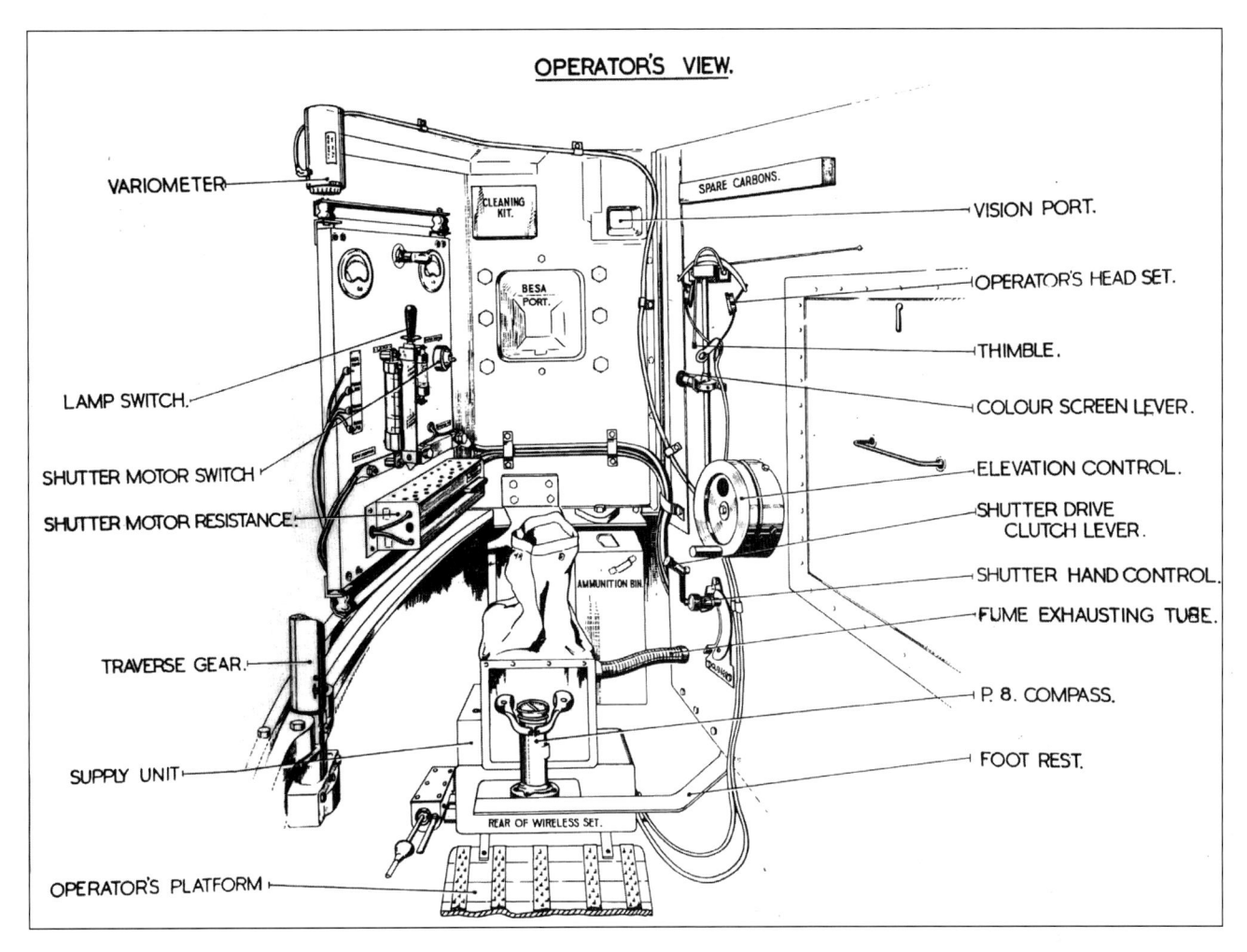

- VARIOMETER
- LAMP SWITCH.
- SHUTTER MOTOR SWITCH
- SHUTTER MOTOR RESISTANCE.
- TRAVERSE GEAR.
- SUPPLY UNIT
- OPERATOR'S PLATFORM
- CLEANING KIT.
- BESA PORT.
- AMMUNITION BIN
- REAR OF WIRELESS SET.
- SPARE CARBONS.
- VISION PORT.
- OPERATOR'S HEAD SET.
- THIMBLE.
- COLOUR SCREEN LEVER.
- ELEVATION CONTROL.
- SHUTTER DRIVE CLUTCH LEVER.
- SHUTTER HAND CONTROL.
- FUME EXHAUSTING TUBE.
- P.8. COMPASS.
- FOOT REST.

forwards through the front slit. A power-operated armoured shutter could rapidly open and close the slit two or three times each second producing a high-frequency flicker, which was not only visually disturbing to the enemy but also very difficult to pinpoint accurately in order to target the source with gunfire.

The operator occupied the remaining cramped space in the left half of the turret, separated from the lamp components by a bulkhead fitted with hatches to allow access when required. From his position he could elevate/depress the light 10° up and down, and also traverse it by rotating the turret using

ABOVE The CDL turret contained a lot – for its time – of sophisticated gadgetry. This is the very cramped turret shown from the operator's position. The BESA MG is not illustrated.

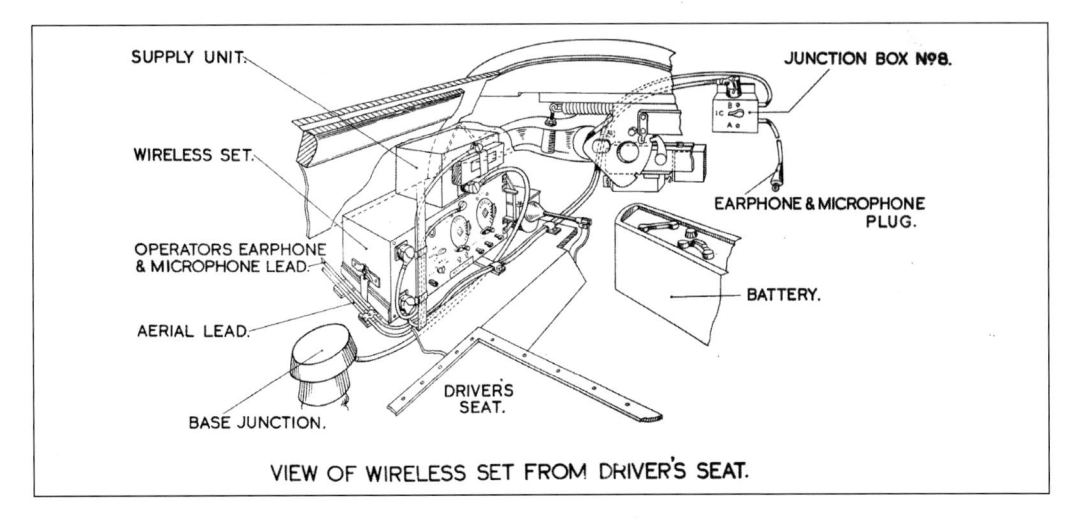

VIEW OF WIRELESS SET FROM DRIVER'S SEAT.

- SUPPLY UNIT.
- WIRELESS SET.
- OPERATORS EARPHONE & MICROPHONE LEAD.
- AERIAL LEAD.
- BASE JUNCTION.
- DRIVERS SEAT.
- JUNCTION BOX No 8.
- EARPHONE & MICROPHONE PLUG.
- BATTERY.

LEFT The turret was too cramped to allow the Wireless Set No 19 to be fitted there in accordance with normal British practice, so it had to be relocated into the hull where it was operated by the driver.

RIGHT The main CDL instrument panel – note the shutter on/off switch and, at the bottom, the shutter speed sliding control.

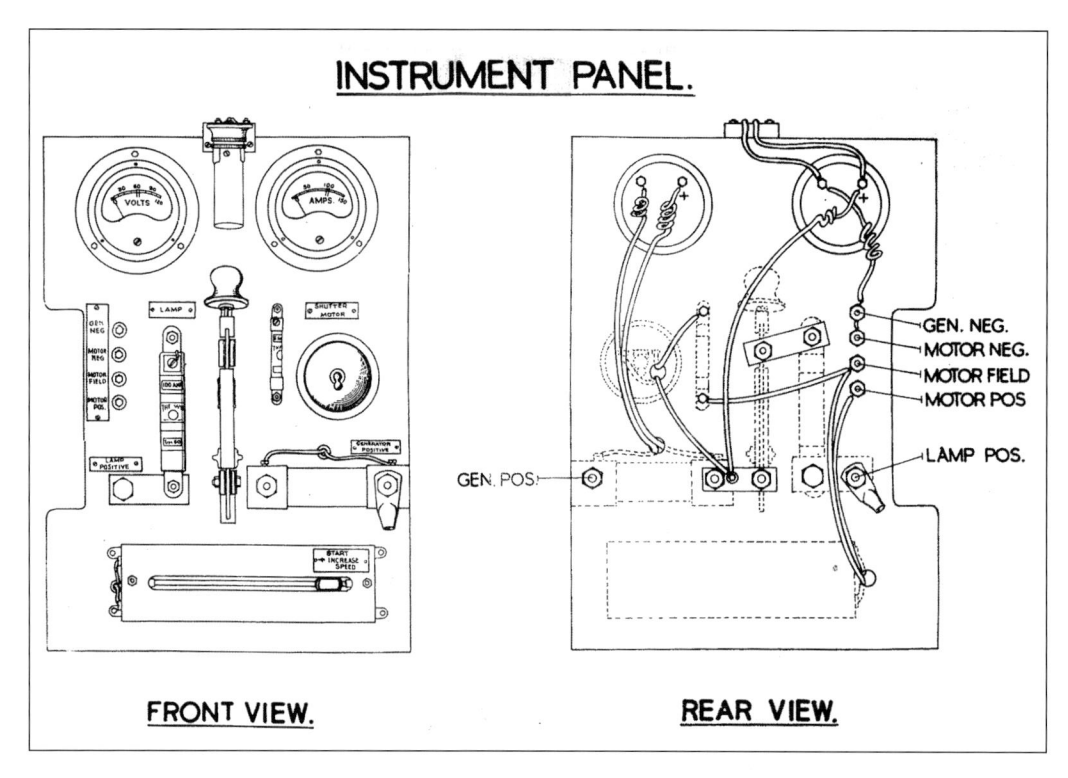

INSTRUMENT PANEL.

FRONT VIEW.

REAR VIEW.

the hand controls – the turret could not actually rotate a full 360°, but only 180° in either left or right from the front. One of the main and potentially dangerous tasks of the operator was to change the carbon elements of the lamp that burned out in use; these had to be replaced wearing tinted goggles and thick gloves, as the heat generated and the intensity of the light risked both burns and blindness. Around the top of the turret was a cylindrical lip, which provided protection to a series of slots used to help cool and ventilate the equipment and operator.

Putting blue or orange colour screens (filters) over the white light produced different effects, including making the tank seem further away than it was (blue) or closer (orange), and two tanks, one using blue and the other orange, could combine their beams to produce white light at the target end. Although no gun was able to be fitted because of space limitations within the turret, a single BESA MG was fitted to give the tank a rudimentary self-defence capability; with only a two-man crew its use was somewhat limited anyway. At a certain point during Matilda production, probably in 1942, the decision was taken to build all new Matildas with three specific modifications to allow the hull to be configured as a CDL, an extraordinary decision unless at that time it was planned that the Matildas would find an extension to their service life purely in the CDL role. These changes were: a rectangular access plate in the hull floor under the fighting compartment secured with six hex bolts; a 'drilled flange' modification to the cross-drive (probably some sort of take-off); and a rectangular access hatch in the rear bulkhead to allow access to the cross-drive modification.

Tactically it was found that a line of tanks could advance together about 40 yards apart, with their flickering pools of light not only distracting the enemy, but also creating what amounted to black holes between the lit areas, allowing advancing infantry to shelter within, all but invisible to the enemy until they were only 50 yards away. To aid the drivers in their task, the normal round headlamps on the hull were replaced by monoslot headlamps in square boxes with a light slit, mounted on each mudguard at the front. The CDL device was classified as top secret, as it had the potential to be used in complete surprise against an unsuspecting enemy. It was probably the difficulties of deciding when to spring the surprise on the enemy that led to it never being used in action, despite a training school formed at Penrith – miles from anywhere – and two complete brigades (1st and 35th Army Tank Brigades) with a number of regiments (11, 42 and 49RTR, 152 and 155 Regt RAC) being trained in its use. After 1943 the CDL device was mounted on to Churchill and Grant hulls, making the Matilda version obsolete.

Mine-clearing Matildas

The story of the development of British flail tanks has been told at length elsewhere, but as the Matilda II formed a fundamental part of the early development work, so that part of it will be retold here. Anti-tank (AT) mines were only developed in the period between the two world wars, as an easy and cheap means of denying ground to enemy tanks – the mere threat of a minefield could be enough to deter tanks. If a tank did come into contact with an AT mine, there would be sufficient damage to at least disable the tank, and as the underbelly or floor was invariably the thinnest armoured part of any tank, crew casualties were also likely to result. Uparmouring the floor was technically difficult and, in any case, in the era when lightweight but powerful anti-tank guns were making their presence felt and threatening the very existence of the tank, there were more important places to put any additional armour on to.

The original idea of what was to become the flail tank is usually accredited to Abraham Du Toit. He was a captain (later major) in the South African Defence Force serving in North Africa and came up with the idea of a device that would cause the mines to explode harmlessly. The way to do this would be to beat the ground in front of the tank, with something that exerted enough force to cause the mine to detonate, while still far enough ahead of the tank not to damage it. The suggested method of doing this was to use rotating chains, known as flails after the devices used to thresh corn. The requirement to be able to clear minefields was clear and urgent, and he was sent to the UK in late 1941 with orders to develop his ideas there, particularly with the AEC vehicles and engineering company working for the Fighting

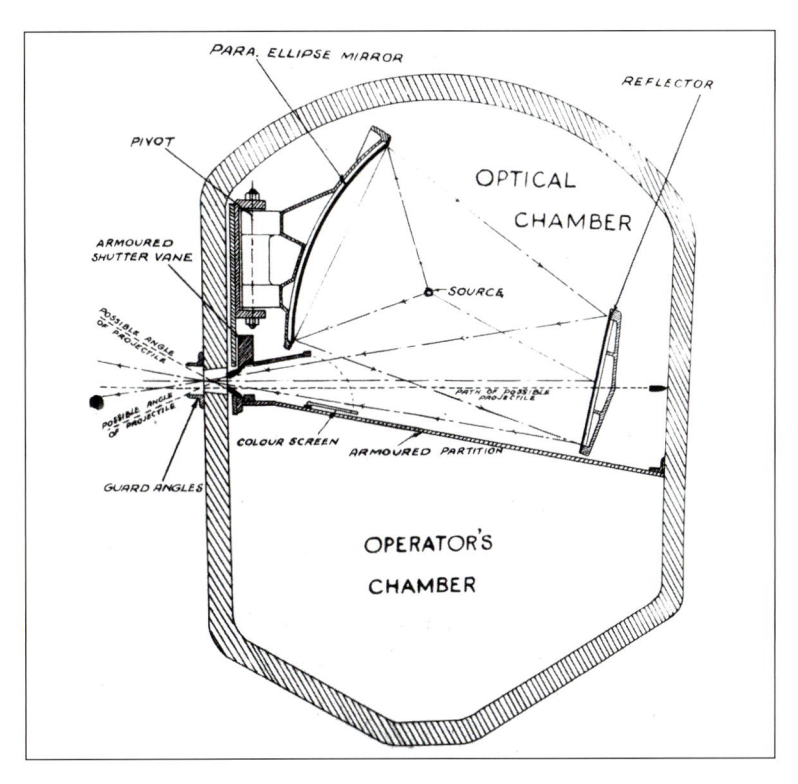

ABOVE Inside the turret, showing how the light from the source was focused by the mirror on to the reflector at the rear of the turret, and then through the narrow slit at the front to reduce the chance of damage.

LEFT A very rare image of a top-secret device in action – a Matilda Scorpion flailing in the Middle East in 1942. The amount of dust raised by the device can only be imagined.
(Merlin Robinson)

ABOVE An equally rare shot of a Scorpion travelling but not flailing; it appears to have been taken by the crew of a lorry as they passed by.

Vehicles Division of the Ministry of Supply. This led to two parallel lines of development.

In North Africa, enough was known of his ideas and suggestions for experiments to begin in his absence, eventually (in August 1942) modifying a Matilda II as the test-bed vehicle; the Royal Engineers, the RAOC and (from September 1942 on its formation) the REME were all heavily involved in the design and trials, with Captain (later Major) Norman Berry RAOC leading the work. Berry had been sent to South Africa in September 1941 where he had met Du Toit and discussed his ideas, before returning to the Western Desert, while Du Toit was sent to the UK.

The Matilda was chosen for a number of reasons; it was a well-understood in-service tank, it was readily available, the front and floor of the tank was particularly well-armoured, and its slow speed was not a handicap when it came to flailing operations, which typically took place at about 0.5mph. Given the code name Scorpion Mk I, in trials the concept was proved and destroyed up to 100% of the mines in its path, although the success rate was less on operations when broken ground caused problems. The flails were also very useful at beating a path through barbed wire, although cutters needed to be added to the devices to prevent the wire wrapping itself around the rotor; it could even be used to dig away at raised defensive earthworks. The rotor for the chains was projected forward of the tank on rigid latticework arms, designed to keep the weight down as the Matilda's performance was being adversely affected by the weight of all the additional components. The drive came from a readily available 30bhp Bedford light truck engine, which was located in a lightly armoured box on the right side of the hull; also inside the box were the controls for the device and the somewhat unfortunate operator, who worked from inside there during flailing operations – a most unpleasant job. The engine tended to overheat and the same must have happened to the crewman sitting alongside it. Some 24 – or possibly as many as 32 – Matildas were converted for use in the Battle of El Alamein of October 1942, as the Germans and Italians were occupying defensive positions protected by many minefields, although it appears that only 12–15 were actually battleworthy on the first day of the attack. One tank used at El Alamein was recorded as having destroyed 47 mines.

An improved version, the Scorpion Mk II, was made, which moved the flail operator into the turret with remote controls for the flail system and also improved the engine cooling and dust filtration. This version was used for the remainder of the North African campaign.

Concurrently with this, Du Toit in the UK was working on another similar Matilda-based device, the Mk I Baron.[5] This retained the turret and the 2pdr gun, partly for simplicity of conversion and partly because it was sensibly thought desirable for the tank to be able to fight as well as flail. The revolving rotor carrying the flail chains was held forward of the hull on two 11ft-long supporting arms attached to either side. Drive for the rotor came from a Chrysler engine. During the first trials, which ended in January 1942, despite showing promise a number of problems were identified. The Chrysler six-cylinder petrol engine used was underpowered and the hydraulic system, based on the Matilda hydraulic power traverse components, was overpressured and also unsatisfactory. By April 1942 the Baron Mk II was ready for trials, using a more powerful 73bhp Bedford engine that used the same coolant system as the host tank, and with a much-improved hydraulic system for raising and lowering the arms to account for uneven

LEFT The flails on the Baron; getting the design of these right took much trial and error.

BELOW A detailed close-up of some of the modifications made to the Matilda hull to mount the Baron equipment.

ground. During the trials it was discovered that the chains produced an uneven beat pattern, and this was finally rectified after much trial and error with a design which used 9/16in cable chain reinforced on the inner half of its length, *ie* nearest the rotor, with two 3/8in steel wire ropes threaded through the links. Work on the Baron Mk II ended in June 1942, having revealed that a yet more powerful engine was needed, along with a lower rotor strike in order to flatten the chain strike, and that using the host tank's cooling system for the flail engine was unsatisfactory.

The final version of the UK Baron was the Mk IIIA which was ready by the end of 1942, in which the turret and gun were

BELOW The Baron was the much-modified turretless UK mine-clearing tank, which was to lead to the successful Sherman-based Crab used in 1944.

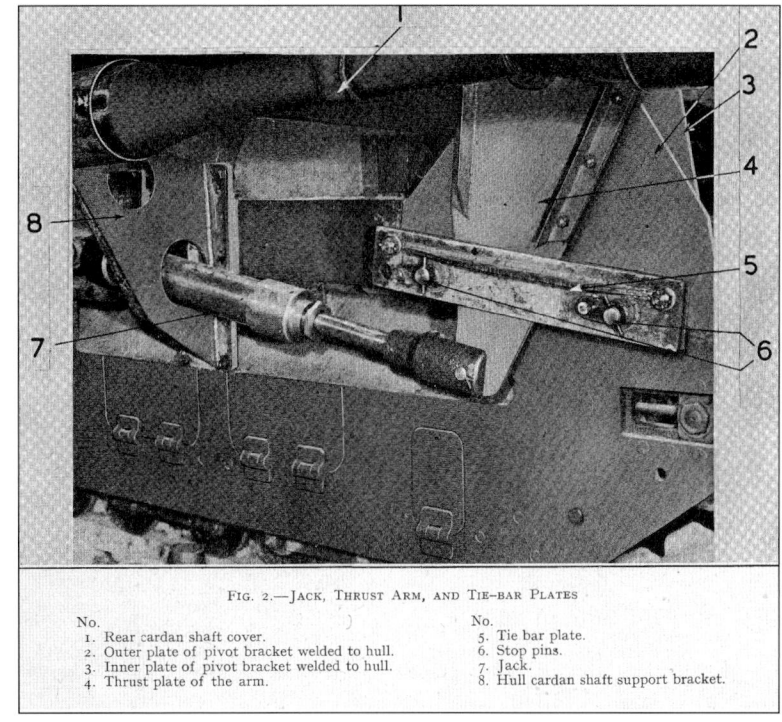

FIG. 2.—JACK, THRUST ARM, AND TIE-BAR PLATES

No.
1. Rear cardan shaft cover.
2. Outer plate of pivot bracket welded to hull.
3. Inner plate of pivot bracket welded to hull.
4. Thrust plate of the arm.

No.
5. Tie bar plate.
6. Stop pins.
7. Jack.
8. Hull cardan shaft support bracket.

removed and replaced by a stepped armoured superstructure, housing the flail (and also radio) operator at the front, with the commander behind and slightly above. This type used two Bedford engines installed one either side of the hull, which had the unfortunate side effect of making the tank so wide that it could not cross the standard Bailey bridge. This led to the understanding that a more battleworthy arrangement meant that the power for the flail had to come in the form of a power take-off from the tank's own engine, and which effectively ended the development on the Matilda; the Mk IIIA was only used for training. Messrs Curran Bros of Cardiff were contracted to build 60 (or 65, details vary) sets of Baron Mk IIIA equipment for fitting to Matildas in the UK. The development of similar flail equipment on other, more modern tanks, notably the Sherman, soon rendered the Baron obsolete. In mid-1943 the RAC section in the WO made enquiries as to whether it would be possible to fit the same apparatus on to US tanks for use during Operation Husky, the invasion of Sicily, indicating how little they understood about the technicalities of the project. The answer was of course that the equipment was specifically designed around the host tank, and while the concept was transferrable, the equipment was specific and was not.

Australian modifications

Owing to their success, the Japanese introduced desperate countermeasures against the Matilda, using mines, sticky bombs and other improvised explosive devices; they lacked an effective anti-tank gun and the standard 75mm field artillery piece was ineffective against the Matilda's heavy armour. It was because of these changing threats that the Australians added protection modifications to their fleet, although not all tanks featured all of these. Among these were:

- Different types of mesh or PSP trackway were welded on brackets about 4in above the engine louvres, in order to prevent them from being damaged by enemy sticky bomb attacks
- Additional POL (petrol, oil, lubricant) can carriers were welded to the front track guards
- Three track links were often fitted into brackets welded on to the roof of the driver's position, either side of the hatch. In some cases, additional links were carried on the hull nose and/or on the hull sides
- Angled plates were welded around the top of the hull to provide a collar to give protection to the exposed turret ring
- Headlamps were often removed
- Armoured extensions made from 1.875in steel were fitted to each front track guard to better protect the idler from damage; these were hinged to allow maintenance
- Additional stowage boxes were attached to the outside of the turret
- Infantry tank telephone on rear left track guard
- A wooden plank was fitted between the front lifting rings to hold stowage on the glacis plate
- Exhaust pipes extended upwards to allow deeper fording.

LEFT Borneo campaign, 1945: a Matilda CS is seen in action on Tarakan, with additional track links providing spaced armour on the hull front. *(AWM089970)*

RIGHT Applying trackway protection screens to the rear hull of an Australian Matilda; note the upturned exhaust pipes. *(AWM092428)*

ABOVE A casualty is carried past a Matilda with a different type of engine deck protection. *(AWM090351)*

RIGHT Borneo, May 1945. Trackway applied to the rear hull and additional track links on the sides. *(AWM090847)*

ABOVE The Japanese 37mm gun could punch holes through the 25mm (1in) side armour but had no chance against the main 78mm armour on the hull and turret front. *(AWM062141)*

RIGHT A preserved Matilda CS with the welded collars added to Australian tanks to protect the vulnerable turret ring area.

127

MARKS AND MODIFICATIONS

ABOVE Armoured track guards were made in Australia to address another specific vulnerability. The lugs on the front married up with the ones on the top of the normal track guard to allow them to be pinned into the 'up' position.

LEFT Fitters welding the collars into place; the exact design varied slightly between tanks. *(AWM084902)*

RIGHT The headlamps have been removed from this tank, and it sports two unusual features: a cylindrical bolster on the nose and a wire cage around the hull top. *(AWM063228)*

LEFT The track guards were hinged to allow maintenance, as demonstrated here. *(AWM092429)*

FAR LEFT A 1st Tank Battalion Matilda in January 1944, with typical additional brackets welded on to the turret to contain ammunition boxes used for extra stowage. *(AWM016491)*

LEFT As an experiment, the Australian Army built this taller, more heavily armoured cupola with narrow vision slits. *(AWM067550)*

LEFT Here is the cupola on trial, where it was found to offer no significant advantages and was never used in action. *(AWM071127)*

129
MARKS AND MODIFICATIONS

ABOVE Two preserved Matildas at Puckapunyal, a 2pdr (front) and 3in CS tank (rear).

Miscellaneous variants

Many other variants of the Matilda were used, often single-vehicle trial vehicles modified from gun tanks, or others only used in small numbers. The table lists all known variants, including some not described elsewhere in the text.

ABOVE The Germans used enough Matildas in both Russia and North Africa to make it worthwhile to print their own handbook for what was known as the Infanterie Kampfpanzer II 748e.

Variant	Use	Remarks
Infanterie Kampfpanzer II 748(e)	German beutepanzer or 'booty tank', captured from the British in France 1940, North Africa 1941–42, Crete 1941 and Russia/Eastern Front from 1941 on	Examples were used not just as temporary gun tanks (particularly in North Africa), but in one case at least, as a prime mover/tractor with the turret removed
50mm self-propelled gun	German	2 converted? Turret removed, 50mm Pak fitted with shield. High Seas Training Command Terneuzen 1941
76.2mm gun	USSR	Attempt to replace 2pdr with Soviet 76mm F-34 gun
6pdr Matilda	Britain (experimental)	At least one hull mounted with a Cavalier/Cromwell 6pdr turret. This required extensive modifications to the turret ring to accept the new turret and was not produced
Baron Mk I	Mine flail (UK)	Name allocated in February 1942; prototype demonstrated 6 June 1942. Chrysler engine mounted on right-hand side of hull. Arms hydraulically raised/lowered. Chain and sprocket drive to flail rotor
Baron Mk II	Mine flail (UK)	Bedford engine replaced Chrysler
Baron Mk IIIA	Mine flail (UK)	Turret replaced by armoured box superstructure housing flail operator and commander. Bedford engine mounted on both sides of hull
Matilda AMRA Mk IA	Anti-mine roller attachment (AMRA)	Experimental Fowler-designed mine roller system. Trialled in North Africa
Matilda Bangalore	Bangalore torpedo carrier/wire cutter	Experimental, single Bangalore torpedo carried on frame of left-hand side of hull
Matilda Black Prince	Radio-controlled tank	1941 experiment using the A12E2 vehicle
Matilda Bridge	Inglis bridge	1942. Not a bridgelayer as such: lightweight bridge pushed ahead of tank on non-driven wheels and tracks from Light Tank Mk VI

Variant	Use	Remarks
Matilda Canal Defence Lights (CDL)	Light projector tank	Used in training only. Mk II and Mk V. Up to 300 converted
Matilda Light Carrot, Carrot, Heavy Carrot	Demolition tank	Experimental use in Obstacle Assault Centre, Light Carrot: 25lb shaped charge carried on front of tank; Carrot and Heavy Carrot: 75lb/600lb shaped charge carried on front of AMRA
Matilda Crane	Changing turrets	Used by CDL units to lift turrets
Matilda Dozer No 1 Mk I, No 3 Mk I	Dozer tanks	Australia. No I used cables to raise/lower blade, No 3 used hydraulics
Matilda Frog	Flamethrower tank	Australia: need identified in late 1942. 80 gallons of Geletrol fuel inside turret, plus additional in tanks on hull. 25 converted in late 1944 and used in action in New Guinea at Labuan on 10 June 1945 and at Balikpapan in July
Matilda Hedgehog	7 × 63lb bomb thrower	Australian design, using naval anti-submarine bombs. 7 × 63lb bombs (each of 37lb Torpex HE) carried in raised box on transmission decks. Range c200 yards. Not used in action
Matilda Lobster Mine flail (UK)	Mine flail (UK)	Experimental
Matilda Murray	Flamethrower tank	Australia: experimental 1945 design to replace Frog using cordite ignition
Matilda Tank Laying Carpet (TLC)	Carpet-laying device	Used in training only
Matilda Torpedo Mortar	2in anti-mine mortar fitted	Experimental
Matilda Trench Crossing device	North Africa	Experimental
Scorpion Mk I	Mine flail (North Africa)	24 modified from gun tanks from around September–October 1942. 12–15 used at El Alamein in October 1942. Flail operator in box on right-hand side
Scorpion Mk II	Mine flail (North Africa)	Modified after El Alamein, with new rotor support booms, no gun fitted, new air filters, flail operator moved into turret
TOG 1	Heavy tank design	Not adopted, but used Matilda II turret

BELOW A captured 'booty tank' in North Africa – the name on the driver's visor is hard to make out but might be 'Arcadia'. Note the penetration through the upper glacis plate.

BELOW 'Oswald', a 50mm self-propelled gun presumably made from one of the 7RTR tanks captured in 1940. The headlamps have been relocated on to the track guards.

RIGHT T18858 was a Ruston & Hornsby-built tank, probably a Mk IV. Despite being built in late 1941, this tank still features the original 'guillotine'-style side-access hatches. [Editor comment: looks to be a captured Russian example on rail flat bearing chalk mark 'Minsk']

RIGHT North African Funnies No 1: this is a TLC, or tank laying carpet, with the carpet still rolled up on the 'bobbin', or drum. *(TM3569C3)*

RIGHT North African Funnies No 2: the TLC about to tackle a barbed-wire obstacle. Laying the canvas over the wire meant that infantrymen could cross it. *(TM3569C4)*

LEFT North African Funnies No 3: light tank wheels and track support this trench- or gap-crossing device. *(TM3569E4)*

BELOW It is hard to say exactly what this modification might be; it was fitted to the rear of 'Grampus II', the ex-7RTR tank sent to the USA in 1940, and bolted on to the rear hull lifting eyes.

BELOW North African Funnies No 4: a crib or fascine supported on the side of this Matilda. *(TM3569F2)*

BELOW Matilda's turret ring diameter and small turret made it incapable of being upgunned to take the 6pdr, so an alternative was tried by fitting an A24 Cavalier-type turret. Overall this was a poor design that reeked of clutching at straws and 6pdrs could be mounted more easily on to newer designs. Note the Australian-style collars fitted to protect the turret ring.

BELOW TOG 1 in 1940 – had it been brought into production, the Matilda turret might have been used as, for its time, it was an advanced design with power traverse and a three-man crew.

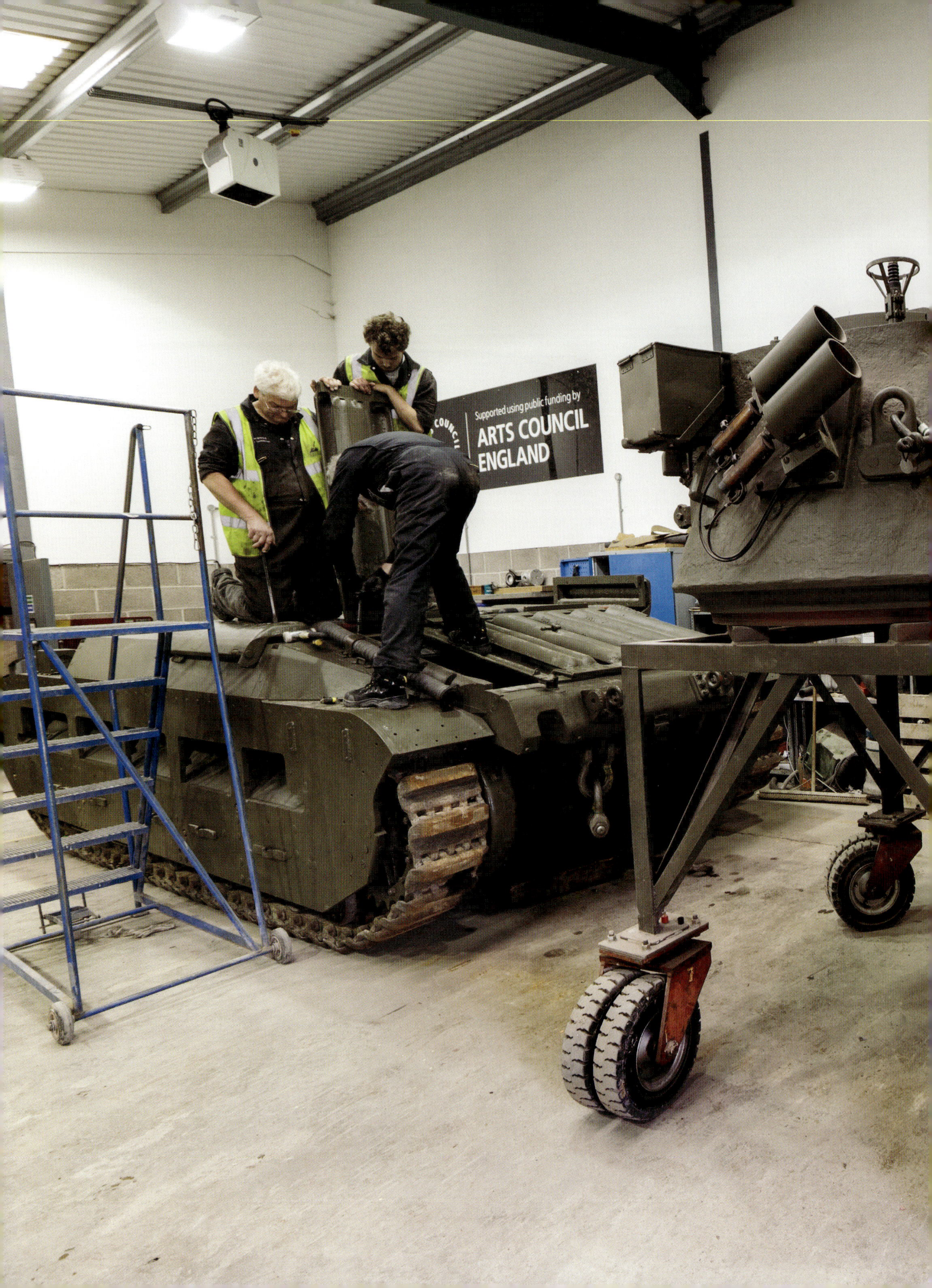
Supported using public funding by
ARTS COUNCIL
ENGLAND

Chapter Seven

The story of the restoration

---•---

Chris van Schaardenburgh, Head of Collections, the Tank Museum

Restoring an eighty-year old tank to pristine 'as-new' condition is not a job for the faint hearted, but the workshop staff and project team at the Tank Museum carried out an outstanding example of museum restoration on their Matilda.

OPPOSITE The completed turret waits on a stand while the crew carry out some final work on the hull. *(TM)*

ABOVE Before: the breech of the 2pdr, BESA MG and gunner's telescope. *(TM)*

The Bovington Tank Museum is the regimental museum for the Royal Tank Regiment and is also the corps museum for the Royal Armoured Corps. The museum is an independent charity, with over 200,000 visitors in 2019. The Tank Museum has been in existence since 1923 when the collection was started for use as a reference collection for the army. Over the years the collection has grown, especially after the Second World War when many captured and Allied armoured vehicles were added to the collection. In the 1970s and '80s an effort was made to get some of the vehicles into a running condition. This collection of running vehicles grew further in the 1990s. These are displayed during events such as Tankfest, Tiger Day and the Tanks in Action displays during the school holidays. In addition, some of the vehicles are used to support the British Army in training exercises or at commemorative events.

Keeping the vehicles moving

Out of a total vehicle collection of over 300 armoured vehicles, the museum operates around 55 mobile vehicles on a regular basis. There are two types of collections that form part of this running fleet: the Historic Running Collection and the Display Fleet. The first of these is only used during specific events like Tiger Day and Tankfest, while the Display Fleet is used more frequently throughout the season, mainly as part of the Tanks in Action displays. The vehicles that form part of the fleet have been selected by asking the following questions:

■ What is the significance of the tank in the history of armoured warfare?
■ Is it a duplicate? If so, can we operate one while we keep the other as the static reference example?
■ What story does this vehicle tell (technology, combat history etc)?
■ Do we have the spares (or the ability to make them) and the knowledge to safely operate the vehicle?

RIGHT Where to start? Jon Kneebone has a look of trepidation as he examines the partially stripped-down engine block. *(TM)*

Many of these running vehicles have been operated for many years, but until recently none had undergone a complete overhaul or restoration, apart from the restoration of our German Tiger 1, which was a Heritage Lottery Fund-supported project, and which was completed by an external contractor. It had become clear that if we wanted to continue to operate this large running fleet, vehicles needed to be completely overhauled as simple maintenance was no longer an option. Even though other vehicles have been partially restored at the museum in the past, the Matilda II restoration has been a unique undertaking and was the first 'nuts and bolts' project from the team in the museum's new workshop.

Why the Matilda II?

The Matilda II tank had been operated by the museum for several years but had developed several mechanical problems which prevented it from further running. Therefore, there was a feeling of responsibility to repair what had become unserviceable while in our care. The Matilda II is also a very significant British Second World War tank, which the leadership of the Tank Museum felt was needed to be kept as an example in a running condition; there is currently no other running Matilda II in the United Kingdom.

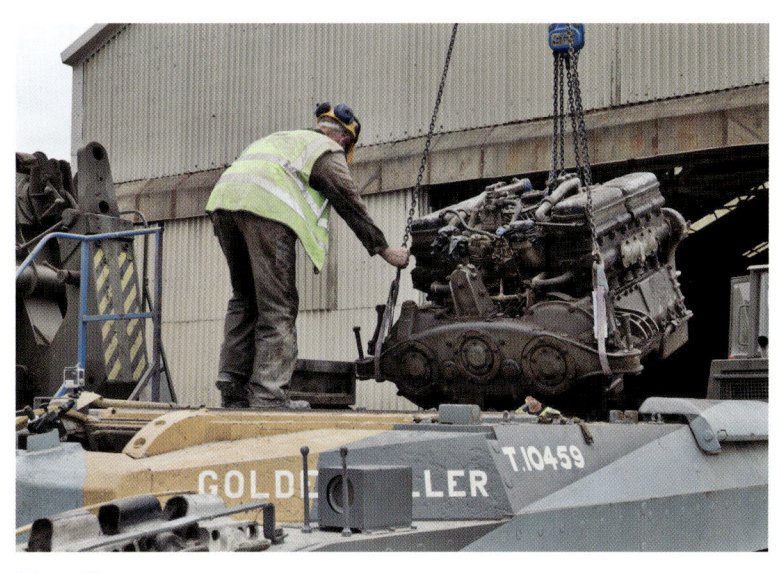

Funding

The Tank Museum was successful in the application for the Prism Fund, so £20,000 was received from Arts Council England. In addition, a £10,000 donation from the David Webster Charitable Trust was received. The total budget for costs (spares, material and external services) amounted to £30,000. In addition to the financial support, the museum received the extremely kind offer of spares from Matt McMahon, an Australian Matilda collector, who donated several key components to the project, saving the project thousands of pounds. This spare parts donation allowed the restoration of both engines.

ABOVE **Before: lifting the Leyland engines out of the hull, with the cross-drive unit nearest the camera.** *(TM)*

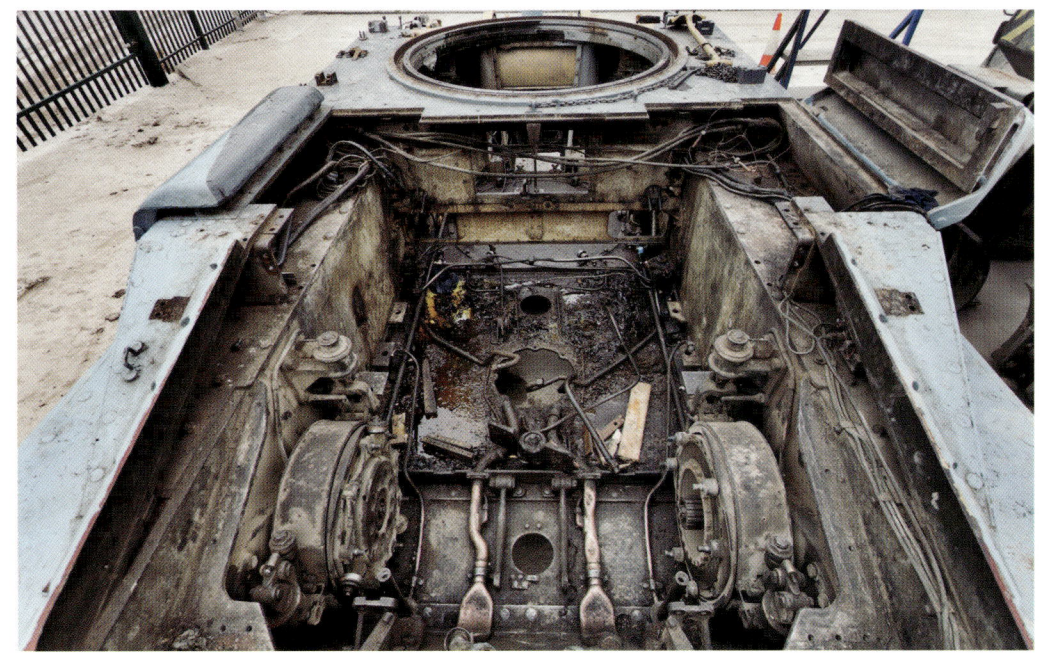

LEFT **Before: more grease and grime, and a good idea of what the engine bay of a service tank ends up like. ...** *(TM)*

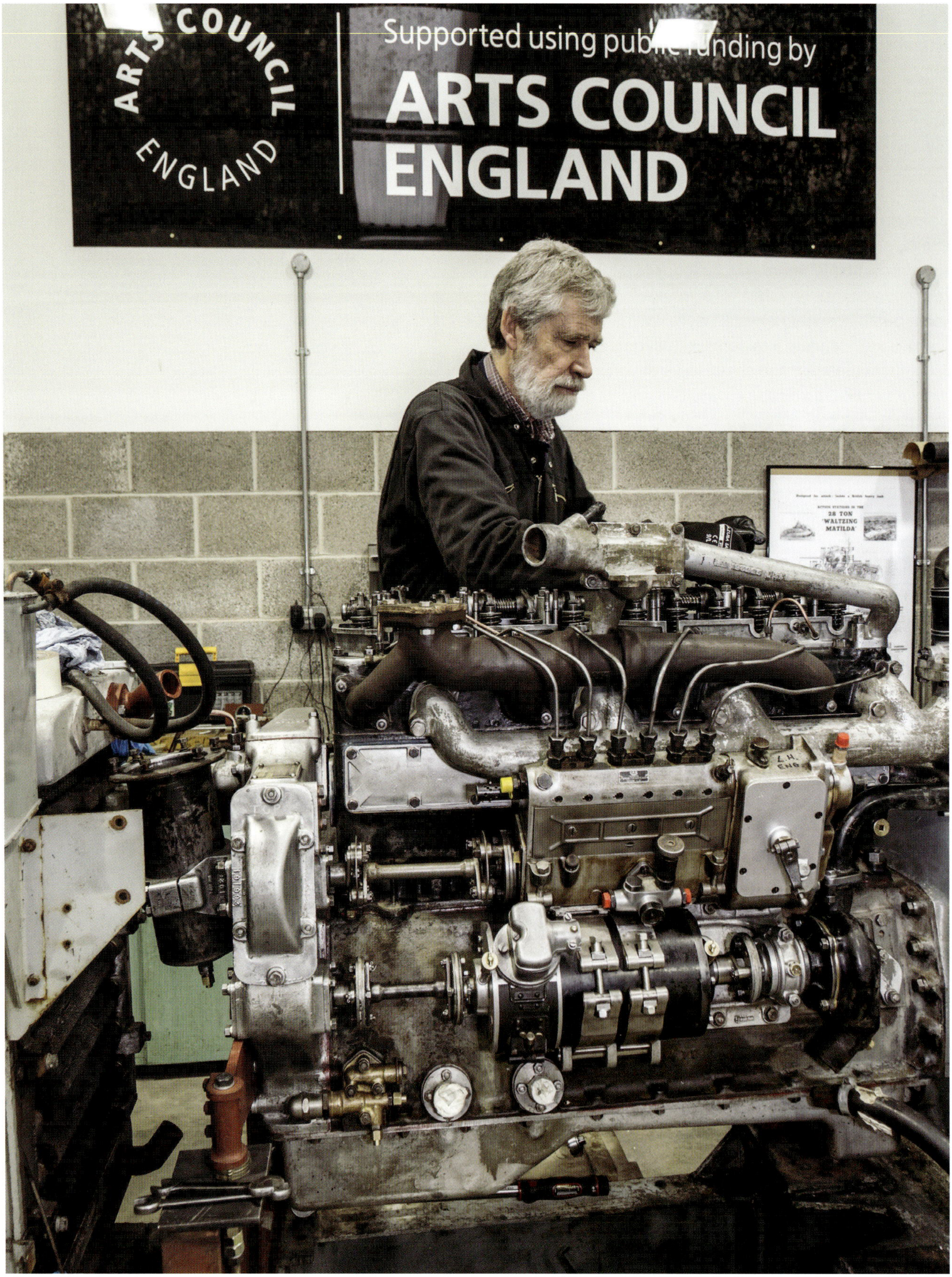
ARTS COUNCIL ENGLAND
ARTS COUNCIL
ENGLAND

OPPOSITE **The rebuilt engine nears completion.** *(TM)*

Condition assessment

The initial belief was that the gearbox had failed. The gearbox had actually been removed for repair, and it then became clear that there were several other mechanical problems with the vehicle. A complete condition report followed, which highlighted the requirements for a complete systems overhaul, while trying to preserve as many of the original features (paint, leather, surfaces) as possible. In hindsight, the condition report needed to be much more detailed and should have included a strip-down of the engines and supporting systems, which early on in the project were (wrongly) assumed to be in a good condition.

The condition report was a combination of an inspection by the workshop technicians, and also involved going through the maintenance and operating records of the particular vehicle. It also involved speaking to the drivers, volunteers and technicians who had operated and worked on the vehicle in the past to fully understand the problems that had arisen over time. Once all the information was collated, a proposal was forwarded to the Tank Museum's Collections Committee that this should be the first in-house restoration project, which was agreed.

Disassembly process

Once the disassembly process started, it became clear that there was much more wrong with the vehicle than the initial assessment had indicated. Firstly, the turret was removed and placed on a stand; this was followed by the removal of the gearbox and engines. Once the tank had been broken up into its main components, these were stripped of their individual fittings such as wiring, internal boxes and operating linkages. Everything was photographed in detail as the strip-down continued, and all items were labelled and placed into the spares store.

ABOVE **Bob Darwood reassembles the reconditioned and rebuilt gearbox.** *(TM)*

LEFT **Just some of the copper plumbing ready to go back into the hull.** *(TM)*

Conservation – or restoration?

Early in the process it was intended only to overhaul all the operating systems and thereby keep the 'feel' of the vehicle as it was. However, as so often during a restoration process, it turned out that many other components were also in need of repair that were not part of the running systems. As noted, the museum was very keen to keep as much original material (and that includes the finishes of surfaces) as possible; unfortunately, someone had (in the 1960s or '70s), covered the entire interior of the vehicle with silver paint, literally covering everything inside. Attempts were made to remove this layer of paint to reveal the original white paint, but this proved impossible; in addition, large areas of the interior paint were completely worn away. So, it was decided to keep the original paint where it was untouched

ABOVE LEFT Before: with the turret removed, the inside of the fighting compartment as it was. *(TM)*

LEFT Before: the turret basket has been lifted out revealing the underside of the RBJ connection and decades of grime and neglect. *(TM)*

BELOW LEFT After: the same space as restoration is nearing completion, and the hull interior is painted once more in its original white. *(TM)*

BELOW After: more components added and the hull is almost ready to be reunited with the turret. *(TM)*

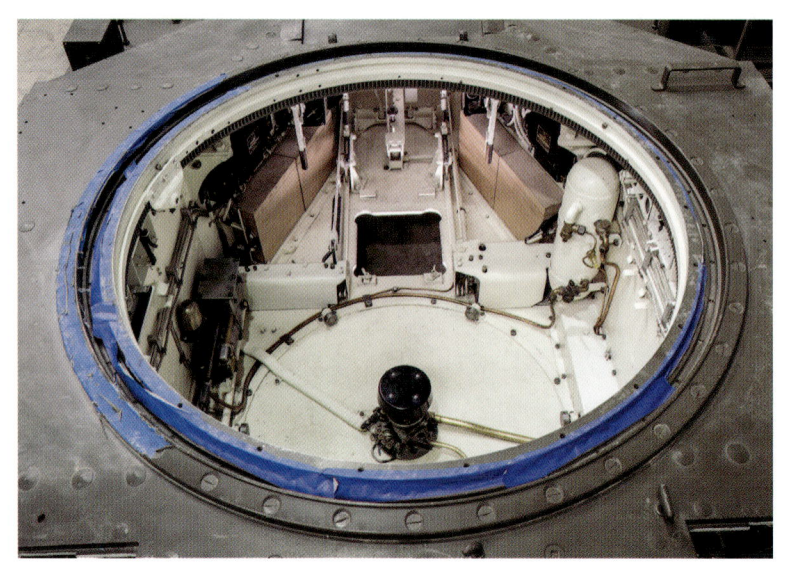

(mainly behind fittings and fixtures) but repaint it where it was removed or painted over.

The discussions on exactly what to replace and what to conserve took a lot of time, but it allowed the team to come up with an approach to the project that suited the situation. Early on in the process there was often reference made to: 'But it needs to look right'; later a lot more enthusiasm was shown for the preservation of existing finishes, even if these were no longer perfect, which served to highlight the age of the vehicle rather than try to make it look brand new once more.

As the vehicle had to be restored to running condition, the safe functionality of key systems such as steering, brakes and the electrical system sometimes required critical components to be replaced in order for them to work correctly, but wherever possible this was done using original parts. There were other considerations, such as the museum's policy to remove potentially dangerous materials (for example, asbestos brake linings), to make the vehicle safer to maintain and operate. In this case, these items were replaced regardless of the condition.

Creating the project team

It took the museum a while to get the restoration team together. Since such a complex project had never been undertaken in house, it was necessary to rotate some members of staff in and out of the project until the right combination of engineering skills, technical understanding and project management abilities was identified. This then allowed the placement of specific volunteers into the team to support the project. During this undertaking the museum was also in the fortunate position of being able to take on apprentices who were used as part of their apprenticeship placements. In the end the project team consisted of:

- Two (paid) workshop technicians
- Five regular volunteers, including a skilled machinist and an engine builder
- Two apprentices.

The project was guided by the Restoration Manager who discussed the project regularly with the Head of Collections.

ABOVE Before: cabling in the turret, with the cover removed from one of the junction boxes. The inside had been painted with post-war silver paint at some point. The earliest Matildas did have silver interiors, but this was changed to white when aluminium paint became hard to obtain. *(TM)*

BELOW The team who completed the restoration – and learned an awful lot in the process! *(TM)*

Causes of mechanical failure

As the project progressed the team began to better understand the failure of the different components; a pattern started to emerge, which highlighted how a lack of maintenance and the wrong type of operation in the past had impacted on the overall condition of the vehicle. Obviously, items like the wiring had become brittle as a result of age, but other components had failed as a result of lack of maintenance. For example, the suspension was greased instead of oiled, thereby blocking the areas that need to be filled with oil. The gearbox had the wrong type of oil, which had damaged the bronze bushes. The compressor had failed because of a lack of lubrication, which then directly impacted on gear changing. Basically, over the years the vehicle had been operated with very limited knowledge of the systems and with very basic maintenance which had caused failures – in some ways this was a microcosm of the factors often commented on in wartime documents, emphasising that the tanks performed better – meaning they were much more reliable – when operated by trained crews with time for maintenance and access to lubricants and spare parts.

The skills required

There was a lot of debate during the project to decide whether some individual components should be rebuilt in house or by external contractors. In the end the vast majority of sub-assemblies were overhauled in house, including the rebuilding of both engines and the gearbox. The museum was extremely fortunate to have two very skilled volunteers as part of the project team: one overhauled the engines and the other made all new bushes for the gearbox. The only components that were overhauled by an external specialist company were the grinding of the crankshaft of one of the engines, the complete overhaul of the air servo and the manufacture of new bushes for the suspension. It also took a while to find the right suppliers for specialist components like correct period wiring, replacement bearings and so on.

Suspension

There were some areas of significant wear on the suspension that needed attention. Each side of the vehicle has five bogie units and one jockey wheel. These are connected to brackets which are in turn cushioned by

BELOW Before: stripping the components of the suspension out. *(TM)*

LEFT Replacing the turret with as much care and attention to detail as the rest of the project. *(TM)*

powerful springs. In addition, there is one idler wheel and one final drive and sprocket per side which collectively form the running gear of the tank. There are a number of pivot points throughout this system that incur wear when the vehicle is used, and as a result there were both bushes and bearings that needed to be replaced to prevent damage to other assemblies. These 'wear parts' would have been routinely replaced when the vehicle was in service. Bearings of the correct type were sourced, and the bushes were deliberately made undersized so that they could be hand-fitted to the relevant suspension pins. This process made allowances for differences in wear and allowed the original pins to be refitted to the vehicle. In the case of the final drives, new shaft oil seals were made – in leather – to match the original and these were trimmed by hand prior to being fitted.

Turret and weapons system

Both the main armament and secondary weapon systems were in desperate need of careful cleaning in order to reveal the engineered surfaces and show areas of original paint. To remove rust, clean off residue and free seized moving parts, the entire weapon system was removed and stripped – including the barrel. In addition, the commander's cupola and the elevation lock on the turret mantlet were inoperative and needed to be removed to repair them effectively. The requirement to carry out this task had a number of benefits for those involved, as the 2pdr weapon system (or a close cousin) is fitted to a number of other British tanks and the team now have an excellent understanding of the equipment and lifting gear required to complete a task of this nature.

Paint

As with the turret, there were some areas within the hull in which the original paintwork had

BELOW Before: shot-blasting the old, hideous and incorrect Caunter camouflage from the hull. *(TM)*

143
THE STORY OF THE RESTORATION

ABOVE Having shot-blasted the hull, the bare metal was primed with red oxide paint, before the correct white paint was reapplied to the whole interior. *(TM)*

ABOVE RIGHT Casting marks on one of the primed armour sections. *(TM)*

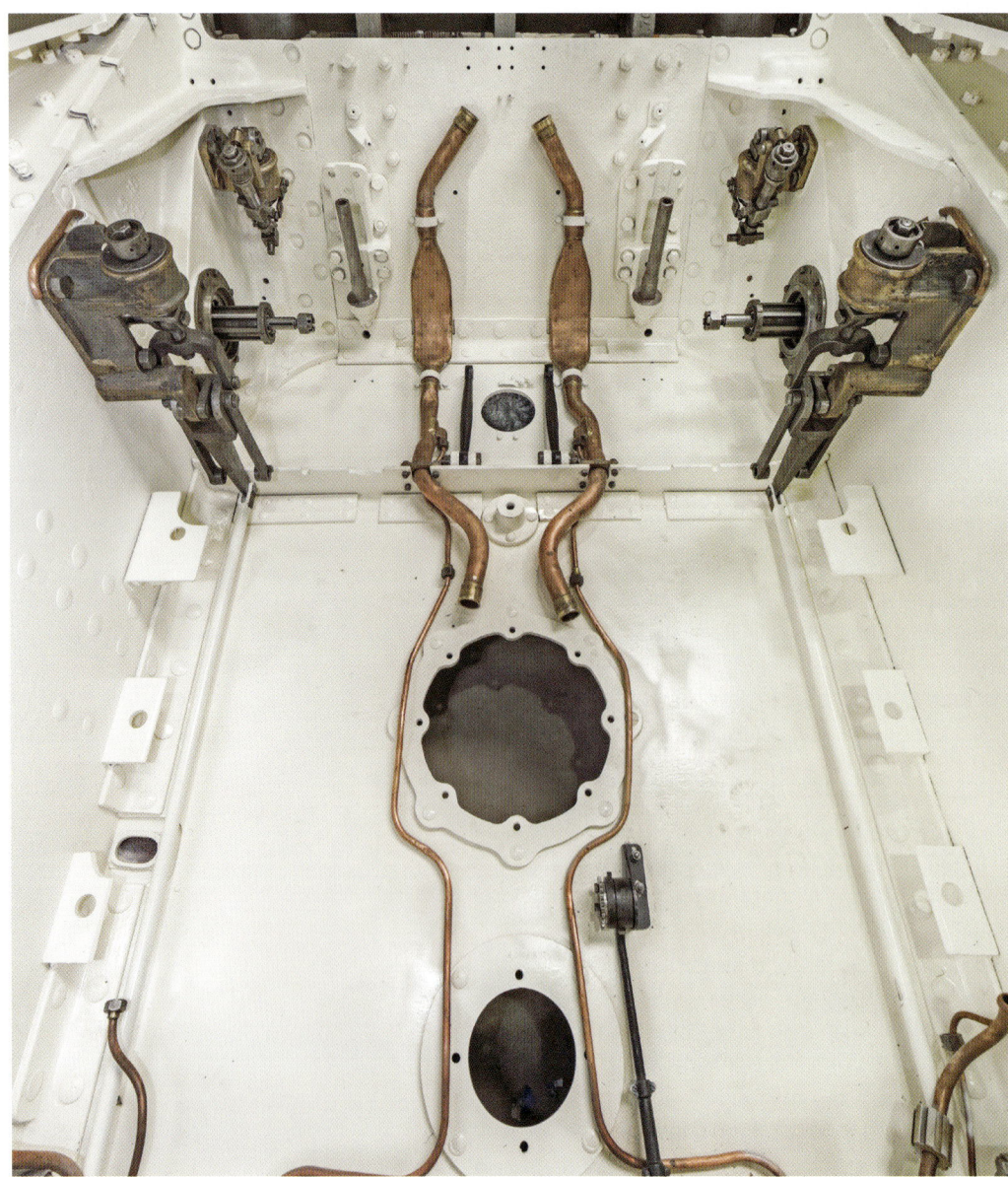

RIGHT That's better! Refurbished components begin to be put back into place. Note the pair of exhaust pipes in the hull centre. *(TM)*

survived. This was mainly found in the forward stowage bins that are located either side of the driver and the team were able to stabilise and maintain it. As the remainder of the hull had been stripped and repainted in the past, the original shade of Khaki Green was sourced and the hull painted to reflect its appearance when it was first made.

Electrical systems

After inspecting the entire wiring system, it was decided to replace all the wiring; over the years the insulation and screening had degraded beyond repair, also several areas had been modified when sections of the wiring had failed without taking care to use original or sympathetic components. It would have been too dangerous to reuse the existing system. However, all original wiring was kept, labelled and placed into storage. Correct period (new) wiring was sourced and used to rewire the entire vehicle in house.

RIGHT The left side of the bulkhead separating the fighting compartment from the engine. *(TM)*

BELOW Quite beautiful. The bulkhead nears completion, with the engine clutch handwheels and their linkages in place. *(TM)*

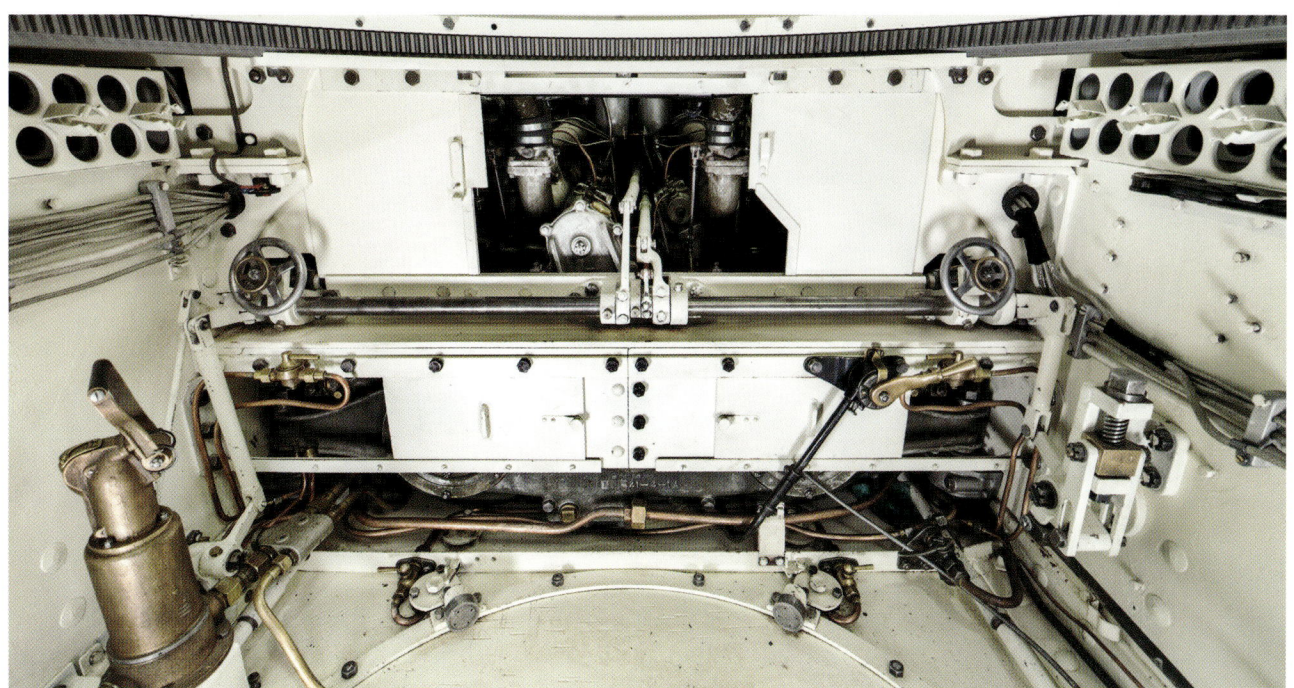

THE STORY OF THE RESTORATION

Work continues as the hull and its myriad components are reassembled. *(TM)*

147

THE STORY OF THE RESTORATION

RIGHT After: the Matilda was never designed to make life easy for the people who had to maintain it! *(TM)*

BELOW Inspecting the inside of the gearbox. *(TM)*

Gearbox

The oil in the gearbox was found to be contaminated, which had caused damage to the internal bushes. The Matilda has a pre-select gearbox which needed all the bands replacing with non-asbestos-containing materials. Many of the internal bushes had to be remade by one of the skilled volunteers, as they had been damaged as a result of the wrong type of oil being used.

The Leyland engines

Although both engines were running when the project started, when they were stripped down they revealed some serious internal problems. Wear and tear on most components was normal, but one of the engines had suffered from damage to the big end and main bearings; that same engine needed a replacement camshaft. Both engines were completely stripped down, cleaned and reassembled using new gaskets and replacement parts where needed. The team was extremely lucky to receive all the worn engine parts, free of charge, from an Australian collector, otherwise the engine repairs would have been made much more difficult, if not impossible. All gaskets containing asbestos were replaced with modern equivalents. The engines

RIGHT After: ready to lift, the Leyland engines about to be inserted into the hull. *(TM)*

BELOW After: going in, the crew take great care not to damage any of the components as the engines are reintroduced into the engine bay. *(TM)*

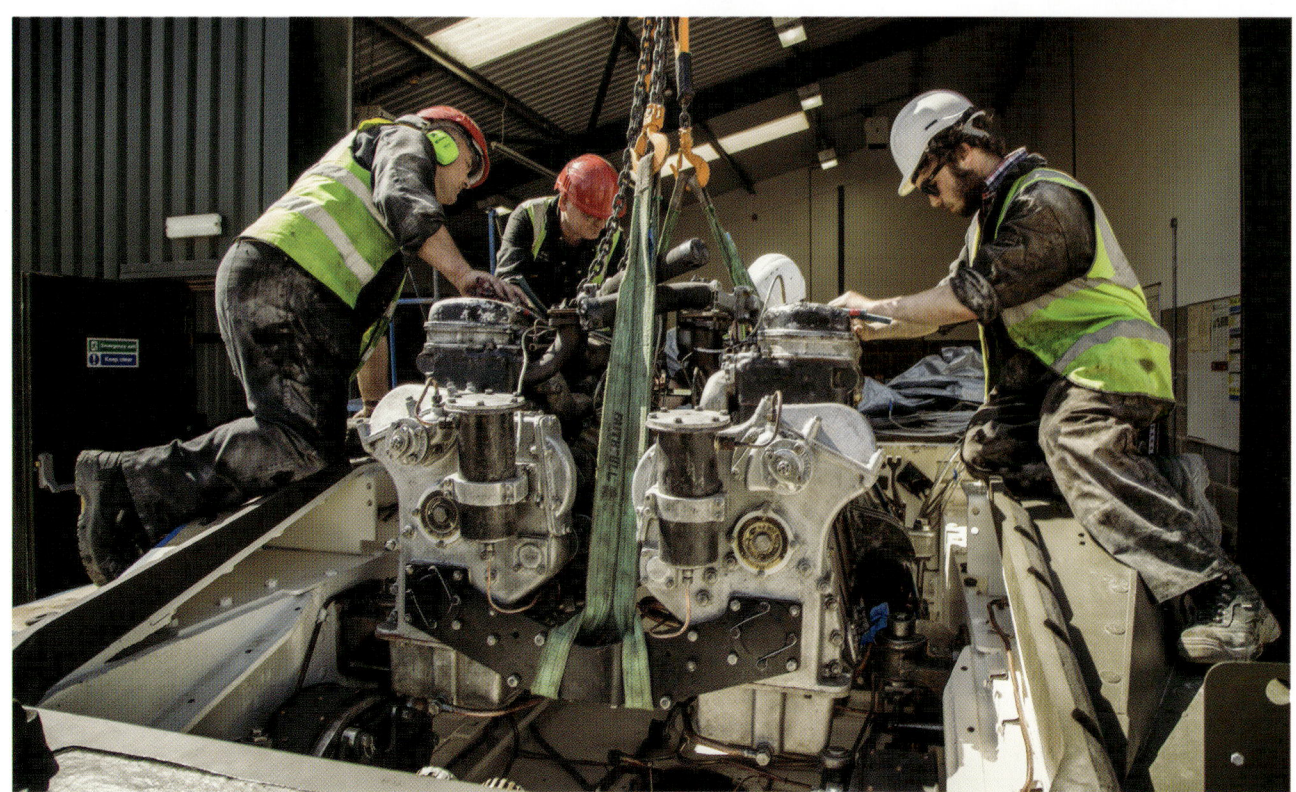

149

THE STORY OF THE RESTORATION

ABOVE After: looking into the engine bay through the manhole cover in the floor. *(TM)*

BELOW The maker's plate, identifying the tank as having been completed on 28 May 1941. She was built in Glasgow by North British Locomotive Co. as part of a batch of 50 tanks, most of which went to the USSR. *(TM)*

were both rebuilt at the museum by an ex-Leyland engineer, who was assisted by the apprentices in order to pass on some of his knowledge. Both engines were test-run before they were refitted to the hull.

Documentation

Each week a report was sent to both the Restoration Manager and the Head of Collections, listing the operations carried out on the vehicle and the personnel who had completed those tasks. This was supported by hundreds of photographs which document every stage of the progress of the project and which will serve as an invaluable reference source for reassembly and the identification of replacement and non-original parts in the future.

The Matilda Diaries

From the beginning the Tank Museum was very keen not only to document the project for future reference, but also to share the progress of the restoration with our visitors. As a result of this *The Matilda Diaries* series was created on YouTube, where workshop staff and volunteers provided regular updates on the project. In the end videos were made, which have so far achieved over 300,000 views. This online project really created a lot of interest in the Matilda II and highlighted the workshop's skills to our online visitors.

Lessons learned

■ The initial time estimate was very optimistic; a much more detailed investigation was actually needed. In the end it took about 2½ years.

- It took a while to assemble the correct project team, with the right combination of skills, experience and project management abilities.
- There was not a good network of suppliers at the start of the project, forcing the museum to do a lot of research in order to find suitable and reliable suppliers.
- It is very important from the start of such a project to establish exactly what level of finish is expected, especially when it comes to the key question of the balance between restoration and conservation.
- The Tank Museum learned an enormous amount from this project which will help massively with the next restoration project.
- The Matilda II was completed in May 2018 and was one of the star vehicles at Tankfest 2018 in June.

ABOVE The newly completed tank, appropriately named 'The Princess Royal', is shown to Princess Anne by Museum Director Richard Smith and Major General Peter Gilchrist in May 2018. *(TM)*

BELOW Finished! The beautifully restored tank is revealed to the public in a demonstration in summer 2018. As a result of the careful restoration she can be expected to remain in a running condition for many years to come. *(TM)*

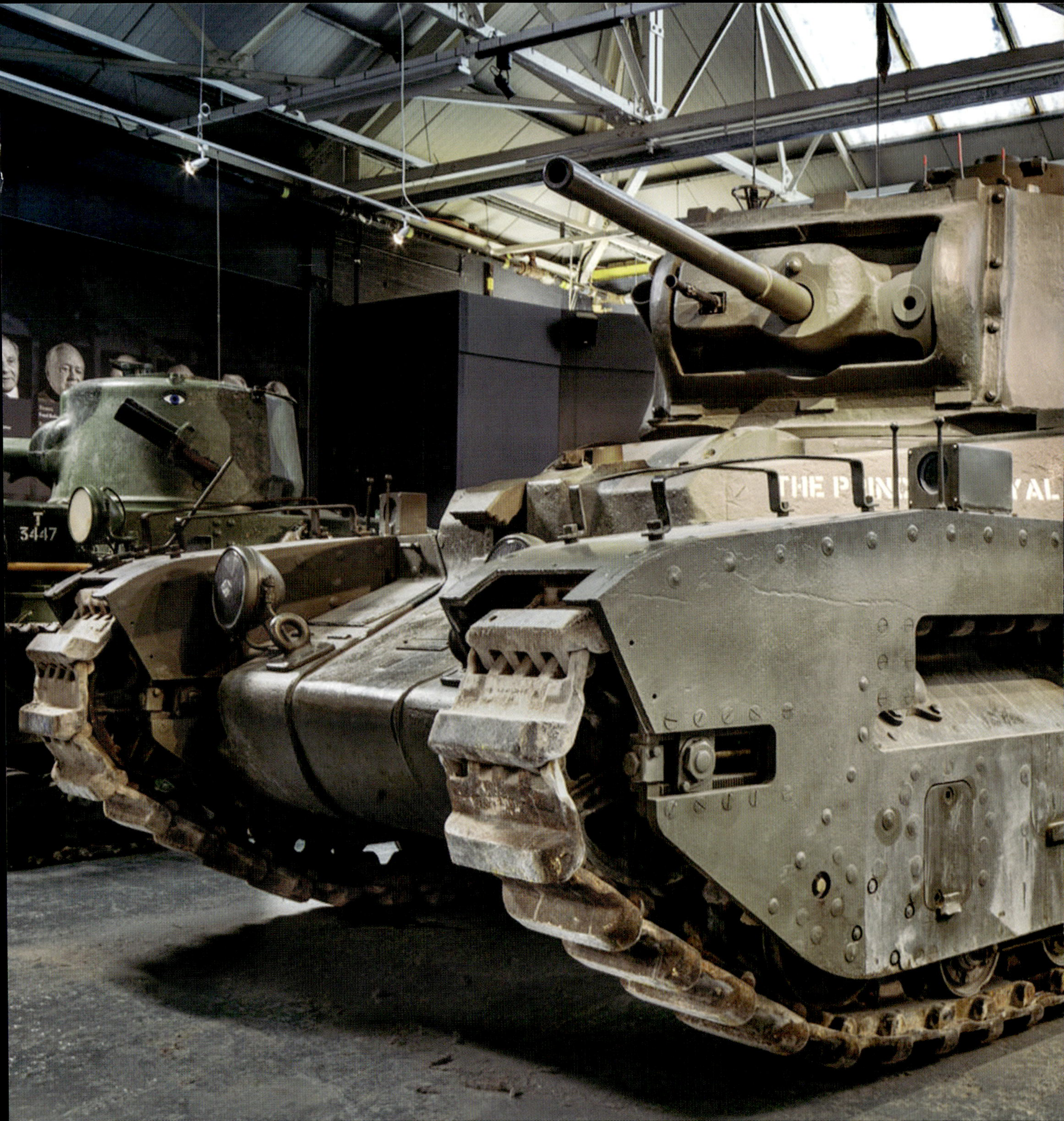
T
3447

Chapter Eight

Matilda walkaround

Only a comprehensive walkaround of the Matilda, both inside and out, will allow the reader to fully appreciate not only the design and layout of the tank, but also the top quality restoration job that has been carried out.

OPPOSITE The magnificent Matilda II as restored and in her place at the Bovington Tank Museum. *(TM)*

ABOVE Looking the part! The tank is in Khaki Green No 3 overall, and although it has not travelled far, the typical staining is already evident underneath the mud chutes. *(TM)*

RIGHT The rear of the tank, showing the wire cage under the rear armour and the bell push in the centre. The ends of the exhaust pipes and silencer boxes are not yet fitted. *(TM)*

ABOVE The Matilda II featured armour on the front that was all but impenetrable by the standard anti-tank guns of 1940, and remained so until the Germans introduced bigger guns and improved ammunition in 1941. *(TM)*

LEFT The track-adjusting mechanism as it would be with a new track. As the track plates stretched in use, the mechanism was adjusted to push the idler wheel forwards, thus taking up the slack. *(TM)*

RIGHT The curved hood over the driver's compartment in the fully closed position. This is the largest hatch of the three provided for the crew, but could become unusable if the main gun barrel was at the 12 o'clock position, preventing escape. *(TM)*

BELOW The armoured hinged covers on the hull top are extremely heavy to lift but, like the rest of the armour, provided an extremely good level of protection. *(TM)*

ABOVE Two 4in smoke dischargers on the turret right side. Based on the breech of the standard .303in rifle, the weapons were fired by the loader from within the turret. *(TM)*

LEFT Looking at the driver from above: this is how he would be driving closed-down, *ie* when the curved armour roof was closed. In practice all the spare space either side of him would be packed with kit and equipment. *(TM)*

ABOVE The driver looking through the periscope – the four slits for the emergency lookout are to the right. One of the three instrument panels is clearly visible. *(TM)*

RIGHT When closed down, the primary means of observation for the driver would be through his periscope, which could be traversed from side to side. If damaged in action he would then use the emergency lookout slits to the right of the periscope. *(TM)*

LEFT A glimpse of the driver from the fighting compartment. The driver could often feel isolated from the other three members of the crew who all shared the limited space in the turret. *(TM)*

BELOW The commander looking through his Vickers Tank Periscope when closed down. Note the leather padding around the circumference of the cupola, and the Wireless Set No 19 in the bottom left, accessible by both the commander and loader. *(TM)*

RIGHT The gunner in his seat and looking through the tank telescope, used for aiming the 2pdr and co-ax machine gun. His right shoulder is in the padded shoulder rest.
(TM)

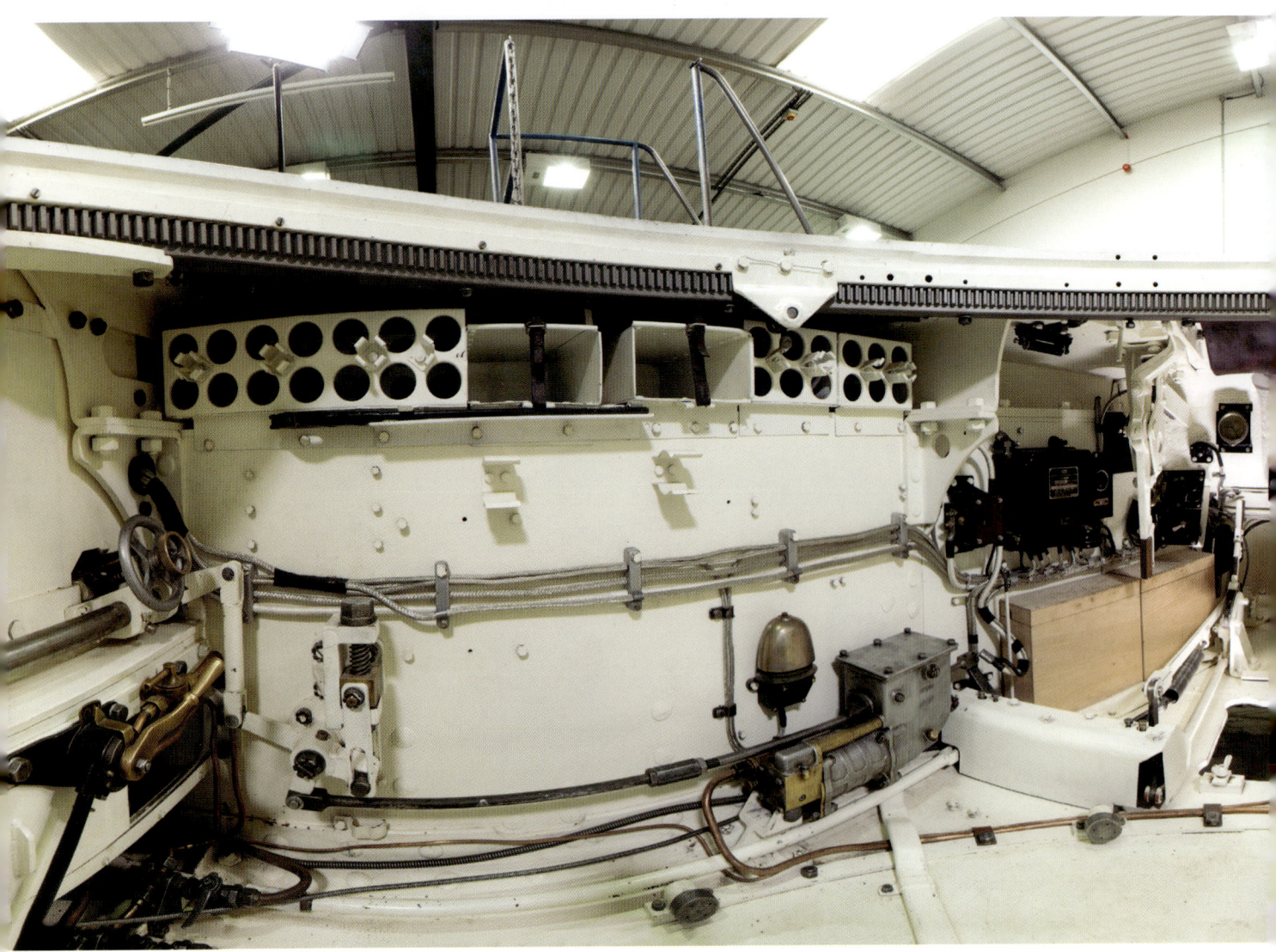

LEFT The loader holding a 2pdr AP shell. The breech is closed and ready to fire. *(TM)*

BELOW A panoramic view of the hull of the tank as she nears completion, from the left rear bulkhead, through the driver's compartment (with the seat and escape hatch removed), to the right-hand bulkhead. *(TM)*

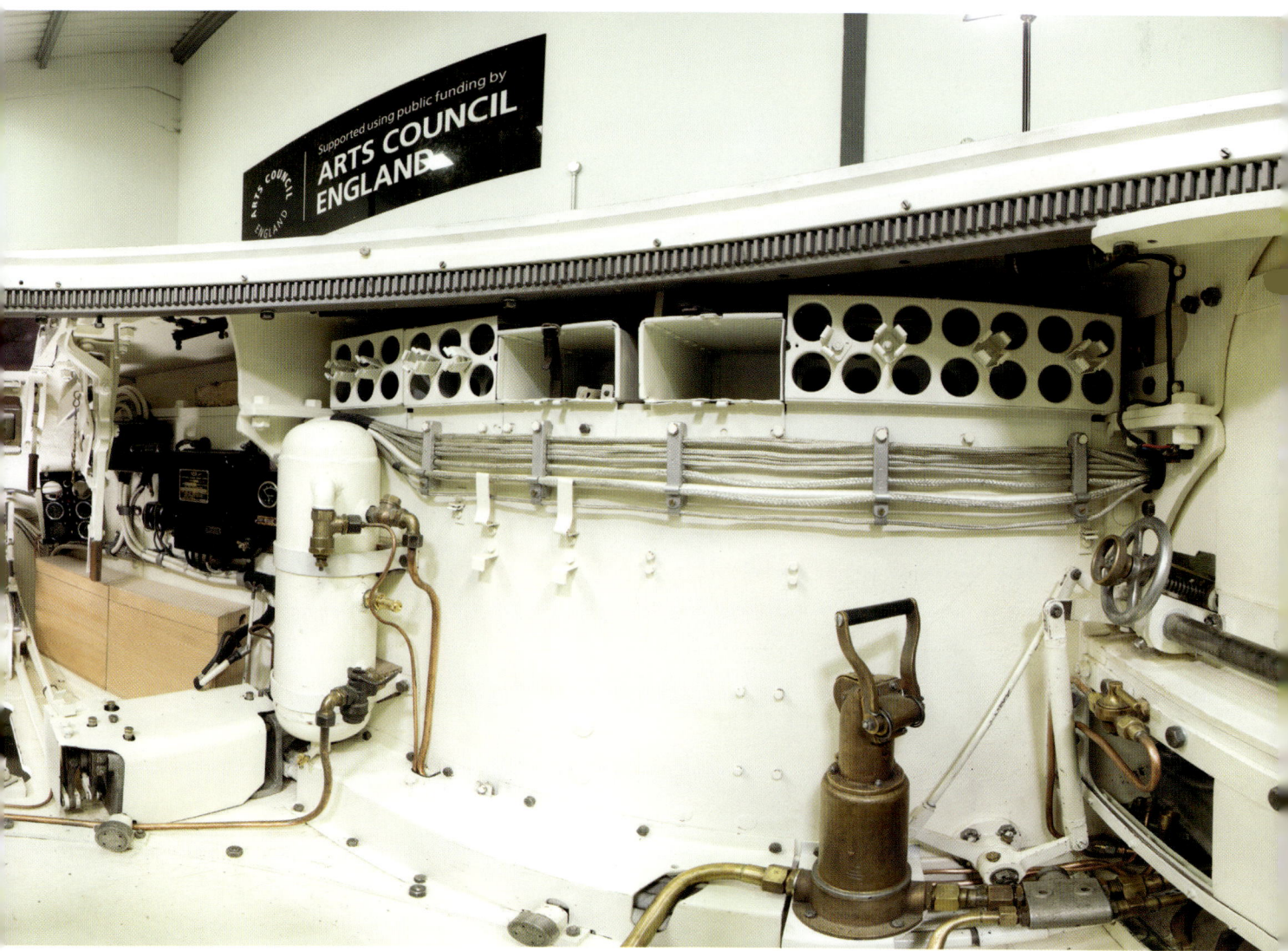

MATILDA WALKAROUND

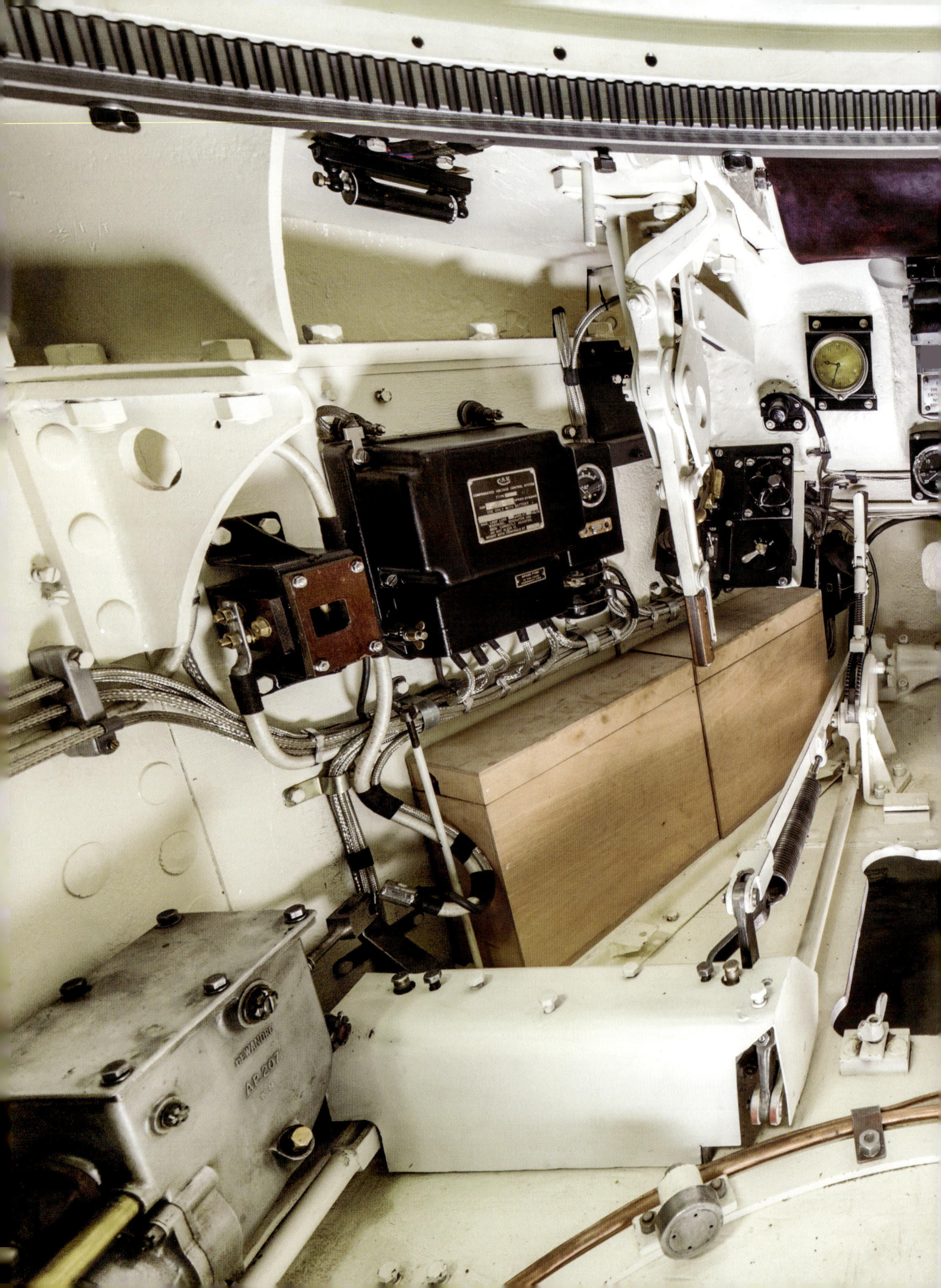
DEWANDRE
AP 207

The driver's compartment, again with seat and escape hatch removed. *(TM)*

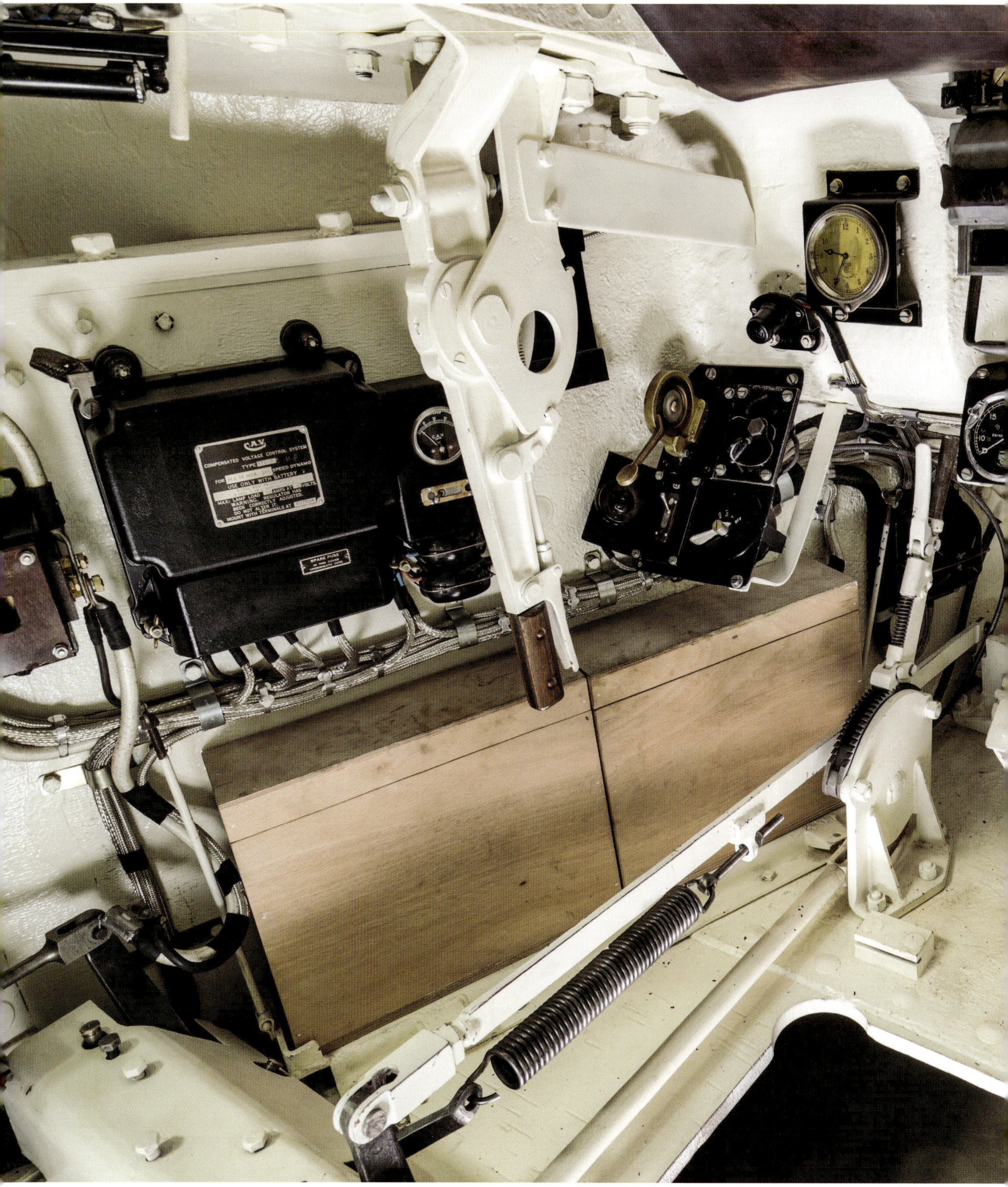
C.A.V.
COMPENSATED VOLTAGE CONTROL SYSTEM
TYPE
SPEED DYNAMO
FOR
USE ONLY WITH BATTERY
VOLTS
AMPS AT
MAX. LAMP LOAD
WARNING. REGULATOR HAS
BEEN CORRECTLY ADJUSTED.
DO NOT ALTER IT.
MOUNT WITH TERMINALS AT
SPARE FUSE

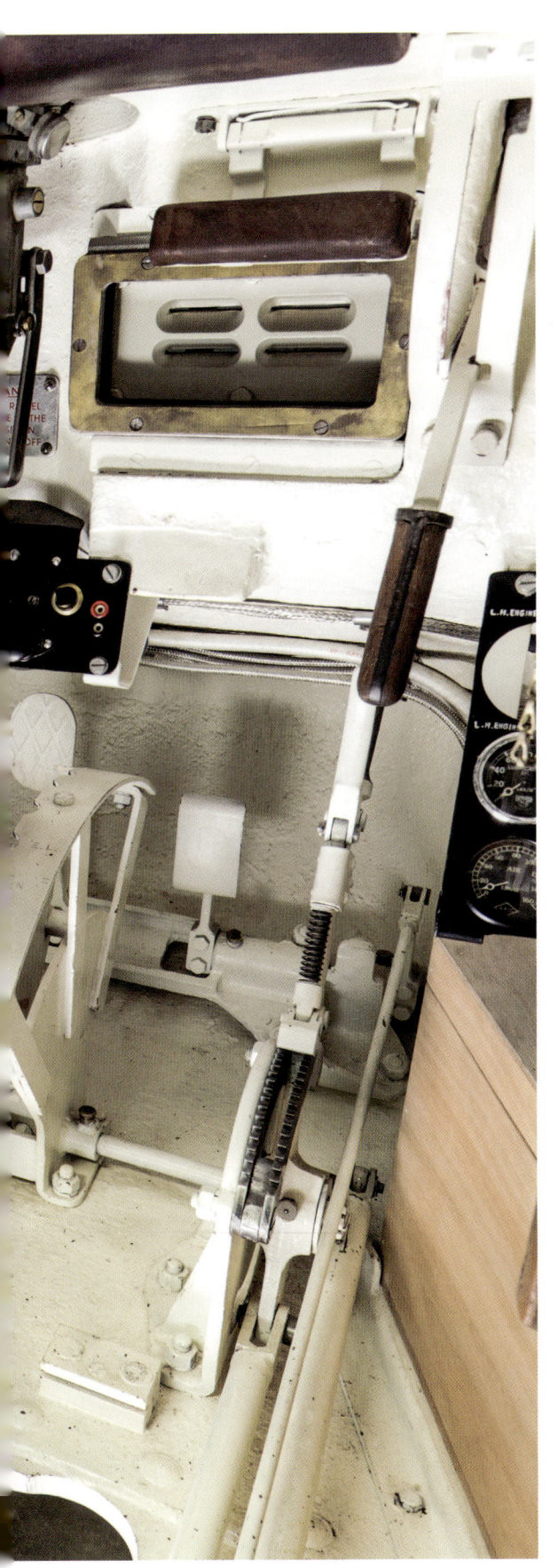

LEFT Left side of the driver's cab. *(TM)*

ABOVE The clock, centre instrument panel with speedometer – optimistically graduated up to 40mph – and the driver's periscope in the centre. *(TM)*

BELOW The left-hand instrument panel with the engine-starting and -stopping controls at the top, and lighting underneath; note the two-position switch for switching the rear lights from red to blue. *(TM)*

C.A.V.
COMPENSATED VOLTAGE CONTROL SYSTEM
TYPE
FOR
SPEED-DYNAMO
USE ONLY WITH BATTERY
MAX. LAMP LOAD
AMPS AT
VOLTS.
WARNING. REGULATOR HAS
BEEN CORRECTLY ADJUSTED.
DO NOT ALTER IT.
MOUNT WITH TERMINALS AT
SPARE FUSE

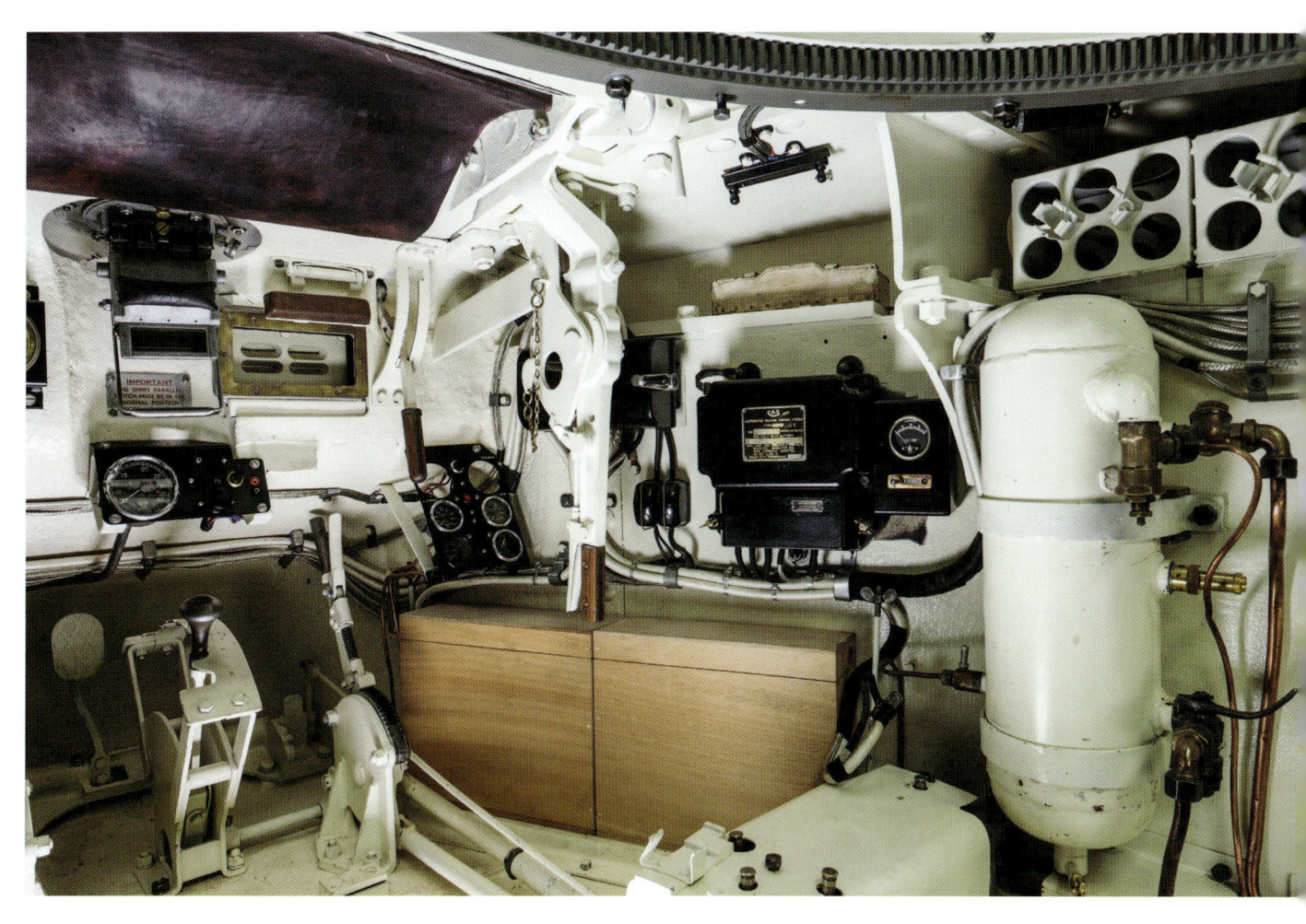

OPPOSITE Right side of the cab. The batteries are in the brown boxes either side. *(TM)*

ABOVE To the rear right of the driver's seat is the compressed-air reservoir for assisting the driver in gear changing, with 2pdr ammunition racks above. *(TM)*

LEFT A close-up of just some of the infamous 'plumbing', with the brass bell for attracting the crew's attention visible at the top. *(TM)*

Endnotes

Chapter 1
1. Also, at this stage many considered Italy's growing militarism and territorial ambitions to be a bigger worry than those of Germany.
2. Tuvia Ben-Moshe, Churchill: Strategy & History (1992) p. 87.
3. Hancock, Design p. 240 & p. 256.
4. Richard Croucher, Engineers at War 1939 – 1945 (1982) p. 6.
5. Although it was widely used by the crews, Vickers never formed part of its official name.
6. The front of the 1917 Mk IV had double this.
7. The first two were made in mild steel.
8. In early tanks it was commonplace for the crew to stand, or to have rudimentary seats at best. As tanks were produced with suspension systems, it became less important for the crewmen to brace themselves when crashing about cross-country, and more important to offer them comfort which would extend their time in action.
9. Experiments in fitting wireless to tanks had started in the First World War, and the first small – a relative term – practical sets began to be developed from 1926. At one stage most engineers agreed that it would be impossible for tanks to transmit and receive transmissions while on the move.

Chapter 2
1. The term 'infantry tank' had been in unofficial use from around 1927, where it referred to the use of tankettes, small, cheap and cheerless two or even one-man machines that carried a machine gun and a small amount of armour.
2. At one stage in 1934 raising another four Army Tank battalions was proposed, but actually bringing the next two battalions into being was not achieved for a number of years: 7RTC were not formed until May 1937, with 8RTC a year later.
3. David French, *Raising Churchill's Army*, p. 34.
4. Probably because of Sir John Carden, the designer, who seems to have used names from his family history as codenames for his projects, hence Matilda and Valentine. He was killed in an air crash two months after submitting the design proposal.
5. One early document refers to it as the 'Tank Medium A11E1', this obsolete designation presumably used because it weighed 11 tons. It was never a medium tank!
6. After Carden's somewhat suspicious death in December 1935, his assistant Leslie Little took over the role of chief tank designer, including the work on the A11.
7. Usually abbreviated at the time as R Tanks.
8. Sensibly, despite Carden's original specification, the army insisted on wireless being fitted.
9. Seven of the 7RTR A12s were attached to 4RTR to bolster their firepower.
10. In late 1942 official sources detailing tank losses in the war up to that point noted that in 1940 a total of 126 Matilda Is and IIs were reported as lost in France.

Chapter 3
1. Vulcan was initially contracted to build ten Light Mk VI tanks on 22 October 1936, and over the next couple of years built another 256 light tanks in three batches.
2. The effectiveness of the side armour is open to debate. In June 1942 the Tank Board recorded an expert comment stating: 'I am convinced that the Matilda II would be much better without a skirt.' This ignores the substantial redesign of the suspension required by the removal of the side armour, and in any case in the following month the tank was withdrawn from front-line service in North Africa.
3. A bell crank is a lever with two arms sharing a common fulcrum at the junction in the centre.
4. Both to keep the silhouette small and to reduce weight.
5. The author is a medium-framed 6ft 2in and can only just squeeze through the turret hatches into the tank. Having small crew members would be a definite advantage!
6. Not including 15 mild steel instructional tanks or the two prototypes.
7. Valentine was of course also an I-Tank, but much better suited to quasi-cruiser use than the ponderous Matilda.

Chapter 4
1. No 7RTR sent six Matilda IIs to assist 4RTR for the Arras operation. Both regiments used the larger tanks to provide fire support for the lighter-armed A11s. The official figures indicate that four more Matilda IIs were in France but not allocated to either 4 or 7RTR, therefore presumably in reserve.
2. B Squadron was initially sent to Port Sudan in late 1940 with 'the pick of the sixteen fittest Matildas in the regiment' from where it moved to East Africa, with the rest of the unit deploying to Egypt three months later.
3. Of course, this was the maximum and was only found at the very point of the hull nose plate, but there was a consistent 75mm on both the driver's vertical plate and the turret front.
4. Sources indicate that in total New Zealand received 34 Matilda IVCS as close-support tanks to operate with their force of Valentines; it is not clear why the 34th tank was not also sent to Australia.
5. No 5 bomb was always launched individually otherwise it could hit the wireless antenna; the others could be launched individually or as a salvo.
6. Presumably using 2pdr HE.
7. From Duncan Crow (ed.), *Armoured Fighting Vehicles of the World, Volume 3* (1971), pp. 77–78.
8. As a final note to this chapter, there is evidence that at least two Matildas found their way to India, although it is not clear why.

Chapter 5
1. Although Leyland designed the engines, the project was overseen by a member of the Mechanisation Board, Mr Daniel Sheryer, ex-Tank Corps.
2. On later tanks (Mk IV onwards) with the so-called balanced electrical system, the series/parallel switch was not fitted, and older tanks had this component removed.
3. Air Raid Precautions.
4. Lakeman AA mountings were first issued in late 1941, with production difficulties causing delays so that units did not receive their full quota until mid-1942.

Chapter 6
1. The RAOC was responsible for much of the maintenance on tanks until the formation of REME in September 1942.
2. Grateful thanks to John Tapsell for detailed information on the CDL.
3. The turret was armoured to an impressive 65mm, the same as the maximum carried on the front of the contemporary Infantry Tank Mk III Valentine.
4. There was also a Type B used on Churchills, and a Type D which was a modified Type A used on Grants. The Type C was designed for use on Landing Craft.
5. The original codename used was Tank Winch, but this was changed to Baron in early 1942.

Bibliography and sources

Bannerman, Mark, *Modelling the Matilda Infantry Tank* (Osprey, 2004)
Crow, Duncan (ed.), *Armoured Fighting Vehicles: British and Commonwealth AFVs, 1940–1946* (Profile Publications, 1971)
Fletcher, David, *Mechanised Force* (HMSO, 1991)
Fletcher, David, *Matilda Infantry Tank 1938–45* (Osprey, 2003)
Forty, George, *The Royal Tank Regiment: A Pictorial History* (Halsgrove, 2001)
French, David, *Raising Churchill's Army: The British Army and the War against Germany, 1919–1945* (Oxford University Press, 2000)
Hill, Alexander, *British Lend-Lease Tanks and the Battle for Moscow* (JSMS, 2006)
Lewin, Ronald, *Man of Armour* (Leo Cooper, 1976)
Liddell Hart, Basil, *The Tanks*, Volumes 1 and 2 (Cassell, 1959)
Macksey, Kenneth, *Tank Force* (Pan/Ballantyne, 1970)
Macksey, Kenneth, *The Tank Pioneers* (Jane's, 1981)
Macksey, Kenneth, *Armoured Crusader* (Hutchinson, 2004)
Perrett, Bryan, *The Matilda in North Africa* (Ian Allan, 1973)
Postan, M.M., D. Hay and J.D. Scott, *Design and Development of Weapons* (Official Civil Series) (HMSO, 1964)
Price, Christopher, *Britain, America and Rearmament in the 1930s: The Cost of Failure* (Palgrave Macmillan, 2001)
Smithers, A.J., *Rude Mechanicals* (Grafton, 1989)
Taylor, Dick, *Mechanical Abortions?* (Unpublished, 2009)
Taylor, Dick, *Firing Now!* (MMP, 2016)

Official publications
Data for Matilda (DTD, 1942)
Field Service Regulations
Fighting, Support and Transport Vehicles and the War Office Organisation Part One (War Office, 1951)
Handbook for the Marks II, II* & IIA Medium Tanks (War Office, 1930)
History and Technical Summary, Tank Infantry Mk I (A11)
Instructional Notes for Students: The 'I' Tank Mk II
Instruction Book for Matilda (Baron)
Leyland Service Manual for Engines E148/149 and E164/165
Leyland Service Manual for Engines E170/171
Matilda I–IVCS Instructional Book, 1941
Matilda IV Stowage Sketches (1941)
MTP 35 Part 52 Infantry Tank Mark II (A12), 1940
Self-changing Gearbox for Matilda: Service Instructional Book
Spare Parts List, Tank Infantry Mk I (Vickers-Armstrongs, 1939)
RAC Liaison Reports
RAC Six-Monthly Reports
Tank Infantry Mk I Instructional Book (1939)
Tank Infantry Mk I Packing Diagrams (1938 and 1939)
Tank Infantry Mk II (AEC Power Unit) Instruction Book (Vulcan Foundry, 1939)

Index

Aberdeen Proving Ground, USA 78
Afrika Korps 6, 63
Ammunition 36, 47, 62, 67-68, 102-104, 108, 161
  HE 17, 63-65, 68, 102, 103
Anti-aircraft guns 58, 69
Anti-tank guns 6, 10. 29, 38-39, 58, 63-64, 70, 126-127, 155
Anti-tank mines 37, 123-126
Armament (weapons) 6, 17-18, 23, 50, 63, 68, 70, 100-107, 112, 133, 143
  anti-aircraft 18
  anti-tank 29, 36, 50
  covers 109
  machine guns 17, 19, 21-23, 28, 30, 36, 48, 64, 99, 101, 107, 112, 160
    cooling 36, 50
  main gun/howitzer 17, 50, 100-103, 114, 143, 156
    recoil system 101-102
  mountings 101, 107
  Russian tanks 54
  smoke grenade dischargers 36, 50, 68, 71, 103, 157
Armit, SSM 'Muscle' 40
Armour protection 6, 18-19, 21-22, 28-31, 35-37, 42, 49, 58-59, 62, 64, 69-70, 79, 82-83, 126-127
  access hatches 23
  cemented tank armour (CTA) 22
  effectiveness 10, 42, 58-59, 64, 126-127, 155-156
  face-hardened armour (FHA) 22
  mantlet 70, 101, 143
  side armour 49, 78, 95
  trackguards 71, 128-129
  track links 126-127
  trackway protection screens 127
Austin, Capt Anthony 36
Australian Army 6, 63, 70-71, 129
Australian Army Tank Museum, Puckapunyal 71, 130

Berry, Capt Norman 124
Books
  Britain, America and Rearmament in the 1930s, Christopher Price 12
  Design and Development of Weapons, J.D. Scott 14
Bridges, Sir Edward 112
British Army 10, 16, 136
  Army Tank Brigades (ATBs) 29, 38, 40, 42, 57, 62
  Field Service Regulations (FSR) 1935 29

  recruitment poster 23
  Royal Engineers 116, 124
  REME 124
  Royal Armoured Corps (RAC) 23, 136
  Royal Army Ordnance Corps (RAOC) 16, 88, 115, 124
  Royal Tank Regiments (RTR) – throughout
British Expeditionary Force (BEF) 38, 40, 42, 62, 98, 115
Brough, Maj Gen Alan 31
Brown, Staff Sgt 115
Browne MC, Capt Douglas 119

Camouflage 58, 115-118
  Caunter 66, 143
Canadian Army 57, 62
Canal Defence Lights (CDL) tanks 6, 119-123
  changing carbon elements 122
  instrument panel 122
Captured tanks 42, 56, 69, 130-131, 136
Carden, Sir John 29-31, 112
Carden, Matilda and Valentine 112
Churchill, Winston 11, 39, 112, 114
Committee of Imperial Defence 10
Communications 37
  antenna 100
  bell and bell push 57, 154, 167
  infantry telephone 126
  Laryngaphone (Checkophone/Parlaphone) 19-20, 36-37
  radios (wireless sets) 20, 22, 36-37, 52, 71, 99-101, 108, 121, 159
Construction 17, 35, 53, 79
  bolted and riveted 82
  built by hand 54
  female factory workers 53
Cooling system and ventilation 49, 52, 82
  airflow through the tank 52
Crew 50, 78
  Australian 71, 73, 90, 103
  CDL operator 121
  commander 18, 20, 28, 37, 50, 67, 71, 106, 126, 159
  driver 19, 36-37, 94, 119, 157-159
  flail operator 124, 126
  gunner 23, 52, 78, 160
  loader/radio operator 52, 78, 100, 126, 159, 161
  Russian 69
Crew positions 52, 82-84, 126
  commander 19, 36, 52, 78, 102, 143
  driver's compartment 19, 22, 36, 49-50, 52, 77, 82-84, 94, 99, 109, 156-158, 161, 165

  clock 99, 165, 167
  controls and instruments 83-84, 165
  gunner 50, 102
  loader 102
  seats 22, 37, 52, 82, 102, 161, 167
Crossing trenches and ditches 114-115, 133
  unditching logs 69
Cupolas 19, 52-54, 106-107, 129, 143, 159
Curran Bros, Cardiff 126
Custance, Brig Edward 31

Darwood, Bob 139
Deliveries 30, 34
  first, to 4RTC Catterick 34
  reference and trials vehicle 36
  USSR (Soviet Union) 6, 67-68
Design and development 6, 10, 12-13, 15-17, 25, 29, 35, 47-48, 97
  A11 ergonomics 36
  costs 30-31
  tank prototypes 16
Diesel, Rudolf 85
Dragon artillery tractor 35
Dunkirk evacuation 39, 42, 62
Du Toit, Abraham 123-124

Electrical systems 99, 141, 145
  batteries 77, 99, 167
  horn 99
  wiring and cables 141-142, 145
Elles, Sir Hugh 47
Engine bay 137, 149-150
Engine cooling 19, 91, 124-125
  radiators and fans 37, 91, 93
Engine deck 35, 71-72, 108, 127
Engine starting and stopping 37, 94-95, 165
  slave-start 54
Engines (powerplants) 13, 17, 20, 28-29, 47, 52, 78, 85-95, 145, 149
  AEC diesel (A183/184) 25, 48-49, 53, 82-84, 85-95, 112, 115
  Armstrong Siddeley V8 19
  block 136
  components 87
  cross-drive unit 92-93, 137
  materials 87
  Ford V8 petrol 31, 35
  Leyland diesel (E148/149, E164/165 and E170/171) 48, 82-83, 85, 87-91, 112, 115, 137, 139, 149
  lubrication 89, 97
  mountings 89
  plumbing 89-91, 139, 167
Exhaust system 57, 70, 82, 115, 127, 144, 154

Fighting compartment 21, 36, 52, 79, 82, 91, 102, 106, 108-109, 140, 145, 159
  bulkhead 145, 161
  fire control 105
  firing grips 106
  floor 79, 105
Finances 10-12, 14, 20, 25, 28, 30
  army budget for fuel: horse fodder 16; petrol 16
  balance of payment deficit 11
  cost of tanks 16, 22
  defence budget 16
  government loan for armaments 11
  Treasury 18; sums allocated annually 12
  Wall Street Crash 1929 11-12, 16
First World War 11, 38
  Armistice 12, 15-16
  Battle of the Marne 38
  Cambrai 1917 28
  equipment lessons 11
  Kirke Report 15
  'Mother' tank 17
  tanks 14-15, 18, 47, 53, 119
Flail equipment 123-126
  engines 124-125; Bedford 124; Chrysler 124
  power take-off from tank engine 126
Foote VC, Lt Col Henry Robert Bowreman 60, 66-67
Franklyn, Maj Gen 38
French, David 29
Fuel 16, 85, 91
Fuel systema and tanks 21-22, 50, 54, 90-92, 109, 126
Fuller, Gen 'Boney' 17

Gardner VC, Capt Philip 'Pip' John 65-66
German Army 34, 39, 58
  horse transport 38
German advance on Moscow 67
German invasion of Poland 10
Guderian, Heinz 38

Hadfields Ltd, Sheffield 49
Harland & Wolff (H&W) 53, 68
Hatches 36, 82, 84-85, 90, 106-107, 121, 132, 156
Hitler, Adolf 38-39
  annexed Czechoslovakia 14
  appointed German Chancellor 10
Hobart, Gen 119
Hulls 6, 23, 47, 49, 78-79, 104, 109, 125, 127, 135, 143-144
  front/nose casting 50, 79, 82-83, 126
  interior 140, 146, 161

Inskip, Sir Thomas 13
Instruction books 48, 91, 130
Italian army 63

Jackson, Gen Sir Louis 15
Japanese surrender 10
John Fowler & Co. 13, 53

Keitel, FM 39
Kneebone, Jon 136

Lamps 99
  De Thoren dazzle device 119-121
  headlamps 37, 79, 83, 99, 119, 122, 128, 131
  rear 165
  searchlights 119
  sidelamps 99
  signalling lamp 99, 102
  spotlights 107, 119
Lend-Lease support to the USSR 67
  Moscow Protocol 67
London, Midland & Scottish Railway 52-53, 116
Losses 41-42, 59, 62; at sea 68

Macksey, Kenneth 66
Maintenance and repairs 25, 97, 129, 142, 148
  engine servicing 90
Martel, Maj Gen Giffard 38

Matilda tanks 113
  A11 Matilda I (Infantry Tank Mk I) 27-42, 47, 112, 114
    description 35-37
    models and mock-ups 48
    prototypes A11E1 31, 33, 53; pilots 'Matilda Senior' 49-50, 112
  A12 Matilda II 6, 30 et seq. ; A12E1 45, 48, 50; A12E1 114; A12E2 48, 50
  Matilda III (Mk IIA) 49, 64, 69, 79, 85, 89, 101, 113
  Matilda IV (Mark II*) 55, 72, 87, 89, 101, 113; IVCS 54, 69
  Matilda V 87, 89, 113
Matilda conversions and variants 71, 130-133
  Australian 71
  Baron and Scorpion mine-clearing tanks 6, 123-126
  Bulldozer 71
  Canal Defence Lights (CDL) 53, 119-123; crane device 120
  CS 54, 57, 62, 65, 69, 101-103, 127
  Frog flamethrower 6, 70-72
  Funnies 132; TLC (tank-laying carpet) 132
  Projector Hedgehog 71-72
Matilda II Restoration 7, 43, 90, 94, 96, 135-151, 153
  condition assessment 139
  disassembly 139-141
  documentation 150
  failure of components 142
  funding 137-138
  Matilda Diaries, YouTube 7, 150
  project team 141, 151
  removal of dangerous materials 141, 148
  skills required 142

McMahon, Matt 137, 149
Mechanisation Board 25, 48-49

Mechanisation Experimentation Establishment (MEE) 30-31, 33-34, 36-37, 114, 116
MG, Abingdon 85
Mine ploughs 37
Ministry of Supply 54, 90
  Fighting Vehicle Division 123-124
Modifications 19, 45, 48, 50, 70, 90, 115, 122, 125
  Australian 126-129

Naming tank types 112-114
  Matilda 11, 30, 42
  semi-official 112
Navigation 107, 119
Night operations 119
  star shells 119
North British Locomotive Co. 13, 53, 59, 72, 150

Operation Battleaxe 66
Operation Compass 6
Operation Crusader 6, 64
Operation Husky 126

Painting 37, 118, 140-141, 143-145, 154
Paterson, Andrew 'Banjo' 112
Payne, Capt 49
Performance 42, 73, 124
  engine output 50
  ground clearance 33, 115
  in snow and ice 69
  range 91
  reliability 25, 27, 31, 37, 42, 86, 142
  speed 18, 22, 28-31, 37, 47, 53, 57, 86, 124
Pope, Brig 42
Production 33-34, 98, 115, 122
  assembly line 51
  contracts 50, 74-75
  exports: Australia 57, 70-73, 90, 107; Canada 56-57; New Zealand 70; Russia (USSR) 54, 57, 67-70, 150; USA 133
  final A11 completed 42
  initial delay 33
  Matilda II halted 54
  orders 33, 37
  reconditioned tanks 73
  re-engined 88
Preserved Matildas 34, 42-43, 107, 127
Princess Anne 151
Production figures 10, 17, 42, 50, 53-54, 67-68, 124
  exports 6, 67-68, 70
  orders 19, 150

Queen of the Desert nickname 10, 63, 67

Rearmament 10-11, 30, 47
  arms race 14
  Ten-Year Rule 10
Red Army 6, 67-68
Registrations (military and civil) 33, 74-75

Rommel, Erwin 38-39
Royal Air Force (RAF) 47, 87
Royal Navy 47
Royal Ordnance Factories (ROF) Woolwich 13, 23, 48, 50
Royal Tank Corps (RTC) 15-17, 19, 34
  battalions 34, 40
  Bovington 15-16, 34
  Catterick 29, 34
  Lulworth 16, 34, 52
Russian Tank Museum, Kubinka 68, 79
Ruston & Hornsby Ltd 53, 132

Seely, Gen 15
Sighting equipment (telescopes) 19, 36, 106, 136, 160
  periscopes 31, 36, 53, 59, 82-83, 106, 158-159
Smithers, A.J. 42
Spare parts 25, 57, 67, 136-137, 142
Specifications 20, 33, 37, 39, 50
  Matilda II 113-114
SS troops 39
Stalin, Joseph 67
Steering system 35, 48, 93, 141
Sticky bombs 73, 126
Stowage 33, 37, 57, 70, 82, 108-109, 126
  ammunition 102, 104, 108, 129
  layout of equipment 109
Studd, Col 31
Sunshield vehicle disguise 115-118;
  Houseboat device 118
Suspension (running gear) 17-18, 21-24, 29, 31, 33, 35, 49, 52, 56, 78, 95-97, 118, 142-143
  Japanese-type 47, 95-96
  lowered 115
  lubrication 142
  mud chutes 18, 21, 23-24, 49, 68, 78-79, 97, 154

Tail skid 57-58, 114
Tank Museum, Bovington 7, 34, 42-43, 90, 94, 96, 103, 106, 119, 135-153
  action events 136
Tank roles, types and classifications 17, 28
  by weight 17
  close-support (CS) 18, 50
  cruiser 13, 24-25, 27-28
  exploitation role 28
  infantry support (I-Tanks) 11, 13, 15, 17, 21, 25, 27 et seq.-
  light 31; reconnaissance 28
  medium 20-25, 28-29, 49, 64
  mine clearing (flails) 123-126
Tanks – British – see also Matilda tanks
  A9 29, 64
  A10 27, 29-30
  A20 project 73
  Centurion 120
  Chieftain 120
  Christie 50, 118

Churchill (A22) 49, 56-57, 67, 73, 102, 123
Covenanter 62, 102
Crusader Mk I 49, 64, 102, 118
experimental Mediums 20-25, 28-29, 64; A7E3 49
Hornet 112
Independent (A1) 22, 112
Medium III 23, 25, 49, 64
Mk V 11; Mk VI 35
Tetrarch 67, 102
Valentine 29, 62, 65, 67-68, 103, 118
Vickers Light Tank Mk 1/Medium I and II 16-22, 47, 96; A2E1 17
Vickers 6-Ton 35
Whippet 12, 25, 53, 112
Tanks – British – official type and mark designations 112-114
  Matilda 53, 57, 59, 113; identifying 90
Tanks – German 38-39
  Matilda (captured) 130
  Panzer III 36, 63; Panzer IV 38, 63
  Tiger 10, 137
Tanks – Russian
  KV-1 68
  T-34 67-68
Tanks – US 126
  M3 Grant 119, 123
  Sherman 126
Taylor, Lt Col Dick 6
Theatres of operation
  Arras 38-42, 56, 62
  Belgium 58
  Borneo 126
  Egypt 63, 116
  El Alamein, Battles of 6, 124
  Far East 6, 70-73
  France 6, 10, 27, 35, 40, 57, 62, 82, 115
  Greece 27
  India 28
  Libya 10, 19, 63
  Malta 57
  Middle East 115, 123
  New Guinea 57, 72
  North Africa 6, 27, 57, 63-67, 130-133
  Pacific jungles 10, 70
  Russia 10, 130
  Sicily invasion 126
  Solomon Islands 98
  Tobruk 6, 63-64
  Tunisia 10
  Western Desert 64, 66, 103
Tilly, Col Justice 15
Tools and lockers 33, 36, 108-109
Tracks 19, 31, 48-49, 54, 56, 79, 95-98, 115, 143
  adjusting mechanism 155
  bearings 143
  bogies 96
  brakes 141
  idlers and sprockets 31, 33, 96, 98, 143

jockey roller 96
materials 97
pins 31, 97-98, 115
spudded 69, 98
trackguard extensions 108
Training 6, 42, 54, 62, 73, 136
  CDL operation 122-123
  driver 93
  mine-clearing flail operations 126
  trade 16
Transmissions 20, 22-23, 49, 78
  clutches 91, 145
  gearboxes 25, 35, 53, 78, 92-93, 142, 148
  louvres 91
  lubrication 142, 148
  pneumatic elements 69
  Reavell air compressor and reservoir 53, 92, 142, 167
Trials 31, 33, 49, 82, 112
  flail mine clearance 124
  gunnery 52, 101-102
  snow 68
  track mark removal 118
  welded steel blocks 69
Turrets 17-18, 22-24, 31, 36, 43, 49-52, 73, 78, 82, 86, 103, 109, 133, 135, 143, 159
  A24 Cavalier 133
  cast 30-31
  CDL 119-123
  layout 102, 105-107
  lookouts 82-83, 104, 158
  removal and replacement 120, 143
  ring collars 71, 127-128, 133
  sub-turrets 21, 23
  traversing 36, 52, 105-106, 133

Vehicle identification/maker's plates 34, 53, 150
Vickers 13, 20, 31
Vickers-Armstrongs Ltd (VA) 16, 21, 23, 47, 95
  River Don works 20-21
Victoria Crosses won 65-67
Vulcan Foundry Ltd, The, Newton-le-Willows 13, 47-48, 51-54, 78, 98, 108, 120
  company logo 13

War Office (WO) 11, 15, 21, 30, 112, 116, 119, 126
Wavell, Gen 115-116
Weapons – see Armament
Wehrmacht (OKW) 39
Weight and weight saving 18, 20, 22-24, 28-29, 35, 53, 79, 96
Wilson, Walter 93
Withdrawal from service 6, 9, 67-68, 72-73
  broken up 54
  obsolescence 52, 63, 70
  replaced 57
  sold as farm vehicles 73
World tank quantities 14